SHORE ACRES

AND OTHER PLAYS

LAST PHOTOGRAPH OF JAMES A. HERNE,
TAKEN NOVEMBER, 1900

SHORE ACRES
AND OTHER PLAYS

BY

JAMES A. HERNE

REVISED AND EDITED, 1928, BY

MRS. JAMES A. HERNE

BIOGRAPHICAL NOTE BY

JULIE A. HERNE

SAMUEL FRENCH
Incorporated 1898
THOS. R. EDWARDS, Managing Director
NEW YORK CITY :: :: MCMXXVIII

SAMUEL FRENCH, LTD. :: :: :: LONDON

CONTENTS

INTRODUCTORY NOTE

The three plays in this volume have been selected for publication because they were the most successful of James A. Herne's productions, and still remain the best known of his dramas; and also because they are representative of his work and reveal its growth from beginning to maturity.

In the fire which destroyed the home at Herne Oaks in 1909, many original manuscripts, press clippings, letters, programs and other data of value were lost. In preparing the brief biography included in this volume, therefore, it has been necessary to rely mainly upon outside sources; but accuracy has been striven for, and definite and authentic dates have been given whenever it was possible to do so.

In preparing this volume, I have been greatly aided by the sympathy and advice of our good friend, Hamlin Garland; and my grateful thanks go to him, and to Dr. Arthur Hobson Quinn, whose enthusiasm and constant encouragement are largely responsible for my undertaking the work. I am also deeply indebted to Mr. R. L. Giffen for his valuable advice and for supplying important data; to Miss Affie McVicker for information regarding exact dates of original productions; and to Mrs. John A. Herne for verifying details regarding the early life of the Ahern family.

KATHARINE C. HERNE.

BIOGRAPHICAL NOTE

James A. Herne, the second son of Patrick and Ann Temple Ahern, was born in Cohoes, New York, February 1, 1839. Some authorities assert that the year was 1840, and the place, Troy, New York, but the date and the locality given here accord with Herne's own statements. Shortly after his birth, the family moved to Albany, where the father was employed for many years in a hardware store.

Patrick Ahern was a South of Ireland man. Small of stature, and wiry of build, he was by nature irascible and intolerant. His idea of parental discipline was a frequent use of the strap. He was religious in a narrow-minded way, and, although brought up a Catholic, was converted to the Dutch Reformed faith in later life. Neither well read, nor a thinker, he seems, nevertheless, to have possessed a shrewd common sense, and he had a pithy way of expressing himself. James A. Herne was fond of quoting his father's sayings. Patrick was honest, thrifty, and, according to his light, a good Christian, but he was never able to inspire his children with any affection, or any real respect for him.

On the other hand, Ann Temple Ahern was adored by her children. James A. Herne held her memory in deep affection, and his delineation of Ann Berry in "Shore Acres," is his tribute to her. In appearance she was a tall, handsome woman, with great dignity and sweetness of manner. She was a devoted wife and mother, and toiled early and late for her little household. She was a devout Catholic.

Besides James, there were six other children; Charles, the eldest, George, John, William, Sarah and Helen. Although the parents were humble people, all their children were highly intelligent, good-looking and magnetic, and three of them contrived to win places in the world: James as an actor and playwright, John as a soldier, and later as an actor, and George as a journalist and business man. While his pay was modest, Patrick Ahern was able to maintain his family in a fair degree of comfort for those days of simple living. The children received a common school education, and strict religious training. The younger boys sang in the choir of the local Catholic church, and sought escape from the irksomeness of this task in playing tricks and teasing each other during the services. The piety of the parents was not inherited by their children, and the somewhat narrow-minded atmosphere of their early upbringing bred in James, at least, an impatience with bigotry, and a dislike for orthodox forms and creeds which endured all his life.

In his boyhood, James wanted to be a sailor, and spent most of his leisure hours wandering along the banks of the Erie Canal watching the passing boats. Once he even started to run away to sea. Discovery, and a sound whipping by his father, cut short this adventure, but James' love for the sea endured throughout his life and is a strong undercurrent in many of his plays.

When he was thirteen, his father took him out of school and put him to work as errand boy in the hardware store. Later James became an apprentice in a brush factory. He was considered exceptionally bright for his age, and people used to remark on his well-shaped head. At such times his father would observe complacently, "James has a head like a forty shilling pot." The owner of the brush factory, a man of wealth and importance, advised Patrick to let the lad finish his schooling, and even offered to assume the expense of educating him. The advice was ignored, and the offer refused by Patrick, who had no vision, and no ambition for his children. So it came about that James was practically self-educated.

It was at this time that his elder brother Charles took James to see his first play at the old Albany Museum, and from that moment the boy determined to be an actor. Fearing the ridicule of his brothers, and another outbreak of parental displeasure, James confided his ambition to no one but his mother, and he continued to plod along at the brush factory. He was twenty years old before he had an opportunity to realize his dream. By this time he had saved up a hundred and sixty-five dollars, with which he intended to purchase a stage wardrobe, having learned that a fine wardrobe was one of the important assets of an actor. But he was induced to finance a barnstorming theatrical company, and his savings promptly vanished.

In spite of this misadventure, the roving, irresponsible existence of the actor continued to have an irresistible charm for the imaginative, restless youth. On his return home, he got a chance to play juvenile parts in James Connor's stock company, and made his first regular appearance at the Adelphi Theatre, Troy, in April, 1859, at a salary of six dollars a week. The part was George Shelby in "Uncle Tom's Cabin." Life, it seemed, had nothing more to offer. To quote his own words, "Twenty years old—an actor, and six dollars a week—why, I had reached the summit of earthly bliss." ("Old Stock Days in the Theatre," by James A. Herne, *The Arena,* September, 1892.)

He now decided, upon the advice of friends, to change the family name, Ahern, to Herne, as being more euphonious, retaining the A. however, as a middle initial. His brothers George and John also adopted this change in name later on.

Herne had a natural aptitude for the theatre; indeed he was what is called "a born actor." During this engagement, he played Horatio in "Hamlet," Cassio in "Othello," and Bassanio in "The Merchant of Venice," in support of various visiting stars, as well as the young lovers in the farces, which, according to custom, always followed the serious play of the evening. But the stock season was brief, and summer found Herne again working in the brush factory. He saved up a few more dollars, went to New York, and invested in two ostrich feathers, and a dress wig. Thus equipped, he joined the stock company at the Gayety Theatre, Albany, where he remained for some years, playing in support of the famous stars of the day. His father had no idea that Herne had gone on the stage, and merely supposed that he was working about the theatre. When Patrick finally learned the truth and saw his son act, he took it philosophically, remarking, "The fools are not all dead yet."

The theatre was closed at the outbreak of the Civil War, and Herne took an engagement with John T. Ford of Baltimore, one of the important managers of the day. The Aherns had already begun to scatter, possibly because of the wanderlust and love of adventure that were inherent in their Irish blood. Charles ran away as a youth and was never heard from again. Helen, the beauty of the family, made a rich marriage, and drifted away from her people. John, a lad of fourteen, went to the war, and finally, Patrick Ahern too, enlisted, and was killed in battle. His death definitely broke up the home, and his wife went to live with relatives in Maine, where she remained until her death.

For several years Herne divided his time between Ford's Washington and Baltimore theatres. It is of interest to note that he spoke the opening address at Ford's Tenth St. Theatre, Washington, where Lincoln was later assassinated. Herne was highly successful, and outside the theatre he lived the careless, pleasure-loving existence of a popular young actor. In appearance at this time, Herne was tall and well-built; he had the mobile features of the actor, but his expression was a trifle sad in repose. He was magnetic, a beautiful Shakesperian reader, and was noted for the finish and naturalness of his acting. Once, during a rehearsal of "Hamlet," Edwin Booth stopped the young actor and asked him where he had found the authority for the reading of certain lines. Herne, in a panic, replied, he had no authority for it, that it had simply seemed to him the proper way to read the speech. The great actor complimented him, saying it was a very fine and unusual reading. Although he was actually engaged to play "utility business," which meant, parts of minor importance, Herne was frequently cast for leads because of his quick study, and he never refused a new part on the score that he did not know it. If necessary, he would "wing it," that is, would memorize it scene by scene, while standing in the wings during the performance. Thus he gained many opportunities for advancement, and soon acquired a considerable repertory. The actor of the old stock theatres received a rigorous training; there were frequent changes of bill, and there were usually two or three plays performed every night—a tragedy, a melodrama, and a farce. The actors were obliged to rehearse daily, and were expected to be familiar with many parts, together with the stage business and the traditional readings of them all, for the visiting stars were exacting disciplinarians. In the course of his stock engagements, Herne played the whole range of drama with such stars as the elder Booth, his son, Edwin, E. L. Davenport and Edwin Forrest. It was an invaluable experience, a great foundation on which to build future achievements, and to the end of his days he was always loyal to the schooling he received in the old stock companies, and proud of his association with them.

Herne idolized the Titan, Forrest, and always declared him the greatest actor he had ever seen, yet he had little sympathy with the tragedies, and the melodramas, frequently bombastic, which formed the stock-in-trade of Forrest and his fellow stars. Although two of Herne's greatest successes as a young man were Claude Melnotte, in "The Lady of Lyons," and Armand Duval in "Camille," his preference was for parts characterized by quaintness, pathos and truth to life. He loved Dickens, and often said that the great novelist taught him to act. He excelled as Bill Sykes, Peggotty, and Captain Cuttle. His love for the sea found an outlet in playing sailor parts. He showed such brilliant gifts in these early days that Mr. Ford begged him to apply himself seriously to his art, to settle down and study, and promised, if he would do so, to make him a second Lester Wallack. But the offer went unheeded. Herne had sufficient money and plenty of friends, and he was content to live in the day. Although successful, a singular lack of ambition

seems to have been his. It was as though, having become
an actor, nothing else mattered. He was a reckless, devil-
may-care youth, with a gift for telling humorous stories, and
a fondness for practical joking that never left him. This
may have been an unconscious effort to escape from the
abiding melancholy which is the tragic inheritance of the
Irish nature. Hamlin Garland once described Herne as having "the saddest face I have ever seen."

After some years spent in stock companies in Baltimore,
Washington and Philadelphia, Herne became leading man
for Lucille Western, whose acting he admired above that of
all the women stars of the day. He toured the country with
her for the next few years, making several trips to California, where he became a great favorite. In 1866 he married
Lucille's sister Helen, who was famous for her beauty. It
was not a happy union, and they were divorced shortly
afterwards. In the early seventies Herne managed the Grand
Opera House, New York, for James L. Fiske. The middle
seventies found him once more in San Francisco, then at the
height of its brilliancy, as stage director of the Baldwin
Theatre, which was under the management of Thomas Ma-
guire, a famous figure in the theatrical world of those days.
The company boasted such illustrious members as James
O'Neill, Rose Coghlan, Lewis Morrison and F. F. Mackay.

The forces which were shaping Herne's life, and giving
it meaning and purpose, were already at work. One morning, Mrs. Melville, a well-known dramatic teacher, came
to the theatre with a young girl, one of her pupils, and asked
Herne to watch her rehearse a scene. Always kindly and
considerate to beginners, Herne consented. The girl was
Katharine Corcoran, the daughter of a young Irish couple
who had come to America in the early sixties. Michael Corcoran, the father, enlisted in the Union forces and died during the War, and his widow was left with four little children. After enduring bitter privations, the little family,
through the good efforts of a relative, came to California,
and here Katharine passed her girlhood. When Herne met

JAMES A. HERNE, FROM A PHOTOGRAPH TAKEN ABOUT 1860

her, she was just past twenty, dark-eyed, vivacious, dowered with sympathy and enthusiasm, and with great natural gifts as an actress. Herne became interested in her at once, and invited her to play Peg Woffington in "Masks and Faces," which he was putting on for his benefit. She made her theatrical début in this part, in November, 1877, and later joined the Baldwin Theatre Company. She and Herne were married, April 2, 1878.

Their marriage was a singularly happy one, a union of minds as well as hearts. Katharine Herne was truly an inspiration to her husband. She encouraged, cheered and advised him. As they worked side by side, through failure and success, he came to depend on her intuitional artistic sense, and always sought and abided by her judgments. His estimate of her powers as an actress is shown by the fact that he wrote all of the leading feminine parts in his plays for her, and she created all but one of them.

Up to the time of his marriage, Herne had tinkered at the work of other men, but had never thought seriously of writing a play himself. One day, however, David Belasco, who was stage manager at the Baldwin Theatre, brought Mrs. Herne the scene of a play he was writing, founded on "The Mariner's Compass." He asked her to show it to her husband and get his opinion of it. The scene was so promising, that, at his wife's suggestion, Herne agreed to collaborate with Belasco on the play, which was first called "Chums," and later, "Hearts of Oak." So it came about that the first actual play-writing which Herne did was on this drama, which was remarkable for introducing a real baby and a real supper on the stage.[1]

The success of this play, first produced at the Baldwin Theatre, San Francisco, September 9, 1879, with Herne as

[1] Prior to "Hearts of Oak," Herne and Belasco had collaborated on two other plays—an adaptation of Gaboriau's "Within an Inch of His Life," and a romantic melodrama, "Marriage by Moonlight," founded on an old play, "Camilla's Husbands." Neither of these plays was successful, and they are not in any sense typical or representative of Herne's work.

Terry Dennison, and Katharine Herne as Chrystal, encouraged its authors to take it East. A few months later
the play opened at the Grand Opera House, Chicago, and
won an immediate success. Later Herne bought out Belasco's
interest, and continued to present the play throughout the
country for the next seven years. Reputation and a comfortable fortune came to the Hernes through "Hearts of
Oak." He had always loved New England, and now he and
his wife settled in Dorchester, a charming suburb of Boston,
where they established a home, and brought up their three
children, Julie, Chrystal and Dorothy.

"Hearts of Oak" won its reputation through its strong
heart appeal, the dominant note which characterizes all the
Herne plays. In a day given over to much that was artificial
and meretricious in the drama, its very simplicity gave it immediate distinction. It was one of the first plays without a
villain, a character up to that time considered an indis-
pensable adjunct of all legitimate drama. Although based
on an earlier play, and partly the work of another hand,
the qualities that made Herne unique are already to be
found in "Hearts of Oak": his love of home, of children,
of simple, kindly people, his quaint humor and his deep vein
of sentiment.

In any estimate of the work of Herne and his wife, it must
be borne in mind that the outstanding features which dis-
tinguished their productions were, the utter simplicity of the
acting, and the perfection of the stage direction. Absolute
naturalness was the key-note of their work. We are ac-
customed to this on the stage today. But "Hearts of Oak"
was, in this at least, years ahead of its time, and Herne and
his wife were pioneers. Their method was a spontaneous
expression with them, and was not developed with the aid
of any premeditated theories. Nor were they aware, in the
beginning at least, that in developing a technique founded
on naturalness, they were working in harmony with the great
movement towards truer and simpler expression in the
theatre, which was beginning to sweep over Europe.

Herne's next play, "The Minute Men," a melodrama dealing with the American Revolution, was a more ambitious effort than "Hearts of Oak." He spared no trouble or expense to have the production perfect in cast, in scenic beauty,
and in historical accuracy. It was first seen at the Chestnut
Street Theatre, Philadelphia, April 5, 1886. But in spite of
the fact that it contained in the character of Dorothy Foxglove, a most charming comedy part for Mrs. Herne, and
in Reuben Foxglove a delightful character part for Herne,
it was not a financial success. The play introduces the only
genuine villain to be found in any of Herne's dramas—Dyke
Hampton. Herne was very fond of Cooper's novels, and
their influence is strongly felt in "The Minute Men," especially in the character of Roanoke, the white youth reared
as an Indian. Picturesque and romantic though "The Minute
Men" undoubtedly is, it is also the most conventional of all
Herne's plays.

The failure of "The Minute Men" made it necessary for
Herne to revive "Hearts of Oak." While on tour he wrote
the first draft of "Drifting Apart," which he called, "Mary,
the Fishermen's Child." Its first production took place at
the People's Theatre, New York, May 7, 1888, with Herne
in the character of Jack Hepburne, and Mrs. Herne as Mary
Miller. "Drifting Apart" deals with the havoc wrought by
drink in the lives of a Gloucester fisherman and his young
wife, and it contains some of Herne's most charming pictures of home life. One scene at least, where Jack dreams
of the death of his wife, Mary, and their child, through
starvation, ranks in tragic power and stark realism with
anything he wrote, and the acting of Herne and his wife
was described as "poignant." But the play was only a
mediocre financial success, although Herne contrived to keep
it going two years.

The Hernes were becoming noted among actors and critics
for the artistry and finish of their productions, but the managers were growing unsympathetic. They told Herne his
plays were "too real," "too good," that "art didn't pay," and

they urged him to give up his ideals and write pot boilers. He began to experience difficulty in booking his productions. He was obliged to play "Drifting Apart" in one-night stands, and in cheap, popular priced houses. These were discouraging days, but an innate doggedness and determination in Herne's make-up kept him fighting, and his wife's faith in him never wavered.

Hamlin Garland, then a young man who had come to Boston from the West, seeking fame as a writer, happened, almost by chance, to see a performance of "Drifting Apart" at an obscure theatre. He was enthusiastic, and sought out the Hernes. An instant friendship sprang up between the three of them. Garland was a radical by temperament, and a zealous advocate of truth and naturalness in all forms of art. In the work of the Hernes he saw a vindication of his beliefs, and he became their loyal champion. Others who now began to rally to the Herne banner were, Howells, the gentle, presiding genius of literary Boston, B. O. Flower, the frail, indomitable editor of *The Arena,* Joseph Edgar Chamberlin of *The Transcript,* and John J. Enneking, the painter. Their recognition put new heart into Herne. He began planning a new play. This was "Shore Acres," destined to be the most successful and the best-loved of all his dramas, and the one in which his spirit seems to have found its fullest and happiest expression.

Up to this time Herne's modernism had been confined principally to matters of technique—dramatic treatment, acting and stage direction. He had made no attempt to introduce his personal view-point or his theories of social conduct into his plays. "Hearts of Oak" and "The Minute Men" are stories, pure and simple. "Drifting Apart" has the drink problem for its theme, but this is only used as an element of dramatic motivation, and none of these plays is, in a direct sense, a criticism of life. In "Shore Acres," however, Herne began definitely to deal with the social and moral problems to be found in the world about him, and this play marks a distinct step upward in his progress as a dramatist

of ideas. This was due, no doubt, in part, to the stimulus
Herne received from the sympathetic minds he now came in
touch with. The group of intellectuals with whom the Hernes
were allied were among the most advanced and fearless
radicals of their day. Their field of vision encompassed the
whole range of art and life, and conversation at the Herne
dinner table included discussions upon such diversified sub-
jects as socialism, impressionism, evolution and the nebular
hypothesis, Ibsen, dress reform, heredity, theosophy, and,
first, last and always, Henry George's theory of the Single
Tax.

It was Hamlin Garland who brought about Herne's con-
version to the Single Tax, and his meeting with the great
humanitarian, George. In common with all right-thinking
people, Herne deplored the existence of poverty in a world
of plenty, but not until he read "Progress and Poverty" did
he become convinced that there was a cure for this condition. He at once became a devoted disciple of Henry George,
and, with the zeal of a crusader, he began to make public
speeches in favor of the Single Tax. Those were the days
when to be radical was anathema. Herne was implored by
his managers to cease his speech-making as being "bad for
business." But he ignored these warnings and continued his
labor of love. He was always fearless in standing for anything in which he believed. He was one of the first to sense
the menace of the theatrical trust and attacked it almost
single-handed. He was also among the earliest actors to
exhort his fellow players to organize.

It was inevitable that what Herne was thinking and feeling so strongly should permeate his work, and it is note-
worthy that the social questions that are woven into the
texture of "Shore Acres,"—land speculation, religious in-
tolerance, and the right of children to work out their des-
tinies independently of their parents' wishes, are issues as
vital today in the life of our people as they were thirty years
ago. The collapse of Martin Berry's ambitious schemes for
sudden wealth has had its recent parallel on a colossal scale

in Florida; the descendants of Sam Warren, the evolution-
ist, suffer persecution in Tennessee, instead of Maine, while
parents, clergymen and teachers argue pro and con over the
rebellious younger generation. In these things also, Herne
was in advance of his time.

Herne started "Shore Acres," or, "The Hawthornes," as
it was first called, in the early summer of 1888. Although he
had the general outlines of the plot in mind, he had not
decided where to lay the action of his play. Mrs. Herne had
spent a few weeks at Lemoine, on the Maine coast, and returned with glowing reports of its beauty and quaint charm.
She urged her husband to go to Maine and absorb its local
color for the new play. Accordingly, Herne and his family
spent the following summer (1889) at Lemoine, and he fell
in love with the place and the people as his wife had done.
He decided to lay the scene of "Shore Acres" on Frenchman's Bay, and during the summer he worked on the first
draft of the play, which was not fully completed for several
years.

The little community of Lemoine was at this period going
through the throes of a land boom, which probably led Herne
to make such a boom the background of his play. Contrary to
the belief, however, which used to be prevalent along the
Maine coast, Herne did not fashion the character of Uncle
Nat after an actual person. The character was suggested by
the part of an old man in a melodrama called "Lighthouse
Cliffs," which Herne had played many years before. None
of the characters in any of Herne's plays is drawn directly
from life, except Ann Berry, although it is true that his
wife's personality inspired many touches in his portraits of
women.

Before the new play could be produced, another idea took
possession of Herne, and clamored to be written. This was
"Margaret Fleming," a sombre, powerful study of marital
infidelity. At the time of its inception, Herne was deep in
the study of the modern European writers. He found Tolstoi,
Zola, Ibsen and Sudermann greatly to his taste, and their

grim commentaries upon social conditions touched a responsive chord. In "Margaret Fleming" Herne found an ideal vehicle for the expression of his convictions about one of the most serious problems of social conduct. The play is relentless, yet profoundly moving; it marks another advance in Herne's progress as a thoughtful dramatist, and it is still considered by many people as his most important contribution to the drama.

"Margaret Fleming" was given a few trial performances at the Lynn Theatre, in Lynn, Mass., opening there July 4, 1890, with Herne as Philip Fleming and Mrs. Herne as Margaret. Howells, Garland, and others who saw the play were loud in their praise, declaring it not only Herne's best work, but an artistic advance upon anything so far produced in the American theatre. In spite of their enthusiasm, the managers of New York and Boston, when approached by Herne, absolutely refused to give the new play a hearing, saying it was too daring. After a year of such rebuffs, Herne and his wife, encouraged by Hamlin Garland, decided to produce the play themselves. They rented Chickering Hall, a small and attractive concert hall in Boston, and with a few deft strokes and at little expense, they turned it into the semblance of a charming, intimate little theatre. "Margaret Fleming" was produced there, May 4, 1891, Mrs. Herne playing Margaret and Herne Joe Fletcher. The play, the simplicity and unconventionality of the production, and the acting of Mrs. Herne created a sensation. So real was the effect produced that spectators declared they felt as though looking through transparent walls into an actual home. Some of the lines, which would be considered merely plain speaking today, were condemned as too frank, and because the drama advocated a single standard of sexual morality it was called "shocking" and "radical." It was widely, and often bitterly, discussed. Artistic Boston flocked to see it and it became the talk of the town.

The direct result of the production of "Margaret Fleming" was an attempt in Boston to organize an Independent

Theatre, sponsored by Hamlin Garland and Mary Shaw, and it also gave an impetus to other movements along the same lines. Actors who longed to get out of routine work, encouraged by Herne's example, began to give special matinees of Ibsen and other advanced dramatists. The American theatre became more hospitable to new forms and new ideas. Indeed, it is not difficult to see in the theatre of today, many results which owe their being to that courageous gesture of the Hernes, and our drama has benefited from what was considered at the time merely "a magnificent failure."

That summer Herne wrote his first and only play to order, "My Colleen." It was a charming comedy of Irish life, and was played for several years by the Irish actor Tony Farrell, and his wife, for whom Herne wrote it.

In the fall of 1891 Herne and his wife decided, for business reasons, to move to New York, and regretfully they sold their pretty Dorchester home and took a house on Convent Avenue, on Washington Heights. His fortune was completely wiped out and Herne was forced to go back into the ranks. He accepted the position of stage director for Klaw and Erlanger, and produced for them a huge entertainment, half melodrama, half spectacle, called "The Country Circus," by Charles Barnard, which ran a season at the old Academy of Music. Meantime, Mrs. Herne tried to get a New York hearing for "Margaret Fleming." A. M. Palmer half-heartedly consented to present the play at a matinee at his theatre. This took place December 9, 1891, with Mrs. Herne as Margaret, supported by members of the Palmer Theatre stock company. The majority of the critics were unsympathetic. The play was revived several times after this, the most important production being at the New Theatre, Chicago, in 1907.

In spite of failure, discouragement and the chilling effect of his return to routine work, Herne still cherished hopes of his play, "Shore Acres." He sent it to manager after manager and between rejections, he would work at it, re-writing a scene here, polishing a line there, touching it up as a painter does a well-loved picture. But not a manager had faith in it. Herne's plays were failures. One prominent manager was willing to risk money on a production, but insisted that a star of his own should play Uncle Nat. It had been Herne's often expressed wish to play one last great part before he died, and he had written Uncle Nat with that idea in mind. Into the character he had put all of himself, his thoughts, his feelings, all that life had taught him, until it had become a living, vibrant thing. He determined that he, and he alone should play the part. So he refused the offer, and one day he found himself out of work and facing a crisis.

A bit of good fortune suddenly relieved the situation. James H. McVicker, owner of McVicker's Theatre in Chicago, and a man of noble heart and mind, had always been more responsive to Herne's ideas than other managers, possibly because he had once been an actor and could understand. In the spring of 1892 he offered Herne a summer's run at his theatre in a repertoire of his plays. This engagement proved to be one of the happiest Herne ever experienced. McVicker was congenial and sympathetic, and, as he gave Herne a guarantee, financial worries were reduced to a minimum for the first time in years, and Herne was able to give his best energies to his work.

"Shore Acres," under the title of "Shore Acres' Subdivision," had its first production at McVicker's Theatre, Chicago, May 23, 1892, with Herne as Uncle Nat and Mrs. Herne as Helen Berry. Later, the title was changed to "Uncle Nat." It ran for several weeks with but fair success. The silent ending which Herne had devised was not used in this production, in deference to the wishes of Mr. McVicker, who, while he admired it greatly, felt it was too radical an innovation, and feared that audiences would not appreciate it and would not wait to see it. Herne therefore consented to let the final curtain fall on the scene where Uncle Nat accidentally fires off the gun. "Shore Acres" was followed by "My Colleen," and the engagement ended with "Margaret

Fleming," for which Herne had written an entirely new last act. This play made a particularly deep impression upon the Chicago critics.

Herne and his wife returned to New York with renewed faith in "Shore Acres," but they were unable to interest the Eastern managers in it and Herne was obliged to enter the ranks once more. In January, 1893, he appeared under the management of Brady and Grismer in a play entitled "The New South," by Clay M. Greene, and gave a memorable performance of a minor part, a wretched, hunted negro criminal.

Now it was that the seemingly miraculous happened. One of the managers who had refused "Shore Acres" a few years previously, was R. M. Field of the famous Boston Museum, which still housed a stock company of the old school. His stage director, Edward E. Rose, however, had always liked the play, and when, early in 1893, Field needed a vehicle for his company, Rose urged its reconsideration. The outcome was that "Shore Acres," with Herne as Uncle Nat, supported by the stock company, opened at the Boston Museum in February, 1893. Its success is history.

Connected with this production is an incident which shows what difficulties the dramatist of advanced ideas encountered in those days. Herne still believed, in spite of McVicker's contention, that his original idea of a silent ending, with the curtain falling upon a darkened stage, was the only true finish for "Shore Acres." Fearing that Field would not permit him to use it, Herne resorted to pardonable strategy. He rehearsed the play with the curtain to fall upon the episode of the gun, as in Chicago. But taking Rose, who was deeply in sympathy with his work, into his confidence, Herne arranged to end the act as written. The opening night Rose stood in the prompt entrance waiting to give the signal for the final curtain. But when the gun episode arrived, he held the curtain, and did not permit it to fall until Uncle Nat, in dead silence, had set the house in order for the night and had climbed up the stairs to bed. The result was as Herne had foreseen. The audience followed his pantomime with rapt attention, and even after the curtain had fallen, was slow to leave the theatre. Critics praised the ending as being one of the most original and moving ever seen, and Herne's methods were vindicated.

"Shore Acres" ran well into the summer, and it is interesting to note that its closing marked the passing of the Boston Museum stock company. The following autumn the play opened at the Fifth Avenue Theatre, New York, and ran until Christmas time, when it was transferred to Daly's Theatre, where it remained until the end of the season. During this run Henry C. Miner became Herne's manager, and their long association was both friendly and profitable.

Herne played "Shore Acres" for five years. His fame as an actor and playwright were at last established, and the artistic principles for which he had fought so long received the serious consideration which is always accorded to success. The happy result was that Herne was freed forever from financial care. He and his wife built a lovely home at Southampton, on Long Island, which they named Herne Oaks, and here they spent their summers with their three daughters, and their small son, John. Here Herne could indulge his taste for quiet, and for the sea. He wrote, he studied, and he spent many hours sailing in his boat, the "Gretchen."

It was during these years of tranquillity that Herne wrote what many consider his finest play, "Reverend Griffith Davenport," or, as it was later called, "Griffith Davenport." It was founded on the novel, "An Unofficial Patriot," by Helen H. Gardener, the noted suffragist and social reformer. The story, which was based on episodes in the life of her father, deals with a Virginia circuit rider and his family, before and during the Civil War. Mrs. Gardener felt that it had dramatic possibilities, and she urged Herne to make a play of it. He was not particularly enthusiastic, and at first attacked it almost perfunctorily, solely because Mrs. Herne saw a big idea in the story. As the play progressed, however, his interest in it grew. The first draft was written at Sayville, Long Island, where the family spent the summer of 1894, and Herne was not pleased with it. During the next five years he rewrote the play several times before he was fully satisfied.

In his use of a Civil War theme, Herne, as in all his plays, departed from beaten paths. His treatment of the subject was foreshadowed in a talk he had with Hamlin Garland many years before, when they were discussing the Civil War and the plays that dealt with it. Herne contended that the field had been worked out, and that the next play on the subject must of necessity deal, not with heroes and battles, defeats and victories, but with the effect of the war upon the lives of a single family or group of people. At that time he had no idea of writing such a play, but the remark was prophetic, for "Griffith Davenport" does indeed deal with the tragic effects of slavery and war conditions upon a devoted family and their neighbors. Into the play, as he went on, Herne put all he had observed during the war-time years of his youth, and much that mature reflection had taught him. The result was a picture of Virginia in the sixties that glowed with truth—a truth of the spirit that went far beyond mere historical accuracy.

In the spring of 1898 Herne's contract with Miner expired, and he decided to discontinue "Shore Acres." The play was still drawing large houses everywhere, but Herne grew weary of playing one part constantly. In the character of Davenport he had written a particularly strong part for himself, and one in complete contrast to Uncle Nat, and in Katharine Davenport there was also a fine opportunity for Mrs. Herne who had not played for some years. Herne offered the new play to Miner, but the manager refused to risk a penny of the fortune he had made out of "Shore Acres" on it, and in the end it was Herne himself who financed the production. "Griffith Davenport" had its premiere at the Lafayette Square Theatre, Washington D. C., January 16, 1899, with Herne as Davenport and Mrs. Herne as Katharine, and two weeks later came to the Herald

Square Theatre, New York. The drama had more sweep than anything Herne had yet attempted; there were forty-two speaking parts, each one a distinctly drawn character, and the play was mounted with the perfection of detail which marked all his productions. But the public was apathetic, and the critics bewailed the fact that Herne was dealing with a "dead issue." Nevertheless, the artistic rewards of "Griffith Davenport" were great. Herne's admirers honored him for not being content to rest on his past achievements; the English critic, William Archer, pronounced the performance, in acting and stage management, the finest thing he had seen on either side of the water, and the novelist, Zangwill, after seeing the play insisted that no one but Herne should direct his dramatization of "Children of the Ghetto," which George C. Tyler was to produce.

So it was that, when the season closed in May, Herne returned to his summer home in an unusually serene and happy frame of mind, sufficiently inspirited to take up a play which he had started the year before. During the summer of 1898, he was urged by his business manager, the loyal and efficient William B. Gross, to make a revival of "Hearts of Oak." He agreed, and started to make a few changes in the play. But before long, his mind ran away with the idea, and he found himself writing a totally new play. He laid "Hearts of Oak" aside and devoted himself to the new drama, which he called "Sag Harbor" after the picturesque old whaling port not many miles from his home. So it happens that "Sag Harbor," Herne's last play, is a lineal descendant of his first, and to the student these two dramas afford interesting comparisons in the growth of his art. "Hearts of Oak" is instinct with a dramatic power and an emotional quality which make it still live, even though its "asides" and its incidental music belong to an older day. In "Sag Harbor" one feels that it is character rather than plot in which the dramatist is interested.

In writing this play Herne took infinite joy, and it is filled with quaint sayings and little human touches drawn directly

from his daily experience. While sailing his boat on Great
Peconic Bay, he became interested in the hardy "bay-men"
as they are called, who earn their livelihood "scallopin' winters, and sailin' comp'ny summers." He was fond of talking
with the "Gretchen's" skipper, the sunburnt, self-contained
Cap'n Peterson, and he treasured up many of his dryly
humorous remarks. Frequently he would anchor and visit
one of the little towns lying on the bay. The village life, so
like that of New England, yet with a distinct flavor of its
own, appealed strongly to Herne, and he seized upon it
eagerly as a background for his play. "Sag Harbor" breathes
the atmosphere of a drowsy Long Island village of twenty-
five years ago, its leisureliness, its vivid interest in other
people's affairs, its utter peacefulness.

This was the only play of Herne's which obtained a hearing without anxiety and travail on his part. After the opening of "Children of the Ghetto," which Herne directed in
the fall of 1899, Mr. Tyler became Herne's manager, and
produced "Sag Harbor" at the Park Theatre, Boston, Mass.,
October 23, 1899, with Herne as Cap'n Dan Marble. It ran
there nearly all winter and then toured the country, drawing
crowded houses everywhere. In the spring the play opened
in Chicago most auspiciously, but the run was cut short by
the serious illness of Herne. He was obliged to close his
season and went to Hot Springs, Arkansas, to recuperate.
Later he joined the family at Herne Oaks. But the break
had come. He was not to be again his vigorous self.

In the fall of 1900 "Sag Harbor" opened at the Republic
Theatre, New York. Its reception was indifferent and it ran
only eight weeks. This was a keen disappointment to Herne,
nevertheless he rallied, and threw himself heart and soul
into the current political campaign. Bryan was running for
President a second time. Herne supported him ardently and
made many speeches urging his election, for he had always
been a firm believer in the Democratic Party and its principles. Bryan's defeat was a keen blow to him.

He continued to play "Sag Harbor" on tour that winter,

but he grew gradually weaker and was forced frequently to rest. A final breakdown came on his return to Chicago in the spring, and once again he closed his season and went home. After making a brave fight for life, he died at his Convent Avenue house on June 2, 1901, of pleuro-pneumonia. He was in his sixty-third year.

Herne was greatly loved by all who knew him. The members of his companies were devoted to him, and he valued nothing so much as the respect and admiration of his fellow players. He was a disciple of Spencer and Darwin, and often declared he was an agnostic; but his nature was deeply spiritual, and tolerance and a feeling for humanity shine through all he did and wrote. In the truest sense, he was "one who loved his fellow men."

JULIE A. HERNE.

SHORE ACRES

A Comedy in Four Acts

By

JAMES A. HERNE.

Dedicated to his children, Julie, Chrystal and Dorothy.

CHARACTERS

MARTIN BERRY, *owner of "Shore Acres," and keeper of Berry Light.*

NATHAN'L BERRY, *"Uncle Nat," his elder brother.*

JOEL GATES, *a grass widower.*

JOSIAH BLAKE, *postmaster and storekeeper.*

SAM WARREN, *a young physician.*

CAPTAIN BEN HUTCHINS, *skipper of the "Liddy Ann."*

DR. LEONARD.

SQUIRE ANDREWS.

TIM HAYES.

YOUNG NAT BERRY.

IKE RICHARDS.

LEM CONANT.

ABE HIGGINS. } *"Kinder work around."*

STEVE BAILEY.

DAVE BURGESS.

GABE KILPATRICK. } *·Fishermen, crew of the "Liddy Ann."*

BILL HODGEKINS.

BOB BERRY.

THE MAIL CARRIER.

ANN BERRY, *Martin's wife.*

HELEN BERRY, *Martin's daughter.*

LIDDY ANN NYE.

MRS. ANDREWS.

MRS. LEONARD.

PERLEY, *Mrs. Berry's hired girl.*

MARY BERRY.

MILLIE BERRY.

MANDY GATES.

BOB LEONARD.

SIS LEONARD. } *The Twins.*

ACT I. View of "Shore Acres Farm," near Bar Harbor.
"Hayin' Time."

ACT II. The Berry farmhouse kitchen.
"The Silver Weddin'."

ACT III. Scene 1. Interior of Berry Lighthouse.
"Havin' an Understandin'."
Scene 2. Exterior of Berry Lighthouse.
"The 'Liddy Ann' in a Sou'easter."

ACT IV. Same as Act II. Fifteen months later.
"Me an' the Children."

TIME—1891.

PLACE—Berry, on Frenchman's Bay, near Bar Harbor, on the
coast of Maine.

SHORE ACRES

ACT FIRST

"HAYIN' TIME"

VIEW of *"Shore Acres Farm," near Bar Harbor.*

SCENE: *Frenchman's Bay, with Mount Desert Island and its range of grandly picturesque hills in the distance. Away off to the right are the stately Schoodac Mountains, veiled in mist.*

On the right of the stage, at the back, on a rocky bluff dotted with dwarf pines, and overlooking the bay, is Berry Light. It is separated from the farmhouse by a shady road, which runs across the stage from left to right. The farmhouse, on the right, is barely visible, being hidden in a profusion of shrubs and flowers. Trees overhang the roof; a white-washed fence divides the door yard from the road. Several shining milk pails are hanging on the fence, and on one of the palings hangs a small weather-beaten mail bag; near it hangs a battered tin horn. The door yard is filled with old-fashioned flowers.

To the left of the stage is an old barn, its doors open, its littered yard enclosed by a rail fence. A dove cote is built into the peak of its gabled roof, and doves come and go leisurely.

Outside the fence, at the upper end, is a pump, beneath which is a trough filled with water. Against the lower end of the fence lies a plough. Trees overhang the roof of the barn, and join those overhanging the house from the other side. At right centre is a gnarled old tree, and beneath it is a bench. Down left, below the fence, is a wheelbarrow.

At the rise of the curtain, and until the act is well in prog-

5

ress, the wind gently sways the foliage with a slight rustling sound. Birds sing, and flit to and fro. The sound of multitudinous insects is the one distinct note of the scene. The bay is calm, quiet, and in the distance a catboat is occasionally seen sailing lazily, appearing and disappearing among the islands. A tiny steam launch appears once, about the middle of the act, and is seen no more. A mowing machine is heard at work in the distance off left. It stops, turns, goes on again, while the voice of the driver is heard guiding his horses, with "Whoa! Stiddy! Get up! Whoa Bill!" (All this must be very distant.)

At the rise of the curtain, MILLIE, a little girl about four years old, is sitting down left near the plough, playing in the sand with clam shells and pieces of old crockery. She wears a quaint little calico dress, and has a small white flannel shawl around her shoulders, crossed in front and tied behind her back. Her shoes are very dusty, her little hands are dirty.

On the road, off stage to the right, a horse and wagon can be heard driving up and stopping outside; and presently the MAIL CARRIER appears, with a mail bag and a basket of groceries. He is a kindly-looking man of middle age, wearing a linen duster, driving gloves and a straw hat. He goes to the bag hanging on the fence, takes two letters from it, and puts in a newspaper wrapped for mailing. He drops the letters into his own bag, and places the basket of groceries beside the fence.

MAIL CARRIER. [Putting his hands to his mouth, calls,] Whoop! Whoop! Whoop!

[At his call, MILLIE leaves her play and runs to him. They are evidently good friends.]

MILLIE. Hello!

MAIL CARRIER. Hello, Millie! I swan I'm afeared I've fergot yeh this mornin'.

MILLIE. Oh! Hev yeh?

MAIL CARRIER. Well, not quite. [*Feels in his coat pocket, gets out a piece of candy as if it were the usual thing, and gives it to her.*]

MILLIE [*Pleased.*] Thank yeh.

MAIL CARRIER. Hain't yeh got a kiss fer me?

MILLIE. I guess so. [*Lifts up her face; he kisses her.*]

MAIL CARRIER. I'll bring yeh a bigger piece to-morry. Good-bye. [*He goes off right, and is heard driving away.*]

[MILLIE *nibbles the candy as she watches him out of sight, then she resumes her play.*]

[*After the mail wagon drives away,* HELEN *enters, left, followed by* UNCLE NAT. HELEN *is a girl of seventeen, with a frank yet thoughtful manner, indicating a girl of advanced ideas. She has golden-red hair and brown eyes; she is picturesquely dressed, and wears a sunbonnet. She carries a small pail full of berries, and a tin cup hangs from a crooked finger.*]

[UNCLE NAT *is a man of sixty, and his large sturdy frame shows signs of toil. His eyes, of a faded blue-grey, have the far-seeing look common to sailors. He wears his yellow-white hair rather long, and he is clean-shaven save for the tippet of straw-white beard that seems to grow up from his chest and to form a sort of frame for his benevolent, weather-beaten old face.* UNCLE NAT *is of the soil, yet there is an inherent poise and dignity about him that are typical of the men who have mastered their environment. He has great cheerfulness and much sly, quiet humor. He wears overalls of a faded blue, a blue checked jumper, beneath which one glimpses a red flannel shirt, and on his head is a farmer's much-battered wide straw hat. His sleeves are rolled back, and he carries a pitchfork in his hand.*]

[*As the scene progresses, one is impressed by the frank comradeship between the old man and the girl. On his part there is tenderness, and a deep interest in her problems; there is*

admiration too for her fine spirit of independence. HELEN
*shows a suppressed feeling of bitterness as she talks. She is
high-spirited and proud, yet simple and direct. They pause
a little above centre as they talk.*]

HELEN. [*Talking as she enters.*] Yes, I know, Uncle Nat,
perhaps I oughtn't. But Father makes me mad when he talks
as he does about Sam.

UNCLE NAT. [*Soothingly.*] Well, now, things'll come out all
right ef you'll only hev patience. You're young, so's Sam.
I told 'im so t'other day. Sez I, "Sam Warren," sez I, "You
hain't got a mite o' sense," I sez.

HELEN. [*In the same manner.*] Father says—if he catches
me speaking to him again, he'll—

UNCLE NAT. You mustn't let 'm ketch yeh! [*Chuckles.*] Law
sakes, ef I couldn't spark a fellah athout my father ketchin'
me at it, I'd bag my head.

HELEN. [*With gentle reproach.*] I can't bear deceit—

UNCLE NAT. Neither kin I, but what yeh goin' to do about
it—give Sam up?

HELEN. [*Determinedly.*] No! [*She crosses to the right, and
sits on the bench under the tree, and says with an undercurrent of defiance,*] I'll never give him up—I'll leave home
first.

UNCLE NAT. [*Teasingly.*] Oh, Nell! You wouldn't hev spunk
enough fer that.

HELEN. [*Half smiling, then thoughtfully.*] Wouldn't I—

UNCLE NAT. No sirree! [*Crosses to the left and places the
pitchfork against the fence.*]

HELEN. You'll see—it'll be his own fault if I do. [*Rising and
going towards him.*] Uncle Nat, if you were my father,
would you—

UNCLE NAT. [*Wistfully, with a tender cadence in his voice.*]
Ef I was yer father, Nell? Ef I was yer father, I'm afeared

I'd let you do jes' about's you'd a mind to. Allus *did* seem
es ef you was my baby anyway, an' I'd give the two eyes
out'n my head to see you an' Sam happy. But I ain't yer
father, Nell—I ain't yer father. [*The last with a regretful
sigh.*]

HELEN. [*softly.*] I sometimes wish you were.

UNCLE NAT. [*Goes to her and places his hands affectionately
on her shoulders.*] Now, hol' on! Thet ain't right. No sirree!
Thet ain't right, an' you know it.

HELEN. Father's changed. [*Leaves him and goes slowly back
to the bench.*] He never takes me on his knee any more.
[*With a slight shade of resentment.*]

UNCLE NAT. [*Smiling, and looking at her admiringly.*]
You're gittin' too heavy I guess.

HELEN. No, it isn't that. Mother's noticed it, and she feels
pretty bad about it too, although she pretends not to see it.

UNCLE NAT. Of course she dooze. She ain't a-goin' to see no
changes in a man she's been married to nigh on to twenty-
five year, not ef she kin help it.

[HELEN *rises, and as she does so she sees* MR. BLAKE'S *buggy,
which is supposedly standing off stage, right. Immediately
her whole manner changes, and she says with an impatient
tone in her voice,*]

HELEN. There's Mr. Blake's buggy again! [*Shrugging her
shoulders.*] He's here about all the time lately.

UNCLE NAT. [*Rather seriously.*] He *is* here pooty consid'ble,
ain't he? What he after I wonder?

HELEN. [*Resentfully.*] Principally—me.

UNCLE NAT. [*Surprised, but rather amused.*] He ain't!

HELEN. [*With finality.*] Yes he is. Father wants me to marry
him.

UNCLE NAT. [*Frightened.*] He don't!

HELEN. [*In the same manner.*] Yes, he does. Mr. Blake told me as much the other day.

UNCLE NAT. My! My! Thet's too bad. I swan thet's too bad. I'm afeared yer father don't understand yeh, Helen. Has he said anythin' to yeh about 't himself?

HELEN. [*Still standing by the bench.*] No, not yet—but he will, and then—well— [*Half savagely.*] He'll find out I'm not Mother—

UNCLE NAT. Tut—tut—tut—there yeh go— Thet's yer father all over again—thet's yer father all over again.

[JOEL GATES *drifts into the farmyard from the road, left. Little* MANDY *drifts in after him.* GATES *is dressed in dark overalls, with suspenders, a soiled white shirt, no vest, and an old drab soft hat. He carries a scythe, the snath under his left arm, the blade to the ground with the point off to the left, and he has a whetstone in his right hand. He looks as if life had battered him mercilessly. He is small and slight, his face weather-washed, kindly; his keen little eyes seem to be as a child's with a question in them, always asking "What is it all about anyhow!—I d'know!" He is never seen without* MANDY. *Her whole little personality is part of his; the nondescript, faded clothing, the rhythm of movement. The far-away look in the old face is repeated in the apple-blossom beauty of the child. He rarely addresses her or seems aware of her presence.*]

GATES. [*In a drawl.*] Good day, Nathan'l.

UNCLE NAT. Hello, Joel!

GATES. [*Talking as he walks across the stage towards the right.*] Why ain't yeh in th' hay field?

UNCLE NAT. Ben there good part th' mornin'. Who be you a-cuttin' fer t'day, Joel?

GATES. Simm'ns. Jes' got done. Goin' t' cut m' own now. Can't afford to lose this weather.

UNCLE NAT. No; too good weather to lose, an' no mistake.

[GATES *is about to exit, with* MANDY *behind him, when he stops abruptly near the bench.* MANDY *pauses also.*]

GATES. Oh, Nathan'l! Will yeh lend me yer gun fer a day 'r two?

UNCLE NAT. [*Reluctantly.*] Yes—I guess'o. What fer? [*Coming down centre.*]

GATES. There's a fox 'r suthin' a-playin' ol' Nick with my chickings.

UNCLE NAT. Thet so? Helen, git me ol' Uncle Sam'l, will yeh? She's a-standin' in her corner in the kitchen. [HELEN *goes into the house.*] Hello, Mandy! [*Chuckles.*] How d'yeh do?—You ben in the hay field too? [*The child nods.*] By George—you're a great haymaker. I'll tell you what—when you git a scythe inter yer hands th' grasshoppers is got to jump over the fence an' no mistake, ain't they, Joel? [*Chuckles.*] Will yeh shake hands with me? [*Urging the child kindly.*]

GATES. Go on—shake hands.

[MANDY *shyly creeps behind her father.*]

UNCLE NAT. Bashful, ain't she?

GATES. [*Reaching around to where the child stands behind him, and pressing her closer to him.*] Yes—she's a shy sort o' critter. Don't never seem t' want t' play with nobody nor nothin' but me.

UNCLE NAT. She's a-growin' ain't she—growin' jes' like a weed. My—my! How like her mother she dooze look, don't she?

GATES. [*With a break in his voice and a catch in his breath, placing his hand on her head and looking at her.*] Yeh. Gits to look more an' more like her every day in the week.

UNCLE NAT. [*Hesitatingly, as if loth to arouse unhappy*

memories.] I suppose—yeh hain't never heerd nothin' of her—sence—hev yeh, Joel?

GATES. [*Out of the depths of pitiful memories.*] No—nothin'. [*With a great sigh.*]

[HELEN *returns with the gun and crosses to* UNCLE NAT. GATES *also crosses to* UNCLE NAT, *leaving* MANDY *in front of the bench. After* HELEN *gives* UNCLE NAT *the gun, she goes over to* MILLIE *who has been playing in the sand, all unconscious of things that have been going on about her, and sits down beside her and plays with her.* MANDY *timidly sits on the edge of the bench; she watches her father intently, with a look of trust and affectionate content which one sees in a dearly loved dog when near his master.*]
[*The attitude of* GATES *and* UNCLE NAT *in the episode of the gun is that of two boys gloating over a treasure.*]

UNCLE NAT. Well—here's ol' Uncle Sam'l. Take good keer of 'r. I set a good deal o' store by Sam'l. [*He hands* GATES *the gun.*]

GATES. [*Putting the stone in his pocket, laying down his scythe and taking the gun.*] Is she—eh—ludded?

UNCLE NAT. Yes, I allus keep 'r ludded.

GATES. Doos she—eh—kick?

UNCLE NAT. She never kicked me, d'know what she might do to a feller she didn't like.

GATES. [*Handling the gun with pride, as though it were a great privilege, his eyes travelling the length of it admiringly, and then looking at* UNCLE NAT *with his face aglow.*] Fit all through the war with 'r, didn't yeh?

UNCLE NAT. Yeh.

GATES. Sixth Maine?

UNCLE NAT. [*His hands clasped behind him, shoulders thrown back, his head high in the air, teeters to and fro on his heels and toes.*] Yeh—Sixth Maine, Company A. Her 'n me 's tramped a good many miles together, one way 'nother. [*His voice is quiet and his face tense with memories.*]

GATES. [*In an awed hushed voice.*] Did yeh ever—kill a rebel 'th her?

UNCLE NAT. [*In a matter of fact tone.*] Don't know. I used t' jes' p'int 'er, shet both my eyes 'n let 'r do her own work.

GATES. [*Reflectively.*] I guess thet's 'bout as good a way as any fer me t'kill thet 'ere fox. [*He is fussing with the gun and unconsciously aims it at UNCLE NAT.*]

UNCLE NAT. [*Taking hold of the gun and pushing it aside.*] Hol' on, yeh danged ol' fool— Didn't I jes' tell yeh she was ludded?

GATES. What yer skeered of? I wa'n't a-goin' to pull the trigger—I was only jes' aimin' 'r.

UNCLE NAT. Well, aim 'r at somebody else.

GATES. There ain't nobody else handy.

UNCLE NAT. I swan thet's too bad.

GATES. Well, good day. [*Takes up the scythe, and puts the gun over his shoulder.*] I'll bring 'r back safe an' sound.

[GATES *goes off right.* MANDY *quietly slips from the bench and slowly drifts after him.* UNCLE NAT *attracts her attention by playfully snapping his fingers at her, and she turns and shows quite a little interest in his kindly friendliness. She passes on, her eyes fixed wonderingly upon him.* UNCLE NAT *is amused and chuckles. After they go off, he seats himself on the bench under the tree.*]

HELEN. Oh, Uncle Nat! Have you and Sam done anything more about your back pension?

UNCLE NAT. Well, Sam got me t' sign some papers over at the Squire's t'other day—but—I d'want him to do nothin' about my back pension. [*With mock indignation.*] What do you an' him take me fur? One o' them 'ere pension grab-bers?

HELEN. [*Going up left.*] Well, Sam says you're entitled to it, and he's going to try and get it for you too.

UNCLE NAT. Sam says lots o' things asides his prayers, don't he Nell?

HELEN. [*Pausing and leaning over the fence.*] I guess he does. [*They laugh together softly with amused understanding.*]

UNCLE NAT. Where yeh goin'?

HELEN. Oh, I don't know. Just for a stroll. [*And much occupied with her problems, she disappears down the road to the left.*]

[UNCLE NAT *rises from the bench a little stiffly, as if checked by a slight rheumatic twinge, goes down left and gets the wheelbarrow. He starts off as if he might be going to get fodder for the noon meal of the animals, when he notices* MILLIE *and says jovially,*]

UNCLE NAT. Well, Millie, d'yeh want a ride?

MILLIE. [*Dropping her play and brushing off her frock, eagerly.*] Yes.

UNCLE NAT. Well, climb into the kerridge an' don't keep the ol' hoss waitin'. Yeh know how to git into a kerridge?

MILLIE. Yes. [*She sits on the edge of the wheelbarrow.*]

UNCLE NAT. Well, I don't know whether yeh do or not. Take a back seat. [*He tips the wheelbarrow gently so that she slides into the back of it. She is a bit startled for a moment.*] You see, I knew yeh didn't know how to git into a kerridge. The fust thing yeh know this ol' hoss'll kick up and knock the dashboard out, an' spill yeh all over the place, an' yeh won't like thet a bit. [*He wheels her off, right.*]

[BLAKE *enters from the barn. He is a man of forty years; he has black hair, and his side-whiskers are close cut. The rest of his face is cleanly shaven. He is dressed in a grey business suit, "store made;" the coat is a single-breasted frock, very slightly cutaway, buttoned with one button at the breast. He wears a white laundered shirt, and a rather high standing collar with a black ready-made tie. His hat is a silk one, old, but not battered, brown at the edges of the crown and brim. His shoes have been home-polished, but are dusty. He has drab castor gloves, not new; he carries a buggy whip, an old white one. He has a black silk ribbon watch guard around his neck, and a gold watch. He is portly and well-to-do, but jovial. He is rather good-looking, and has the air of a contented, cheerful business man, shrewd, but not cunning or mean; he is always smiling. He passes through the gate of the barnyard, and goes right centre.]*

[He is followed by MARTIN, *a heavy robust man of fifty. He is slow and deliberate in manner and speech. His face and hands are weather-beaten, his hair is sandy-grey and cropped, and he has a short stubby beard. He wears pepper-and-salt trousers tucked into his boots, a black vest, and an open, white, home-made and home-laundered shirt with collar attached. His shirt sleeves are rolled up a trifle, showing red flannel beneath. He has a black silk sailor handkerchief, and a black soft hat, well worn. He carries a jackknife in his right hand, and is opening and shutting the blade with his thumb as he walks along, "clicking" it. His left hand is behind his back, and his head is down, as if in deep thought. He stops inside the rail fence.]*

[At the same time enters from the house, PERLEY, *the "hired girl," a strong muscular girl of about twenty, in a calico dress, with her sleeves rolled up to her shoulders, showing her red powerful arms. She pays no attention to* BLAKE *or* MARTIN, *and goes to the mail bag, takes it down, takes out the paper, crosses over and gives it to* MARTIN, *who mechanically looks at the address as if he knew what it was, as it is a regularly "subscribed for" paper. She crosses back to the basket of provisions, puts the bag into the basket, stands with her back to the men, with her hands on her hips, and*

*looks up and down the road for a moment. She then takes
up the basket and goes into the house.*]
[*The dialogue between* MARTIN *and* BLAKE *has gone on
right through the action, from the moment they entered.*]

BLAKE. No, sirree. I tell yeh, Martin, the day o' sentiment's
gone. We're livin' in a practical age. Any man's liable to
go to bed poor 'n wake up a milli'naire. Ef I'd hed a friend
to give me such a boost and such advice's I've given you,
I'd hev owned half the State o' Maine, I believe.

MARTIN. [*At the lower end of the fence, and facing the
audience; putting the paper in the watch pocket of his vest.*]
Why, yeh see's I told yeh, Mother left the place to me 'n
Nathan'l, an' we sort o' promised 'er we'd never sell it an'—

BLAKE. Sentiment! All sentiment! Any man thet'll hang
on to an old farm jes' 'cause— [*Goes to the pump, takes the
cup and pumps water into it*] he sort o' promised his dead
mother he'd never sell it, ain't got no business to live in
this bustlin', go-ahead, money-makin', devil-take-the-hinder-
most day of ours— [*Drinks*] thet's all I've got to say.
[*Laughs. Pours the balance of the water into the trough,
replaces the cup and wipes his mouth.*]

MARTIN. [*Casually.*] P'r'aps you never sot much store b'your
mother, Mr. Blake.

BLAKE. I never hed no mother—thet is not to speak of. You
know all about thet as well as I do. [*He returns to* MARTIN.]

MARTIN. Thet mus' be the reason yeh can't understand—

BLAKE. [*Patronisingly.*] I kin understand this. [*Leaning with
his back to the fence, both elbows on the top rail.*] "Shore
Acres" is a good enough farm as Maine farms go—yeh
manage by hard work to make a livin' fer yerself an'
family—

MARTIN. [*Defensively, nodding his head at* BLAKE.] A good
—comfortable—livin'! [*He puts his foot upon the middle
rail.*]

BLAKE. [*Admitting the correction good-naturedly.*] A good comfortable livin'! [*Switching the whip up and down.*]

MARTIN. [*With quiet dignity.*] An' pay my debts.

BLAKE. An' pay—your debts.

MARTIN. [*Complacently.*] Don't owe no man nothin', an kin sleep nights.

BLAKE. [*Patronisingly, agreeing with him.*] From sundown to cockcrow—I ain't a-goin' to dispute thet, thet's a-l-l right. Well, now, you happen to hev a hundred an' sixty rod, more or less, of about the sightliest shore front to be found on the coast. Yeh didn't know thet till I told yeh, did yeh?

MARTIN. No, I didn't. [*Climbs up, sits on the rail fence, facing the house, and sticks the knife into the rail between his legs.*]

BLAKE. Well! This shore front makes your land val'able. [*Turning and putting his foot on the bottom rail.*] Not to plant potatoes in—but to build summer cottages on. I tell yeh, the boom's a-comin' here jes' as sure as you're born. [*Carried away by his own enthusiasm.*] Bar Harbor's got s' high, yeh can't touch a foot of it—not by coverin' it with gold dollars. This has got to be the next p'int. [*Goes to the bench, right, and sits down.*]

MARTIN. [*He is impressed by* BLAKE'S *enthusiasm, but there is caution in his immediate response.*] Seems so—the way you put matters.

BLAKE. Seems so? 'Tis so. You pool your land in with mine— [*He talks with a confident, good-natured, yet shrewd business air. He lays out a plan on the grass with the end of his whip.*] We'll lay out quarter-acre lots, cut avenoos, plant trees, build a driveway to the shore, hang on to all the shore front an' corner lots—sell every one o' the others, see!!! They'll build on 'em an' that'll double the value of ours—

see!—they'll have to pay the heft o' the taxes 'cause they've built; we'll be taxed light 'cause we didn't—see?

MARTIN. [*In the same manner.*] I d'know as I jes' see.

BLAKE. [*Confidentially.*] If we can get holt of half a dozen just the right sort o' fellahs—city fellahs—yeh know—fellahs that hev got inflooance to bring folks down here—we can afford to give 'em each an inside lot, here an' there, provided they'll guarantee to build, lay out their grounds, an' help to make the place attractive. That'll give us a kind of starter—see? [*Chuckles.*]

MARTIN. [*Warming a bit at* BLAKE'S *confident statements.*] Seems es ef thet wouldn't be a bad idee.

BLAKE. *Bad* idee? It's *the* idee! [*Rising and going to* MARTIN, *confidentially.*] Let me show you—

[*He takes a notebook from his pocket, and begins to show* MARTIN *some calculations he has jotted down. They become so absorbed in this that they do not notice* GATES, *who enters right, followed by* MANDY.]

GATES. [*Smiling ingratiatingly.*] How d' do? [*If encouraged he would stop, but they merely nod.*] I hear you fellahs is a-goin' to boom things here 'n the spring. [*He goes quite close to* BLAKE *and* MARTIN *who are deep in discussion. He tries to peer over their shoulders, and raises his voice as if they were deaf.*] Is thet so thet Jordan Ma'sh's comin' down here to go inter business? [*He pauses, inviting a response; again braces up a bit and makes another effort, now in a manner implying that he is doing them a great favor.*] I wouldn't mind sellin' thet seven acre o' mine—ef I thought I could git rich out 'n it.

[BLAKE *looks over his shoulder as if a puff of wind or something had disturbed him, then pointedly resumes his talk with* MARTIN. GATES *is crestfallen, and turns away.*]

GATES. Gosh! How some folks kin get stuck up 's soon as they git a little mite rich—I never see— [*He shuffles off*

left, with mingled dignity and resentment, followed by
MANDY.]

BLAKE. I tell yeh, Martin, I've got the scheme! You go in
with me an' in less than a year I'll make you so rich you
can live in Bangor. Move your mother's remains up there,
an' have 'em buried in one o' them fine cemet'ries, an' put
a handsome stun over her as you'd ought to do.

MARTIN. Nathan'l an' me 's ben savin' up fer a stun. I guess
we've got most enough now to git one—money's scurse with
us—we don't see much *real* cash.

BLAKE. I'll tell you what I'll do. I'll take a mortgage on the
farm for the money to start you—an' you kin sell the lots.

MARTIN [*Hesitatingly.*] I'll talk to Nathan'l an' Ann.

BLAKE. Talk to 'em—of course—but don't let 'em talk you
out of the scheme. There's a good deal of sentiment in
Nathan'l.

MARTIN. It'd make me pooty rich, wouldn't it?

BLAKE. Rich? Well, I guess. Yeh wouldn't hev to be bor-
rowin' nobody else's chaise to go to meetin' in.

MARTIN. Seems es though it hed ought to be done, don't it?
Yet it seems a kind o' pity to—

BLAKE. To get rich, eh? [*Laughs.*] Say, look a-here! Honest now—wouldn't you like to live better 'n you do? Now
honest Injun, wouldn't yeh?

MARTIN. [*A bit warmed by* BLAKE'S *suggestions.*] I suppose
I would.

BLAKE. Of course yeh would, an' yeh'd like to have your
family live better. Helen'd ought to hev a real good symin-
erry eddication—she's worth it, she's a bright han'some girl
—she'd ought to be a bookkeeper or suthin'. [*Complacently.*]
I was a-tellin' her t'other day 'bout your a-wantin' her 'n me
to git married, an'—

MARTIN. [*Showing interest.*] What'd she say?

[BLAKE *purses his lips and shakes his head dubiously.*]

MARTIN. Did yeh offer her the piannah, as I told yeh to?

BLAKE. Y-e-s—

MARTIN [*Nonplussed.*] I thought she'd 'a' jumped at the piannah. She's so fond o' music.

BLAKE. I offered her everything I could think of. I offered to build her a house, an' let her paint an' paper it any way she'd a mind to.

MARTIN. [*Pondering.*] I guess I'd better talk to her myself. She giner'ly does what I tell her to.

BLAKE. Yes, but you see girls are beginning to think they've a right to marry who they please.

MARTIN. [*With pride in* HELEN, *and pride in his own power to control her.*] Not *my* girl.

BLAKE. [*Going right, with a shade of resentment.*] I'm afraid I'll never git very close to her so long 's young Doc Warren's around.

MARTIN. [*Angrily.*] Doc Warren!—She don't keep company along o' him no more? [*As if in doubt.*]

BLAKE. Don't she?

MARTIN. I guess not. I told her I didn't want she should— thet's allus ben enough.

BLAKE. Them free thinkers is hard to git shut of. They're dangerous to young folks' religion.

MARTIN. Helen's ben riz a stric' Babtis'—I guess she'll stay so; she's a pious girl.

BLAKE. Them's the wust when they do change. Sam Warren was *raised* respectable enough. His father and mother were Presbyterians.

MARTIN. [*His memory carries him into the past, and a smile creeps into his face as he answers patronisingly,*] Ol' man Warren was a good-natured honest ol' soul an' all that—but I never thought he had any too much sense.

BLAKE. No! If he had he wouldn't have worked himself to a skeleton tryin' to make a doctor out of his boy. [*Laughs.*]

MARTIN. [*Nodding his head wisely.*] The mother had a good deal to do with thet, I guess.

BLAKE. Six o' one an' half a dozen o' the other. What she said was law with the ol' man and what he said was gospel with her. They thought the sun jes rose an' sot in their Sam, an' now look at 'im. First he read Emanuel Swedenborg, an' he was a red-hot Swedenborgian—then he got hold of Spencer an' Darwin an' a lot o' them kind o' lunatics an' began to study frogs an' bugs an' things. [*He laughs.* MARTIN *laughs too, but not so heartily as* BLAKE *does.*] Why, sir! One mornin', a spell ago, as I was goin' to Ellsworth, I seed him a-settin' on his hunkers in the middle of the rud, watchin' a lot of ants runnin' in an' out of a hole. [*Both roar with laughter at this.*] D'yeh remember thet free lecture he gave with the magic lantern in the school house, on evolution 's he called it?

MARTIN. Yes, some of 'em wanted to tar an' feather 'im thet time.

BLAKE. Oh! Pshaw! That wouldn't 'a'done! [*A slight pause.*] Now he's come out as a home-a-pathic physician— [*Laughs.*] He ain't a doctor—he's a pheesycian— Goes around wantin' to cure sick folks with sugar shot—by George! [*Both laugh heartily.*]

MARTIN. L'see—ain't he a-tendin' ol' Mis' Swazy now?

BLAKE. [*Carelessly.*] Yep! Doc Leonard give her up, an' they had to have him. [*Starts to go off right, then stops.*] Oh, I'm goin' to git rid o' all my hawgs. I'd like you to have them two shoats, they're beauties!

MARTIN. [*Preoccupied.*] I guess I've got all I want.

BLAKE. Well, think over thet there land business. If you want to get rich, now's your chance—if you don't, I can't help it. Good day! [MARTIN *nods.*] Good hay weather. [*Scans the sky.*]

MARTIN. Fust-rate.

BLAKE. [*As he goes off right.*] Most through?

MARTIN. Finish this week ef the weather holds.

BLAKE. [*Outside.*] Good day!

MARTIN. Good day! [*He looks after* BLAKE, *then slowly and thoughtfully enters the barn, head down, hands behind his back.*]

[HELEN'S *voice is heard off left. She talks as she enters; she has an arm around* YOUNG NAT, *a handsome boy of fourteen. He is an errand boy in* BLAKE'S *store. He wears knickerbockers, and a cap with no visor. He has the air of being spoiled and thoroughly selfish.* HELEN'S *manner towards him is one of amused and affectionate tolerance.*]

HELEN. [*Laughing indulgently.*] La, Nat! What good would my marrying Mr. Blake do you?

YOUNG NAT. Lots o' good. You could coax money out o' him, an' give it to me.

HELEN. [*Shocked.*] Oh! Nat Berry! [*Shakes her finger at him.*] Would you take that kind of money?

YOUNG NAT. I'd take any kind o' money. 'Tain't no worse than weighin' yer hand with the sugar, is it?

HELEN. [*As if talking to a child, placing her hands to his face.*] Well, Natty dear—

YOUNG NAT. [*Pushing her hands away.*] Don't call me Natty. Gosh, don't I hate thet! Mother makes me so 'shamed every time she comes up to Blake's. This is the last suit o' knickerbockers she gits on me. Gosh, wouldn't I have lots o' things ef you'd marry ol' Blake! [*Putting his arms around*

JULIE HERNE AND JAMES A. HERNE, IN SHORE ACRES, ACT I

her, coaxingly.] Say, Nell, will yeh? Marry ol' Blake—do. Jes' 'this once an' I'll never ask you again. Will you? I'll do as much fer you some day! Will you?

HELEN. No, I won't! I don't want to marry Mr. Blake.

YOUNG NAT. [*Reproachfully; going right.*] Ain't you selfish!

HELEN. Aren't you selfish!

YOUNG NAT. You'd marry Doc Warren mighty quick ef Father'd let you.

HELEN. [*Smiling proudly.*] I guess I would.

[SAM WARREN *enters by the road, right, at the back. He is tall, handsome and manly, with an open honest face, and a frank manner. He stands for a moment, leaning over the fence, listening to* YOUNG NAT *with an amused smile.*]

YOUNG NAT [*Coming towards* HELEN.] Hands like a black-smith, poor's Job, proud as a peacock an'—[*With awe*]— don't believe there's any Hell.

HELEN. [*Quietly smiling.*] Well, neither do I.

YOUNG NAT. O-O-O-h!—Nell Berry! I'll tell yer father, an' then you'll find out!

[SAM *comes down and takes* YOUNG NAT *by the ear and twists it playfully.* YOUNG NAT *howls.*]

SAM. What do *you* think about it, Nat?

YOUNG NAT [*Crying.*] Ouch! L' go my ear!

HELEN. [*Going to* YOUNG NAT *and folding him in her arms.*] Ah!

YOUNG NAT. An' you let go of me, too. [*Pushing her away and going up centre.*]

HELEN. Sam! You've hurt him. You're too rough. Don't cry, Nat.

SAM. I didn't mean to hurt him, Nell. He's more mad than hurt I guess, aren't you, Nat?

YOUNG NAT. [*Crying.*] None of yer business! I'll get even with you fer this some day, you see if I don't! I wish I was big enough, I'd show you whether there's any Hell or not, you great big blacksmith, pickin' on a little fellah like me! [*He goes off left, crying.*]

[SAM *laughs and crosses to right centre, watching him.*]

HELEN. [*With gentle reproach.*] You shouldn't tease Nat so, Sam. You know he doesn't like you. [*She sits beneath the tree on the bench, right. She is vibrating with content and happiness in the presence of the man she loves.*]

SAM. [*Sits down on the plough lying against the barnyard fence.*] That seems to be a general complaint around these parts. A fellow that knows some things his great-great-grandfather didn't know is an object of suspicion here. [*As he talks, he picks up a handful of sand and lets it slip through his fingers.*]

HELEN. [*Smiling.*] Well, what are you going to do about it?

SAM. [*Cheerily.*] Keep right on knowing. Just as long as they build printing offices, we've got to know, that's all there is about that.

HELEN. I'm afraid—[*Laughs softly.*]—my reading is going to get me into trouble.

SAM. How so?

HELEN. [*Still amused.*] Why, the other day I was trying to tell Father something about evolution and "The Descent of Man," but he got mad and wouldn't listen.

SAM. [*Laughing.*] Family pride! You know, Nell, there are lots of people who wouldn't be happy in this world if they couldn't look forward to a burning lake in the next. [*Takes a book out of his pocket and carelessly flips over the pages, looking at her as he talks.*]

HELEN. Kind of sad, isn't it?

SAM. Oh! I don't know! They take a heap of comfort preparing to keep out of it, I suppose.

HELEN. [*Seeing the book in* SAM'S *hand, rises and goes towards him.*] What book's that? [*Trying to read the title on the cover.*]

SAM. [*Rising.*] "A Hazard of New Fortunes."

HELEN. Have you read it?

SAM. Yes.

HELEN. [*Eagerly, reaching for it.*] May I read it?

SAM. Yes, I brought it for you. [*He gives her the book.*]

[HELEN *delightedly takes the book and begins eagerly scanning the pages as she turns and goes back to the bench under the tree, speaking as she goes.*]

HELEN. I've been longing for this book. I read a fine article about it in the Boston paper. [*Sits down and looks at* SAM *with a joyous smile.*] Thank you ever so much, Sam.

SAM. [*Pointing to the book.*] That's a book you won't have to hide. Your father'll listen to that. If he was a speculating man, now, it would do him good.

HELEN [*Turning the leaves of the book, and pausing here and there at a page as something interesting catches her eye.*] How's poor old Mrs. Swazy getting along?

SAM. [*In a matter-of-fact way.*] First-rate. She'll pull through this time.

[*As the scene progresses,* SAM *moves about restlessly, as though preoccupied with something. He is never far away from* HELEN *and always has his eyes and attention focused upon her.*]

HELEN. [*Looking up at him with awe and wonder.*] Oh! Sam! After they'd all given her up— [*Proudly but ingenuously.*] Well, they'll have to acknowledge that you're a great physician now.

SAM. [*Laughs.*] Great fiddlesticks! Why, the folks around here wouldn't let me doctor a sick kitten if they could help it.

HELEN. Why, you'll get the credit of this!

SAM. Yes! Me and the Lord! [*Laughs.*] I'm satisfied so long as the old lady gets well.

[HELEN *is still sitting on the bench, glancing over the book, a look of contentment and happiness upon her face.* SAM, *who has been leaning against the barnyard fence, goes to her thoughtfully, his whole manner changed. He stands slightly above her to the left, puts one foot on the bench, leans on his knee and bends over her, and says in a rather quiet tense voice*]

SAM. Nell—I want to tell you something.

HELEN. [*Without looking up, says gayly as* SAM *pauses.*] Something good, I hope.

SAM. [*In the same manner.*] Don't I always tell you good things?

HELEN. [*With a teasing little laugh, looking up at him over her shoulder.*] Most—always, Sam!

SAM. [*Quietly, looking down into her eyes.*] I'm going away. [HELEN *seems stunned. The joy passes out of her face; her eyes are still upon him, but all the happiness is gone from them. The book drops from her hands and falls to the ground. She slowly slides along the bench away from him as though to study him better. She is pale and frightened, and in a dry voice with a low cry of pain, she says:*]

HELEN. Oh!—Sam! [*Then, feeling it cannot be true, she leans towards him and adds in a very appealing voice,*] Honest?

SAM. [*Quietly.*] Honest. What's the use of my staying here? [*Sits down left of* HELEN.] Nobody'll speak to me except Nathan'l—and your mother—and you. [*Putting his arm around her.*]

HELEN. [*Drawing away from him, endeavouring to over-come her emotion.*] Don't, Sam— Please don't.

SAM. [*With a dry laugh.*] And *you're* half afraid to.

HELEN. [*Brokenly.*] No! I'm not afraid—only you know —Father says—

SAM. [*In the same manner.*] I know—they all say it. Blake says I've got dynamite in my boots. Just because I can't believe as they do—they won't any of 'em look at me if they can help it. So I'm going out West, where a fellow can *believe* as he likes and *talk* as he likes—

HELEN. [*With awe, her eyes upon him.*] To—*Chicago?*

SAM. [*Amused.*] Oh no—o! A fellow may *believe* what he likes in Chicago, but he mustn't *say* too much about it. I'm going a-w-a-y out West. Montana—or somewhere out that way.

HELEN. [*Innocently, in a pathetic voice.*] Oh my! I'll never get so far as that, will I?

SAM. [*Not heeding her, rising and walking up centre.*] I want to get where I can sprout a new idea without being *sat* on.

HELEN. [*In a crushed voice.*] Yes, of course—you're right.

SAM. Where I won't be hampered by dead men's laws and dead men's creeds.

HELEN. [*Turning to him in a chiding manner.*] Why, you don't blame Father for believing as *his* father believed, do you?

SAM. No. But I *do* blame him for sitting down on me just because I can't believe the same way. I tell you, Nell—[*He picks up a pebble.*]—one world at a time is good enough for me; and I've made up my mind that I'm going to *live* while I'm in this one—[*He throws the pebble as far as he can reach, watching its flight*]—and I'm going to do something more than practice medicine in Berry. Sitting around, waiting for patients—[*Rather contemptuously*]—such as old Mrs. Swazy. [*He puts his hands in his pockets and turns down centre.*]

HELEN. [*Getting up from the bench and going to him, centre.*] Yes. But—what's going to become of *me?*
[SAM *goes to her with arms outstretched, and enfolds her lovingly.*]

SAM. [*Tenderly.*] You! You're going to stay right here with your mother, till I get started. Then I'm coming back to get you and take you out there and show those western fellows a *real* Yankee girl. [*Amused.*] You know, Nell, the newspapers used to print pictures of them with pants on and a stove pipe hat!

HELEN. [*Making a pitiful effort to be cheerful.*] Yes! But they don't do that now, Sam.

SAM. No, they do *not* do that now. You girls have come to stay, there's no getting around that fact, and we cranks are going to help you stay here. [*He notices the book lying on the ground.*] Let me show you something in that book.
[*They walk over to the bench,* SAM's *arm remains about* HELEN. *She sits down, he picks up the book and sits at her left, and they both become deeply absorbed in reading.*]

[MARTIN *enters from the barn, leading a horse by the halter to water him at the trough.[1] His head is bent and he is in deep thought, pondering upon the idea of getting rich which* BLAKE *has suggested to him. He does not see* HELEN *and* SAM *until he turns to re-enter the barn. When his eyes rest upon them, so content and absorbed in each other, he pauses amazed, and his face flames with bitter resentment. He is unable to speak for a moment, then he blurts out harshly,*]

MARTIN. Sam Warren, hain't yeh got no more pride than to come where yeh ain't wanted?

[1] *NOTE:* If it is not convenient to have a horse, Martin can come in with two heavy stable buckets, one in each hand, which he fills with water from the trough.

[SAM *and* HELEN *start in surprise.* HELEN *shyly draws away from* SAM. SAM *looks up with a very affable air and says pleasantly and respectfully,*]

SAM. Hello, Mr. Berry! Yes sir, I have.

MARTIN. [*In the same manner.*] Well, what yeh doin' here, then?

SAM. [*Looking at* HELEN *slyly as if it were a good joke.*] I thought—I *was* wanted.

MARTIN. [*Taking a menacing step towards him.*] Didn't I tell yeh yeh wa'n't?

SAM. [*Smiling, but rather reluctantly.*] Yes sir,—*you* did!

[SAM *plays this scene very quietly, never losing his temper; plays it as if something else of more immediate importance were on his mind.*]

[*The scene throughout is pitched in a quick staccato, which reaches its height in* HELEN'S *cry of terror as the two men clinch. Then there is a pause, and the rest of the scene, until* MARTIN *leaves the stage, is completed in tense low tones that are portentous of trouble. There is active hate on* MARTIN'S *part.* SAM'S *attitude is one of simple manly poise.*]

MARTIN. Well, ain't thet enough?

SAM. [*Pleasantly.*] Yes, I suppose it is—but I thought that —maybe you'd like to know— [*Rises and goes towards him.*]

MARTIN. [*Goaded by* SAM'S *manner, fiercely.*] I don't want to know nothin'! An' I don't want *her* to know nothin' thet I don't want her to know! [*Indicating* HELEN *with a nod of his head.*]

SAM. [*Making another effort to conciliate him.*] Why you see, Mr. Berry—you can't help—

MARTIN. [*Breaking in and shouting at him.*] I'm a-bringin' up my family! An' I don't want no interference from you —nor Darwin—nor any o' the rest o' the breed! [*With a passionate sweep of his arm. He half turns as if to go.*]

SAM. [*Smiling.*] Darwin's dead, Mr. Berry—

MARTIN. [*Turning and interrupting, resentfully.*] Them *books* ain't dead.

SAM. [*Very positive and very much satisfied with his statement.*] No! "Them books" are going to be pretty hard to kill.

MARTIN. [*Sharply, turning to* HELEN *who is still seated on the bench.*] What book's thet yeh got there now? [*Indicating the book with a wrathful toss of his arm.*]

HELEN. [*Very gently.*] One of Sam's books, Father.

MARTIN. [*Glaring at* SAM.] Well, give it right straight back to Sam. I don't want nothin' to do with *him* nor his books.

SAM. [*Kindly, correcting him.*] It *is* my book, Mr. Berry, but it was written by a man—

MARTIN. [*His temper rising steadily, flashes at him.*] I won't hev yeh a-bringin' them books here! A-learnin' my daughter a pack o' lies, about me an' my parents a-comin' from monkeys—

SAM. [*His eyes twinkling with suppressed amusement, answers soothingly.*] La bless you, Mr. Berry! That was ages ago!

MARTIN. [*Is goaded to the extreme by* SAM'S *manner.*] I don't care how long ago it was, I won't hev it flung in my children's faces.
[HELEN *is much distressed by her father's bitter temper, and she suddenly attempts to calm him, and approaches* MARTIN *who has been standing near the barnyard gate. She timidly holds out the book to him, and says pleadingly:*]

HELEN. Father, I wish you'd let me read you this little bit—

MARTIN. [*With ugly stubbornness, checks her with a sweep of his arm, as though pushing away some harmful or noxious thing.*] I don't want to hear it. I read *The Bangor Whig,* an' *The Agriculturist,* an' the Bible, an' thet's enough. There ain't no lies in *them.*

SAM. [*Ironically.*] No, especially in *The Bangor Whig!*
[*Here the staccato changes to a deep ominous murmur.*]

MARTIN. [*Peering at* SAM *through half-closed lids, mutters,*]
I'm skeered of a man thet ain't got no religion.

SAM. [*With quiet assurance.*] But, Mr. Berry, I *have* got a
religion.

MARTIN. [*Doubtfully, in the same manner.*] What is it?

SAM. [*His manner becoming serious, in a voice warm with
feeling, pointing off with a sweep of his arm.*] Do you hear
those insects singing?

MARTIN. [*Rather puzzled, mumbles.*] Yes—I hear 'em!

SAM. [*Seriously and calmly.*] Well, that's their religion, and
I reckon mine's just about the same thing.

MARTIN. [*With supreme disgust and contempt in his voice
and manner.*] Oh! Good Lord! [*He starts for the barn with
the horse.*]

HELEN. [*With tender appeal, swiftly following him.*] Father,
why won't you ever let Sam tell you—

[MARTIN, *goaded to the breaking point, turns upon* HELEN,
*dropping the halter and allowing the horse to go into the
barn.*]

MARTIN. [*Hardly able to control his rage.*] Look a-here,
Nell! I've had all the words I'm goin' to hev with *you*—
[*Shaking his closed fist threateningly.*] But by the Eternal,
I ain't a-goin' to hev thet fellah a-comin' here preachin' his
infidelity to my family. [*Frantic with rage, he now says more
than he intends to, deliberately and fiercely.*] If you *want*
him, you *take* him, an' clear out!

[SAM *approaches quickly, intensely moved by what* MARTIN
has said.]

SAM. Do you mean that, Mr. Berry?

HELEN. [*Her head high in the air, her whole attitude one*

of noble defiance.] I will! [*As though accepting the challenge.*]

MARTIN. [*Looks at* HELEN, *quite broken, all the fire of his passion in ashes, and murmurs thickly,*] Yeh won't?

HELEN. [*Proudly, her eyes full of burning tears, her voice vibrating with emotion.*] Won't I? You'll see whether I will or not! [*There is a challenge in her voice too.*]

SAM. [*Moving towards* MARTIN, *intensely excited by his words.*] Mr. Berry—if you'll say that again—

MARTIN. [*Springs at* SAM *and clutches him by the throat.*] Damn you!

SAM. [*Swiftly seizes* MARTIN'S *wrist with his left hand, drawing back his right hand to strike.*] Damn you!

HELEN. [*With a cry of terror, covering her face with her hands, calls out appealingly,*] Oh! Sam—don't!
[*The sound of* HELEN'S *voice brings both men to their senses, and they relax their hold upon each other. They stand silent for a moment, both a little ashamed. Then* MARTIN *says in a heartbroken manner,*]

MARTIN. D'yeh mean to steal my child from me?

SAM. [*Quietly, adjusting his collar.*] I'm not going to *steal* her, Mr. Berry—I'm going out West to *earn* her!

MARTIN. [*Speaking through his teeth, vehemently.*] Sam Warren, I hated you afore—but *now* you've shamed me afore my own child. Git off'n my farm an' don't yeh never set foot on't agin— [*Quite low and passionately.*] It's dangerous fer both on us.
[MARTIN *wearily drags himself into the barn.*]
[HELEN *stands dazed and heartbroken.* SAM *leans against the fence, his hands in his pockets, his head bent, deep in thought. There is a moment's pause.*]

[ANN [1] *bustles cheerily out of the house. She is a woman of forty-five, handsome in a wholesome, motherly way. She is dressed in a freshly laundered, becoming calico dress, and her sleeves are rolled up beyond the elbows, showing a pair of shapely arms. She is quick and energetic in all her movements. To her, home is the most desirable place in the world, and she rules it with all the skill and love of a typical American housewife. Her manner is pleasant and happy. She is always smiling and always sees the best side of everything. Nothing disturbs her; she meets all the problems of her daily life with a quiet and unobtrusive efficiency.*]

ANN. Well Helen, I was jes' a-wonderin' what'd become o' you. Sam Warren! I hup Martin hain't seen yeh; I say, hain't seen yeh.

SAM. Yes, he has—

ANN. Didn't he hev a tantrum; I say, a tantrum?

HELEN. [*Concealing her true feelings, listlessly.*] No, Mother, he didn't say much—not as much as—

ANN. I want to know! Well, there must ha' ben sumpthin' powerful on his mind; I say, on his mind.

SAM. I guess there is now, if there wasn't before. [*Sadly.*]

ANN. Well, Nell, blow the horn. Dinner's all sot an' I don't want it to git cold. Sorry I can't ask yeh to stop, Sam; I say, I'm sorry I can't ask yeh to stop. [*She goes into the house.*]

SAM. Thank you, I don't think I'd enjoy the meal. [HELEN *and he look at each other, her eyes fill with tears.*]
[HELEN *goes up to the fence, picks up the horn hanging there and blows it twice. Then she turns back to* SAM, *letting the horn slip from her hand to the ground.*]

[1] *NOTE:* Ann begins all her speeches slowly, increasing in rapidity as she progresses. She is in the habit of repeating the final words of all her speeches emphatically, as though the person she were addressing had not heard her.

SAM. [*Slowly.*] Well, Nell, I suppose you and I might just as well say good-bye now as any time—

HELEN. [*Again quite overcome at the thought of parting with him, holds out her hand, which he takes.*] Good-bye, Sam. [*Cries.*]

SAM. [*Very tenderly.*] Good-bye, Nell. [*Draws her to him.*] Don't cry! I don't know how soon I'll get away, but just as soon as I can I will. I'll try to see you before I go—if not —I'll—

HELEN. [*Pleadingly.*] You can't take me with you, can you, Sam?

SAM. [*Wistfully.*] No, Nell, I can't. I haven't got money enough. I ought to have a hundred dollars more than I've got to get away myself. [*Meditatively.*] I wonder if Blake'd lend me a hundred dollars.

HELEN. [*Still struggling with her tears.*] I wouldn't ask him —he'd only refuse you. [*She breaks down and clings to* SAM *like a child.*] It's going to be awful lonesome—

SAM. [*Deeply moved.*] I know—it's going to be pretty lonesome for me too. There, now— [*Taking both her hands in his.*] I thought this was going to be one of those partings without tears—[*Trying to cheer her up*]—nor promises— nothing but just confidence.

HELEN. [*Making an effort to overcome her grief.*] All right —Sam. [*Lifting her head and taking a deep breath to get hold of herself, bravely but still with a slight break in her voice.*] If I don't see you before you go, good-bye. [*Goes to the house, as if to go inside, stops at the door and turns as though struck by a sudden thought.*] I don't think you'd better come here again, Sam. I don't want to quarrel with Father if I can help it— [*With a note of fatality.*] I'll have to some day I know—but I want to avoid it just as long as I can. [*She smiles and tries to brave it out, but it is plain that she is silently crying.*]

SAM. [*Stands a moment, looking at her tenderly and longingly, as though loth to leave her. He cannot control his own feelings. He turns away abruptly as he says*] Good-bye, Nell, keep up your courage, my girl. And remember, it isn't as though it was forever, you know. [*He goes off right above the house.*]

HELEN. [*Her eyes follow him off.*] Good-bye, Sam. [*Waves her hand as if in response to him and calls after him.*] Take good care of yourself, won't yeh?

SAM. [*Speaking off stage, as though from a little distance.*] I'll take care of myself, you take care of yourself.

[HELEN *turns slowly away and drags herself broken and weary into the house.*]

[*There is a brief pause, then* MARY BERRY, *a lively girl of about 10, comes running from the road, left, into the yard. She has a little bunch of wild flowers in her hand. She is skipping gayly, and just as she is about to enter the house,* BOB BERRY, *a sturdy little fellow of about 8 years with rosy cheeks and dancing eyes, runs on excitedly from the left, with his schoolbooks tied in a strap, and says,*]

BOB. Mary, Mary, take my books in the house, I'm goin' in swimmin'. [*He throws the books into her hands and runs off right, above the house.*]

MARY. [*Calling after him,*] Bob Berry, if you go in swimmin' I'll tell yer Ma.

BOB. [*In the distance, off right.*] Tell if yeh want to—ol' tattle tale.

MARY. [*Running into the house.*] Ma, Ma, Bob's goin' in swimmin'—

[IKE RICHARDS, LEM CONANT, ABE HIGGINS *and* STEVE BAILEY, *farmhands, enter from the left. With them is* TIM HAYES, *the hired man, a good-natured, red-headed Irishman. They are playing with an old football, laughing and scuffling in a friendly way.*]

[GATES, *with* MANDY *in his wake, follows the men on, and watches them, keenly interested.*]

GATES. Give me a kick.

TIM. [*Good-naturedly.*] Let the ould man have a kick. [*The others jeer at this.*]

ABE. He can't kick it, he's too old.

GATES. [*Enraged.*] Too old, am I? You jes' see. [GATES *seizes the ball and gives it a tremendous kick which sends it flying down the road. The men cheer him derisively.* GATES *picks up a chip and puts it on his shoulder.*]

GATES. [*To* ABE, *assuming a defiant attitude.*] If I'm too old, you jes' knock this chip off'n my shoulder.

[ABE *hesitates, but the other men urge him on, at last forcing him into the fight. He and* GATES *have a brief, rough-and-tumble wrestling match, which ends when* GATES *ducks* ABE *in the water trough.*]

[*The men greet* ABE's *defeat with shouts of laughter, and he hurries somewhat sheepishly into the house, followed by the others.* GATES *looks after them, wagging his head triumphantly.*]

GATES. [*Calling after them.*] Too old, am I? They don't build houses like they used to. An' they don't make boys like they used to, nuther! [*With an air of high satisfaction he goes off, down the road, lower right, followed by* MANDY.] [*Enter* UNCLE NAT *along the road, upper right, wheeling* MILLIE *in the barrow.* MILLIE *has a line through the rod of the barrow, and is pretending to drive.*]

UNCLE NAT. [*Talking as he enters.*] An' after that they lived in peace and died in Greece, an' was buried in a pot of honey.

MILLIE. What's the else of it, Uncle Nat?

UNCLE NAT. There ain't no else to it. Besides, this hoss don't do 'nother stroke of work till he gets his oats. [*He wheels the barrow down stage below the bench, right.*]

MILLIE. [*Climbing out.*] Wait till I unhitch yeh—

UNCLE NAT. This is a new fangled hoss. He can hitch himself up and unhitch himself, and currycomb himself and get his own oats, an'—[UNCLE NAT *goes to the trough and starts to wash his hands.*]

MILLIE. [*Following him up to the trough.*] Hossy want a drink?

UNCLE NAT. No—hossy don't want a drink. Hossy wants to wash his hands so thet he can set down to the table like a clean respect'ble hoss. [MILLY *splashes water in his face. He staggers back, pretending to be drenched and shaking the wet off.*] Is thet what yeh call givin' hossy a drink?

MILLIE. [*Chuckling.*] Yep.

UNCLE NAT. Well, the fust thing yeh know, this hoss'll duck yeh in the hoss trough.

MILLIE. No he won't.

UNCLE NAT. Won't he? You jes' see if he won't. [*He talks to* MILLIE *in the manner of one child talking to another.*] You can't throw water in a hossy's face without makin' him mad no more than yeh can give a elephant a chaw o' terbacker without makin' *him* mad. Did yeh ever give a elephant a chaw o' terbacker?

MILLIE. No!

UNCLE NAT. Well, don't yeh try it, cause I knowed a boy in a circus once that give a elephant a chaw o' terbacker, an' he didn't see thet boy agin fer more n' a hundred years. But he jes' remembered it an' he blew water all over him. I tell yeh, elephants has got good memories— [UNCLE NAT *takes a clean bandanna handkerchief out of his pocket and wipes his hands. He is about to enter the house, when he is stopped by the voice of* MARTIN, *who comes from the barn and pauses outside the barnyard gate.*]

[MILLIE *resumes her play in the sand.*]

MARTIN. [*Casually.*] Nathan'l.

UNCLE NAT. [*Kindly.*] Hello, Martin.

MARTIN. Be yeh hungry?

UNCLE NAT. [*Still mechanically wiping his hands.*] Not powerful, but able to git away with my rayshuns 'thout no coaxin' I guess. Why? [*Taking a step towards* MARTIN.]

MARTIN. [*Still casually.*] 'Cause I'd like to talk to yeh— [*Studying his face closely*]—an' I d'know's I'll hev a better chance.

UNCLE NAT. [*Cheerily; putting his handkerchief back in his pocket.*] I d'know's yeh will, Martin. [*He moves a few steps down right;* MARTIN *is up left centre near the barnyard.*]

MARTIN. [*Hesitates, picks up a stick, takes out a jackknife and whittles it, looking intently at the stick and walking down a few steps towards* UNCLE NAT. *He seems rather to dread saying what is on his mind.* UNCLE NAT *looks at him furtively; this unusual request puzzles him; he is apprehensive that it is of* HELEN *and* BLAKE *that his brother wishes to talk, and a look of disapproval sweeps into his eyes. His face grows a bit stern, but his manner is kindly and attentive. After a pause* MARTIN *blurts out abruptly,*] Mr. Blake's been here.

UNCLE NAT. [*Gazes at him curiously, looks off right as if he could still see* BLAKE'S *buggy there, picks up a straw and chews it, and says carelessly,*] Hez 'e? [*Seats himself on the wheelbarrow.*]

MARTIN. [*Seating himself on the stable bucket which he has turned bottom upward.*] Yes. He argues that we'd ought to cut the farm up into buildin' lots.

UNCLE NAT. [*Is dazed by this. It is so sudden and unexpected that he scarcely gets its full meaning, as he murmurs in a low tense voice,*] Dooze 'e?

MARTIN. Y-e-s. He says there's a boom a-comin' an' the land's too val'able to work.

UNCLE NAT. [*Murmurs mechanically,*] Dooze—'e—?

MARTIN. Yes. He wants I should pool in with him, an' build cottages an' sell 'em at a hundred per cent more'n they cost, an' git's rich's Jay Gould.

[*Slowly it comes to* UNCLE NAT *that his brother is saying—* "*Sell the farm.*" *He grows cold—there is a heavy painful lump where his heart was beating a moment ago. His eyes grow dim and tired—there is no sunshine—no more music in the day. Sell the farm—the dear fields with all their slopes and undulations, the great old silver birches guarding the orchard from the pastures, the gnarled oaks along the rocky shore. He knows in a thousand aspects this old farm, summer and winter, always affable and friendly to him, and it is here he has learned to know God and love him. He answers casually enough in a tone of wonderment,*]

UNCLE NAT. I want t' know 'f he dooze. [*A moment's pause.*] Where d's he talk o' beginnin'?

MARTIN. [*Blurting out half defiantly, half shamefacedly.*] Out there at th' north end o' the shore front—an' work back t' his line.

UNCLE NAT. [*The numbness passes and there is a tingling in his veins. Tense set lines come into his face and his voice grows vital. He talks with his usual clear cadence and gentle rhythm.*] Yeh don't mean up yonder? [*Pointing with his thumb over his shoulder, right.* MARTIN *looks up and nods.*] Not up at the ol' pastur'?

MARTIN. [*Slowly.*] Y—e—s—

UNCLE NAT. [*In a tense voice.*] Dooze 'e calk'late to take in the knoll thet looks out t'Al'gator Reef?

MARTIN. [*As before.*] Y-e-s—I s'pose he—dooze.

UNCLE NAT. [*Rising, speaking quietly, but with a quiver of smothered feeling in his voice.*] Did yeh tell him—'bout—Mother's bein' buried there—?

MARTIN. [*Sulkily.*] He knows all 'bout thet jes' as well as you do.

UNCLE NAT. [*With significance, but very simply.*] Dooze.
Well—what's he calk'late to do with Mother?

MARTIN. He advises puttin' on her in a cimitery up to Bangor.

UNCLE NAT. [*A deprecating shadowy smile flits across his face; he shakes his head slowly and replies,*] She'd never sleep comfort'ble in no cimitery, Martin—Mother wouldn't.

MARTIN. Blake says thet's the choice bit o' the hull pa'sell.

UNCLE NAT. [*Gently persuasive.*] Then who's got so good a right to it as Mother has? Yeh don't begrutch it to her, do yeh, Martin?

MARTIN. I don't begrutch nothin'. Only, Blake says folks ain't a-goin' to pay fancy prices fer lots 'thout they hev their pick.

UNCLE NAT. [*Gently reproachful.*] D'ye think any fancy price had ought to buy Mother's grave, Martin?

MARTIN. Thet's sent'mint!

UNCLE NAT. [*As though rebuked.*] Is it?

MARTIN. Yes, it is—Blake says—

UNCLE NAT. [*Nodding his head, with a little sad, half-smile.*] Dooze—well— [*He sighs.*] P'r'aps 'tis— [*There is a pause; then, as though a flood of memories had suddenly rushed over him.*] You don't rec'llect much about Father—do yeh, Martin?

MARTIN. No.

UNCLE NAT. You was so young—[*His eyes look far off down the years, and he tells the story simply and directly and the clear cadence and soft rhythm are like the colours in a picture*]—a baby a'most, the evenin' him an' Si Leech was lost tryin' to save the crew o' thet 'ere brig—thet went to pieces on the reef yonder. [*Indicates over his shoulder with a nod of his head.*]

MARTIN. [*Under the spell of* UNCLE NAT'S *mood, is touched, and replies very gently,*] No. Mother'n you never seemed to care to talk much about thet.

UNCLE NAT. Mother an' me seen the hull thing from the p'int o' thet 'ere knoll— [*With a slight indication of his head over his shoulder.*] After it was all over she sent me hum—told me to take care o' you—said thet I needn't come back—thet she'd stay there an' wait fer him. 'Twa'n't no use t'argy with Mother, y'know, an' so I went. I put you in yer cradle an' sot down alongside o' yeh. I'd know as I ever passed jes' sich a night—seemed s'kinder l-o-n-g. [*Pause.*] Jes' as soon as it was light enough to see—I went back to find out what'd come o' her—I didn't know but what she might hev—but she hadn't—she was there—jes' where I left her—I don't believe she'd moved an inch the hull night. It had been a-rainin'— [*Pause.*] Her eyes was sot in her head and starin' right out to sea—ef I'd 'a' met her any other place but there, I swear I wouldn't 'a' know'd 'r. I took her by the hand to sort o' coax 'r away, "Nathan'l," she says, "when I die—I want yeh should bury me right here on this spot—so's ef Father ever *dooze* come back—he'll find me waitin' fer him." I hed to turn 'round an' look at 'er—her voice sounded so kinder strange—seemed as ef it come from way off somewheres. [*Pause.*] She lived a good many years after thet— but I don't believe she ever missed a day 'thout goin' over t' thet knoll. I allus sort o' imagined she wa'n't never jes' right in her head after thet night. [UNCLE NAT *is lost in memories for a moment. Then catching his breath and pulling himself together, he continues,*] Well, Martin, there she is. We buried her there at last—you an' me did. I d'know, but seems to me—ef I was you—I'd kinder hate to sell thet fer a buildin' lot. Thet is, I'd want to be pooty partic'lar who I sold it to.

MARTIN. [*In the manner of a spoilt child, closing his knife with a sharp click.*] I'm tired o' lightkeepin'.

UNCLE NAT. [*Warmly, with quick understanding.*] I don't

blame yeh. Why didn't yeh say thet afore? Yeh needn't do
it no longer. Tim an' me kin take keer o' the light jes' as
well's not. I only sort o' hang onto it 'cause father had it put
there, an' the Gover'ment named it after him—he used to
think so much o' that.

MARTIN. [*Defending himself.*] You *give* me your interest
in the farm anyhow—made it all over to me the day I was
married.

UNCLE NAT. [*Warmly with a fine spirit of conciliation.*] I
know it an' I hain't never regretted it. I ain't a-regrettin'
of it now.

MARTIN. [*Peevishly.*] You seem to kind o' shameface me
for wantin' to sell it.

UNCLE NAT. Didn't mean to, Martin—it's only nat'ral thet I
should feel kind o' bad to see the ol' place cut up—but law
sakes! Who'm I thet I should set my face agin improvements
I'd like to know?—[*Laughs.*] You've got a wife, an' children, an' a family, an' all thet. Mr. Blake mus' be right. So
go 'head an' build, an' git rich, an' move up to Boston ef yeh
want to. Only, Martin—don't sell thet. [*Indicating over his
shoulder, right, with his head.*] Leave me thet, an' I'll build
on't an' stay an' take keer o' th' light, as long's I kin—an'
after thet—why—well, after thet—yeh kin put both on us
in a cimitery ef yeh hev a mind to.

[*His voice trails off into silence.* MARTIN *stands downcast.*
UNCLE NAT *remains immovable, self-hypnotised by the recital
of his story—somehow all the sting of it has passed and he is
at peace. He is still contemplating the remote days of his boyhood, and he stands there picking a bit of string into fine
shreds too deeply absorbed to be aware of the life about him.*]

[MILLIE *is lying asleep on the sand.*]

[ANN *enters briskly from the house.*]

ANN. Sakes alive! Martin Berry, ain't you a-comin' to yer

dinner to-day? I say to-day? [*Goes up centre and looks off right.*]

MARTIN. [*Slowly, starting towards house.*] Yes, I was jest a-comin'. [*As he crosses to the house, he says very gently,*] Nathan'l, dinner's waitin'. [*He goes slowly and thoughtfully into the house.*]

ANN. [*Looking up the road and calling,*] Bob—B-o-b! Bob B-e-r-r-y— Come out o' thet water— Come to yer dinner! —Yer back'll be all blistered! [*She sees* MILLIE *lying asleep and goes down to her.*] Bless thet child, she's clean fagged out! Come to Ma, precious. [*She takes* MILLIE *tenderly in her arms.*] Come Nathan'l, your dinner'll be stun cold. I say stun cold. [*She goes into the house with the child.*]

[UNCLE NAT *stands deep in meditation.*]

THE CURTAIN DESCENDS SLOWLY

ACT SECOND

"The Silver Weddin'"

The *Berry farmhouse kitchen.*

SCENE: *A quaint old New England farmhouse kitchen of the better class, used partly as a living room. There is a large window centre, full of pots of growing flowers. Beneath the window is a table upon which* HELEN *places cups and saucers and from which she serves tea during the dinner. To the right of the window is a wooden sink with an old-fashioned hand pump, and there is a large stove to the left of the window, upon which a kettle is boiling and pots are stewing. Behind it is a woodbox. On the shelf back of the stove stands an old-fashioned cuckoo clock.*

A sturdy old open stairway is against the left wall, and at the back of it is a row of pegs, where hang UNCLE NAT'S *old army coat and cap, and* HELEN'S *jacket and tam-o'-shanter. There is a door leading to the woodhouse to the left of the stove. Standing parallel to the stairs is a long dining table, covered with a white linen cloth. Against the side of the stairs is a heavy old-fashioned mahogany sideboard, from which* HELEN *later takes small articles, such as tumblers, and salt and pepper holders. At the foot of the stairs a door opens into the sitting room. There is a worktable, right, below the sink, covered with material for making bread, and on it are several loaves of bread fresh from the oven. Below the worktable is a door leading outside. To the right, between the door and the sink is an alcove where stands a large old-fashioned dresser, holding dishes, pans, and various kitchen furnishings, also several large pies.*

At the rise of the curtain, ANN, HELEN *and* PERLEY *are in the midst of extensive preparations for dinner.* MILLIE *is down*

44

right, by a chair, making doll's bread, very intent on her work. ANN *is hot and flustered. She is dressed in an old-fashioned black silk dress, open at the neck, with a white lace collar. The skirt is pinned up, showing a white petticoat underneath trimmed with home-made lace, and there is a big white apron over all.* PERLEY *is cool and unconcerned.* MARY *and* BOB, *with aprons over their best clothes, are sitting on the stairs, polishing spoons and forks.* HELEN *is setting the table. She is dressed daintily in a simple muslin frock, and also wears a large apron to protect her dress. She is grave and thoughtful; the memory of the encounter with her father is still sharp upon her. She moves about, doing her work with swift deft touches.*

ANN. [*At the stove, stirring the cranberry sauce.*] Sakes alive! I hup another silver weddin' won't come in this house in a hurry; I say, in a hurry. [*She goes to the table, and starts sharpening a carving knife, preparatory to cutting a large loaf of bread which is on the table.*]

HELEN. [*At the foot of the table, as she finishes placing the knives and forks.*] Ma, I've arranged all the presents on the centre table. [*Smiling. She is very tender and sympathetic in her attitude towards her mother.*] The sitting room looks like a jewelry store. [*She goes to the sideboard, left, and takes from it a glass jar holding teaspoons, and places it on the centre of the table.*]

MARY. Oh, let's go'n see! [*Runs off into the sitting room.*]

BOB. Yes, let's do. [*Follows* MARY.]

HELEN. Aren't you proud of them, Mother?

ANN. [*Seriously.*] Helen, you know what the Bible says about pride's one day havin' a fall. No, I ain't proud. [*Turning and coming down slowly towards the centre of the stage, absentmindedly drawing the carving knife across the steel as she talks.*] Of course, it's nice to be so remembered by everybody, an' there's a good many nice presents there—some I ben a-wishin' fer. But I think I value yourn an' the young uns an' Nathan'l's an' Martin's the best o' the lot. Not thet I ain't grateful, but, somehow, the nearer— [*Fills up, hastily brushes away a tear with the back of her hand, and turns to the stove to hide her emotion. Lifts the griddle and pokes the fire.*] How like the Ol' Harry this fire dooze burn! Seems es ef everythin' went agin me to-day; I say, to-day. [*Calls.*] Tim! [*To* PERLEY, *sharply.*] Tell Tim I want him. [*Puts the griddle back on the stove, and closes the damper.*]

[PERLEY *goes down to the door, right, opens it, and calls* TIM, *each time in a different and higher key.*]

PERLEY. Ti-m—T-i-m—T-i-i-m-m—

TIM [*Outside, in the distance.*] More power to ye, but it's the foine loongs ye have in ye! Fwat is it?

PERLEY. Mis' Berry wants y-o-u. [*Goes back to her work.*]

ANN. [*To* PERLEY, *handing her a saucepan of potatoes.*] Mash them 'taters; I say, mash them 'taters.

[PERLEY *gets the potato masher, takes the pan of potatoes to the sink, peels and mashes them, adding butter, salt and a little milk.*]

[TIM *appears at the door in his shirt sleeves.*]

TIM. Fwat is it, ye Andhrewscoggin' mermaid, ye? [*He starts to come into the room.*]

ANN. [*Stopping him, peremptorily.*] Scrape yer feet, Tim Hayes, an' don't track the hull cow shed over my clean floor; I say, clean floor. [*She is standing near the window, centre.*]

TIM. [*Wipes his feet on the door mat, and speaks ingratiatingly.*] Yis ma'am. I will ma'am. Fwat can I do for ye?

ANN. I want you should split me a handful of fine wood; this 'ere fire's actin' like the very Ol' Nick to-day; I say, to-day.

[TIM *goes into the woodhouse, and reappears almost immediately with a handful of small wood which he gives to* ANN, *who puts a few pieces on the fire. He returns to the*

*woodhouse and during the next scene he is heard splitting
wood.*]

PERLEY. [*Who has now finished mashing the potatoes;
speaking through* TIM'S *business.*] What yeh want I should
do 'th these 'ere 'taters?

ANN. Put 'em in a veg'table dish an' set 'em in the ov'n to
brown; I say, to brown.

[PERLEY *puts the potatoes into a vegetable dish, smooths
them over, shakes two or three spots of pepper on them, and
puts them in the oven. She takes plenty of time over this.*]

[ANN *stirs the cranberries, tastes them, lifts up the kettle and
sets it back, and puts the griddle on the hole.*]

[UNCLE NAT *appears at the top of the stairs, dressed in a
new "store" suit. He looks very important and proud, and
glances down expecting all eyes to be upon him, but nobody
notices him. He comes down a few steps. His new boots hurt
him, and he pauses and bends his feet on the toes, as if to
ease the boots, murmuring to himself "Gosh, but these shoes
do hurt!" He straightens up, comes down a few more steps,
and again eases his right boot and, making a wry face, he
slips his foot partly out of the boot, and finishes the descent
limping, but with a comfortable sense of relief. When he is
well towards the left centre of the stage, he stands, anxious
to be noticed.*]

UNCLE NAT. [*In a jubilant tone.*] Well, Helen, I got 'em on!

HELEN. [*Coming down to his left, and speaking delightedly.*]
Oh Uncle Nat! Ma, look! Isn't he sweet?

ANN. [*Stops in her work at the table in front of the window, and comes down right of him.*] Well Nathan'l, how nice
you do look; I say, look.

[PERLEY *comes forward a few steps and gazes at him admiringly.*]

UNCLE NAT. How do they fit me?

ANN. Jes' es ef they was made—

HELEN. [*More critically.*] Turn round, Uncle Nat. [*He does so with an air of great importance, and is very happy over the impression he is creating, for it is many a long day since he had a new suit of clothes.* HELEN *smooths the back of his coat down with her hand.*] The waist might be a trifle longer. Don't you think so, Ma?

ANN. [*Inspecting him carefully with her arms on her hips.*] Oh! Do you think so? Seems to me's ef 'twas meant to be jes' thet way. [*Goes back to the stove.*] I say, jes' thet way.

HELEN. Well, maybe it was. [*A pause. She returns to her work at the table.*]

UNCLE NAT. [*Fingering his vest.*] Helen, there's a button come off this vest a'ready. I guess they're jes' stuck on. I wish you'd sew 'em on with thread, by 'n' by.

HELEN. All right, Uncle Nat, good strong thread.

UNCLE NAT. [*With a complete change of manner, full of businesslike importance.*] Well, how be yeh gettin' along— I hope yeh hain't sp'ilt nothin' sence I ben away. Helen, will you get me my apron. [*He takes off his coat and places it carefully over the back of a chair, and comes down centre.* HELEN *gets him a woman's checked apron.*] I want you should tie it in a bowknot so that when the company comes, I can get it off handy. [*He stands with arms outstretched;* HELEN *ties the apron around him just beneath his shoulders. He pushes it down.*] Not too high-waisted, not too high-waisted. [*He pushes his foot back into the boot and limps to the stove.*] How's the ol' cranberries gettin' on? [*Slight pause.*] Who sot these cranberries on the back of the stove? [*Looks around at them all accusingly.*] Don't yeh know nothin' in this house, or don't yeh? [*Lifts up the saucepan and puts it on the front of the stove. Tastes the cranberries, and says reproachfully,*] Oh Ma, I'm sorry yeh put more sugar in the cranberries, yeh got 'em too sweet. I had 'em jes' right when I left 'em. [*Nobody answers.*] Ma, did you put any more sugar in them cranberries?

ANN. [*Busy at the table, right, speaking over her shoulder.*]
I didn't put no more sugar in 'em.

UNCLE NAT. Well somebody has. Helen, did you put any
more sugar in them cranberries?

HELEN. No, Uncle Nat.

UNCLE NAT. Well, somebody did. [*Turning to* PERLEY *in an
accusing manner.*] Perley, did you put any more sugar in
them cranberries?

PERLEY. [*A little resentfully, drawling.*] I hain't teched 'em.

UNCLE NAT. [*Testily, imitating her drawl.*] Well, *some*body's
teched 'em. Cranberries couldn't walk off the stove and get
into the sugar bucket by themselves.

PERLEY. They wuz a-scorchin', an' I sot 'em back, thet's all
I done.

UNCLE NAT. [*In disgust.*] Well I wish you'd let 'em alone.
I'd ruther have I don't know what around me than a lot of
women when I'm a-cookin' of a dinner. [*Taking the saucepan off the stove, and setting it in the sink.*] Nell, dish out
them cranberries and set 'em t' cool some place 'r other, will
yeh?

HELEN. Yes, in a minute. [*Gets a preserve dish from the alcove, dishes out the berries, and sets them on the table at
the window.*]
[BOB *runs on from the sitting room.*]

BOB. Ma, can we play store with the presents?

ANN. Yes, play with 'em all you like, but don't break any of
'em; I say, don't break any of 'em.

BOB. Oh, we won't break 'em. [*Runs off.*] Mary! Mary! Ma
says we can play with 'em.

UNCLE NAT. [*With happy expectancy.*] Now, les' see how the
ol' turkey's a-gettin' on. [*Goes over to the stove, sees the
damper is shut, and says indignantly,*] Now, in the name of

common sense, who shut up thet damper! [*Opens the damper with a jerk.*]

ANN. Yeh must 'a' done it yerself.

UNCLE NAT. Upon my word, a man can't leave a stove out of his hands five minutes without somebody a-foolin' with it. [*He opens the oven door and looks at the turkey, his face aglow with admiration. They all stand around him, very much interested.*] By George, ain't he a beauty? [*In a grieved tone.*] Who turned him on his back? I had him on his side.

HELEN. You want him to brown all over, don't you?

UNCLE NAT. See here, who's cookin' this turkey, you or me? [*Smacking his lips.*] Get the platter, he's done. Ef he stays in there any longer, he'll be burned to a crisp. [HELEN *gets a platter from the dresser.*] Ma, you get me a dishtowel. [ANN *gives him a dishtowel. All is bustle and excitement as he lifts out the dripping pan, and sets it on top of the stove.* UNCLE NAT *is left and the women are right of the stove.*]
[TIM *comes in from the woodhouse with an armful of wood, both large and small pieces, which he dumps into the woodbox, afterwards brushing the chips which cling to his sleeve into the box. He stands and looks admiringly at the turkey.*]

UNCLE NAT. [*Glowing with pride.*] What do you think of thet for a turkey, eh Tim?

TIM. As they say in ould Ireland, that's a burrd!
[*He goes over to* PERLEY, *who stands near the sink, right, throws his arm around her, and hugs her roughly and quickly. She hits him with a dishcloth, and he runs out down right, laughing, followed by* PERLEY *hitting the air with the dishcloth, trying to reach him. After he goes, she returns coolly to her work at the sink. This byplay is unnoticed by the others, who are intent on the turkey.*]

UNCLE NAT. [*To* ANN *and* HELEN, *chuckling; speaking through* TIM's *business.*] I wonder what they call a turkey in Ireland, a critter? Give me a large fork. [HELEN *gives him one.*] Now a big spoon. [ANN *gives him one.*]

ANN. [*As* UNCLE NAT *starts to lift the turkey out with the fork and spoon.*] Be careful. Don't stick the fork into the turkey; ef you break the skin, the juice'll all run out; I say, run out.

HELEN. Be careful, Uncle Nat, don't drop him.

UNCLE NAT. [*Puts the turkey back in the pan, turns from one woman to the other, and says with gentle exasperation,*] Say, if you can find anythin' to do about the house, I wish you'd go an' do it an' leave me alone. Yeh've got me s'nervous, I don't know whether I'm standin' on my head or my heels. [*Gets the turkey into the platter, and says joyously*] There he is! Now put him in the oven to keep warm, while I make the gravy. [*Proceeds to stir the gravy in the dripping pan.*] Nell, pour a little water in there, careful now. [*She pours some into the pan from the tea kettle.*] Thet's enough. Thet'll do— Thet'll do! [*He pushes the kettle spout up.*]

HELEN. [*Protesting.*] Why, Uncle Nat, you won't have half gravy enough! [*Attempts to pour more in.*] Ma, I wish you'd look at this.

UNCLE NAT. [*Turning to* ANN.] Ma, you attend to your own business.

[*While* UNCLE NAT *is talking to* ANN, HELEN *pours more water into the pan.* UNCLE NAT *turns and sees her doing it, and he pushes the spout up and burns his fingers.* HELEN *drops the kettle on the stove.*]

UNCLE NAT. Now you've done it, Nell! You've got enough gravy to sail a boat in. [*Blowing his scalded fingers.*]

HELEN. Well, you want to thicken it with some flour, don't you? Here! [*She takes the dredging box and sifts in the flour.*]

UNCLE NAT. [*Making the best of it, stirs in the flour as she sifts.*] Thet'll do— Thet'll do— Thet'll do! Do you want to make a paste of it? Oh, Nell, don't put so much in, you've got it all full o' lumps now. [*Unconsciously blowing his scalded fingers, holding them up in the air, and then again blowing them.*]

HELEN. All right, Uncle Nat. Make the gravy yourself. [*She returns to her work.*]

UNCLE NAT. [*After a slight pause. He is now stirring the gravy.*] Now gimme the giblets, an' I'll stir 'em in an' make the giblet sass. [*There is no answer. He speaks a little louder.*] I say, some one o' yeh gimme the giblets, an' I'll make the giblet sass. [*The three women stop in their work and look at one another, as if to say "What are we going to do now?"*] Come, hurry up! [*A pause,* UNCLE NAT *blows his fingers.*] Gimme the giblets I tell you! [*Silence.* HELEN *crosses over to* PERLEY. UNCLE NAT *gets impatient.*] Will yeh gimme the giblets, Ma?

ANN. I don't know where they be.

UNCLE NAT. They're in the choppin' tray, wherever you stuck it.

ANN. [*Holding up the empty chopping tray, and showing it to him.*] No they ain't nuther; I say, nuther.

UNCLE NAT. [*As he continues to stir the gravy.*] Well, they was there. What yeh done with 'em?

ANN. I hain't done nothin' with 'em.

UNCLE NAT. [*Getting testy again.*] Well, *some*body's done suthin' with 'em. [*Turning to* HELEN.] Hev you seen 'em, Nell?

HELEN. No, Uncle Nat.

UNCLE NAT. Well, *somebody's* seen 'em. [*Turning to* PERLEY, *accusingly.*] Perley, hev you been a-monkeyin' with them giblets?

PERLEY. [*Who has been trying to escape observation by vio-*

lontly scouring a pan at the sink, blurts out.] I fed 'em to the chickings.

UNCLE NAT. [*Dropping the spoon with utter exasperation.*] Well, of all the durn gawks I ever see you beat all! Thet ends the dinner! No giblet sass. Me a-settin' down fer half an hour a-choppin' giblets fer you to feed to the chickings. Perley, yeh're a nateral born gawk.

ANN. [*Crossing to the table.*] Oh, Nathan'l, give me a hand with this table, will yeh?

UNCLE NAT. [*Going to the lower end of the table.*] What yeh want to do with it, Ma?

ANN. Oh, jes' set it out a piece from the stair.

UNCLE NAT. [*As they move the table slightly towards centre.*] Be keerful, Ma, it fell down last Washin'ton's birthday. [*Crossing to the window and looking out.*] Looks a leetle like a shower. I hope it won't keep any of the company away.

ANN. Oh, I guess not. They ain't nuther sugar nor salt; I say, nuther sugar nor salt.

[MILLIE *by this time has made all the dough into little loaves on a tin plate, and she now takes the plate to* ANN. *She has managed to get herself pretty well messed up with flour.*]

MILLIE. Mama, please bake this for dolly'n me.

ANN. Powers above! Look at thet child! What'n the name of all possessed hev yeh ben a-doin' with yerself? I say, a-doin' with yerself?

MILLIE. Makin' bwead for dolly 'n me.

ANN. [*Smiling indulgently.*] Well, I should say you hed. Nathan'l, tend to thet baby; I say, thet baby. [*She takes the plate of dough from* MILLIE.]
[*During the following scene,* ANN, HELEN *and* PERLEY *busy themselves with the dinner things.*]

UNCLE NAT. Yes, ef I didn't tend to her, I'd like to know who would. [*Crosses to the sink, takes a clean towel and pumps water on one end of it. He then goes centre to* MILLIE.] Upon my word, Millie, this is too bad. Here's company a-comin' and you think we've got nothin' to do but run after you young uns every five minutes of the day. We put yeh all three this mornin'—why didn't yeh stay put? Mussy, mussy, mussy, what a dirty child!

MILLIE. That ain't dirt, it's bwead.

UNCLE NAT. [*Getting down on his knees, and beginning to clean her hands with the wet end of the towel.*] Well, it's mighty dirty bread. Who'd yeh 'spose'd eat bread from such dirty hands as those? Who you makin' bread fer?

MILLIE. Dolly.

UNCLE NAT. [*Drying her hands.*] Well, it's a good thing that dolly's only got one eye. She'd never eat bread from such dirty hands, not unless you kept it on the blind side of her. [*Washing her face.*] My sakes alive, why, you'd scare all Mama's visitors out o' th' house with such a dirty face.

MILLIE. [*Talking through the towel.*] Bob's got a false face.

UNCLE NAT. What's that?

MILLIE. Bob's got a false face.

UNCLE NAT. [*Drying her face.*] Hez he?

MILLIE. Yes. [*Talking through the towel.*] I wish you'd buy me a false face, will yeh, Uncle Nat?

UNCLE NAT. You don't want no false face, you want yer own sweet pooty little clean face. [*Kisses her.*] Now shake yer frock. [*She shakes it in his face.*] Don't shake it in my face. Stand over there and shake it.

MILLIE. Ain't I a nice clean child now, Uncle Nat?

UNCLE NAT. You're the nicest cleanest child in the hull State of Maine.

[*As* UNCLE NAT *finishes making* MILLIE *tidy, the noise of*

*approaching wagons is heard in the distance, and now all
the guests except* BLAKE *arrive outside, amid great bustle and
laughter, as if they had finished the journey in a race. Instantly all is excitement indoors.*]

UNCLE NAT. Hello, Ann, here they be! [*Crosses up left.*]
Helen, take my apron off. [*She does so.* UNCLE NAT *puts on
his coat quickly, and hurries off, right, leaving the door open.
He is heard greeting the guests outside.*]

ANN. Mussy on me, an' I ain't fit to be seen to a nigger clambake; I say, clambake! [*She takes her apron off.* HELEN
unpins her dress, and smooths it down.]

[HELEN *and* PERLEY *go to the window.* BOB *and* MARY *run
in from the sitting room.* MILLIE *goes to the door, right.*]

CAPTAIN BEN [*Outside.*] Hello, Nathan'l— Many happy returns o' the day!

UNCLE NAT. [*Outside.*] Don't git things mixed, Cap'n. This
ain't *my* fun'ral. [*All laugh.*] Step right in. Tim an' me'll
take care o' the hosses.

[*All the guests enter together, laughing and talking.* CAPTAIN
BEN HUTCHINS *comes first. He is a jolly man of about fifty,
half-farmer, half-skipper, with iron-grey hair and a full
beard; he wears a blue suit with brass buttons and a peaked
cap. He is accompanied by* LIDDY ANN NYE, *a motherly
widow in half-mourning. They are followed by* SQUIRE AN-
DREWS, *a very tall, wiry, distinguished-looking man about
seventy-five. He is well-preserved, and has very grey hair
and a pink face. He is very deaf, and carries a tin ear--
trumpet which has seen much service. With him is* MRS. AN-
DREWS, *a tall woman with white hair; she is dressed in good
taste. The* DOCTOR, MRS. LEONARD, *and the* TWINS *enter last.
The* DOCTOR *is a genial country physician. His wife is a trifle
overdressed; as her husband is a professional man, she feels
a bit above the farmers' wives. The twins are nicely dressed;
the boy is in knickerbockers, and the little girl wears a white*

dress, trimmed with lace. The DOCTOR *and the boy take off their hats as they enter. All the guests scrape their feet on the mat. They all speak at once.*]

DOCTOR. Many happy returns of the day, Mrs. Berry!

MRS. LEONARD. Returns of the day, Mrs. Berry, I'm sure.

SQUIRE ANDREWS. Many happy returns of the day, Mis' Berry!

MRS. ANDREWS. I wish you many happy returns of the day.

CAPTAIN BEN. May ye live another twenty-five years, an' invite us all agin.

MRS. NYE. Well, Ann, I swan yeh look younger'n yeh did twenty-five years ago, an' no wonder!
[*As they speak, they are all endeavouring to shake* ANN *by the hand.*]

ANN. [*Shaking hands with them all, excited and happy.*] Don't come near me, if you don't want to get yer clothes spattered. This ol' stove sputters like I'd know what today. I'm greasier'n a pig. I'm 'bleeged t'yeh all fer comin'; I say, fer comin'.

CAPTAIN BEN. Oh! Ketch any of us missin' one o' *your* dinners! [*All laugh.*] I was tellin' Mis' Nye thet ef I had a cook like you aboard the "Liddy Ann," I'd stay t' sea the year 'round. [*Laughs.*]

MRS. ANDREWS. The boot's on the other leg. We're obleeged to *you* fer askin' of us.

SQUIRE ANDREWS. [*With the horn at his ear.*] What do you say?

MRS. ANDREWS. [*Through the trumpet.*] I said Mis' Berry's lookin' well.

SQUIRE ANDREWS. Oh yes—she allus looks well.

ANN. Well, ef you'll all step into the settin' room an' lay

off yer things, I'll run upstairs an' try to make the *bride* presentable.

ALL. [*Laughing.*] Certainly, certainly, by all means! [*They all go off through the door leading to the sitting room.*]

ANN. Children, take the twins in an' show 'em the presents, an' let 'em look at yer noo red albyum. [*She goes upstairs followed by* PERLEY.]

[BOB *and* MARY, *one on each side of the* TWINS, *lead them by the hand in the direction of the sitting room. The* DOCTOR, *who is going out last, is stopped by* MILLIE, *who has a dilapidated doll, with no clothes, no hair, one eye, one arm and half a leg gone, in her arms.*]

MILLIE. Tan 'oo ture my dolly, Doctor?

DOCTOR. Cure your dolly? I guess so. What appears to be the matter with her? [*Taking the doll, and entering into the mood of the child.*]

MILLIE. She's sick.

DOCTOR. Sick! [*Looking the doll over.*] I should say she was. What's come of her other eye?

MILLIE. She swallowed it, an' it's down in her little tummick.

DOCTOR. Is *that* so? My, My! She *is* in a bad way. Well, come along, and let's see what we can do for her. [*He goes out after the others, leading* MILLIE.]
[*During this scene,* HELEN *has been busying herself with the table, putting on the bread, butter, cranberry sauce, etc.*]
[MARTIN *and* BLAKE *enter through the door, right.* BLAKE *is in his best black suit, and* MARTIN *is dressed in his Sunday clothes.*]

MARTIN. [*Speaking as he comes in.*] Where's Ma, Helen? [*Crosses over to the row of pegs at the back of the stairs and hangs up his hat.*]

HELEN. [*Coldly.*] She'll be here in a minute. [*Shows that*

*she and her father have not been on the best of terms since
the quarrel with* SAM. *She is not rude, however.*]
[*As* BLAKE *notices* HELEN'S *manner, he draws back and
pretends to be wiping his feet on the doormat, so as not to
hear what passes. He does not enter the room until* MARTIN
crosses the stage for his exit.]

MARTIN. [*Pauses, and looks at* HELEN.] Hain't you got over
the sulks yet?

HELEN. I'm not in any *sulks,* but I can't laugh when you
stick pins in me. [*She crosses over to the stove, kneels down,
opens the oven door and looks at the turkey.*]

MARTIN. I don't want to stick pins into yeh, Nell. You give
up Sam Warren, an' you an' me'll never have a word.

HELEN. [*Speaking over her shoulder and temporarily stopping her work, trying to hide her feelings.*] He'll not trouble
any of us much longer, I guess.

MARTIN. [*Pleased.*] Hev yeh forbid him a-seein' of yeh?

HELEN. *You* have, haven't you?

MARTIN. Yes.

HELEN. Well?

MARTIN. An' ef he knows when he's well off, he'll do as I
say. Company's come, I see.

HELEN. [*Rising.*] Yes, they're in the sitting room.

MARTIN. [*As he goes out, left.*] Come along, Mr. Blake.

BLAKE. I'll be there in a minute.
[*As* MARTIN *reaches the sitting room, he is heard saying
genially,*]

MARTIN. Be yeh all here?

THE GUESTS. [*Outside.*] Many happy returns of the day!

BLAKE. [*Whose eyes have been fixed on* HELEN *from the
moment he entered.*] Well, Helen!

HELEN. [*Pleasantly, but distantly.*] How do you do, Mr. Blake.

[*During this scene,* HELEN *goes to the sideboard, gets the tumblers and salt cellars, and begins arranging them on the table. She is at the left of the table;* BLAKE *stands right centre.*]

BLAKE. I suppose you'll be hevin' a silver weddin' of your own one o' these days, eh?

HELEN. [*Carelessly.*] I don't know, I'm sure.

BLAKE. Did Sam tell yeh about wantin' to borry a hundred dollars o' me?

HELEN. [*Interested for the first time.*] No. When?

BLAKE. Yesterday afternoon.

HELEN. [*Eagerly.*] Did you lend it to him?

BLAKE. No, but I told him I'd give him a thousand if he'd pick a fuss with you, clear out, an' promise never to come back.

HELEN. [*Smiling scornfully.*] What'd he say?

BLAKE. [*Pauses deprecatingly.*] Said he'd—see me in Hell fust.

HELEN. H'm! [*As if to say "I knew he'd say just that." She turns and busies herself near the head of the table.*]

CAPTAIN BEN. [*Outside.*] I said fifty fathom.

THE GUESTS. [*Outside.*] Oh! We didn't understand yeh, Cap'n Ben.

BLAKE. [*Insinuatingly.*] Has yer father said anything to yeh about me *lately?*

HELEN. [*With a bitter little laugh.*] No, he doesn't say much to me *lately* about anything, or anybody.

BLAKE. Well! I've got the biggest scheme fer gettin' him an' me rich! I'll tell you what I'll do with you,

HELEN. [*Proudly.*] I don't want you should do anything with me, Mr. Blake. [*Crosses to the dresser, right.*]

BLAKE. Your father's set his mind on you an' me gettin' married, y'know.

HELEN. My father had better mind his own business. [*She picks up a pie and wipes the under part of the plate with a dishtowel.*]

BLAKE. His *own* business! Great Scott! D'yeh mean to say it ain't his business who his daughter marries?

HELEN. That's just exactly what I mean to say. [*Crosses to the table, left, with the pie, and sets it on the table.*]

BLAKE. [*Gives a long low whistle.*] Well, Sam Warren *has* filled your head with his new fangled ideas, an' *no* mistake.

HELEN. [*Filling up with tears.*] Never mind Sam Warren, Mr. Blake. I can talk for myself.

BLAKE. That's just why I think s'much of you. Helen, I'm goin' to be awful rich. I'll give you half of every dollar I make for the next twenty years, if you'll marry me.

HELEN. [*Kindly, but with finality.*] No, Mr. Blake, I can't marry you. [*She is left of the table;* BLAKE *is right, close to the table.*]

BLAKE. [*Wistfully.*] Too old, I suppose?

HELEN. [*Sighing heavily.*] No, it's not that. That wouldn't make any difference to *me*.

BLAKE. Too orthodox? [*With large generosity.*] You needn't go to meetin' if you don't want to. You can read all the novels you've a mind to. [*Beaming and enthusiastic, with a warm spirit of sacrifice.*] I'll read *them books* with you.

HELEN. [*With a hopeless little laugh.*] Oh, Mr. Blake, you don't understand me. [*Crosses to the sink, taking off her apron.*]

BLAKE. [*Intensely.*] No, nor you me. I never set my mind on a thing yet I didn't get.

HELEN. [*Scornfully.*] I'm afraid you've done it this time, Mr. Blake. [*Gives her apron a vigorous and emphatic shake as she hangs it up on a peg by the sink.*]

BLAKE. No, I haven't. I'm goin' to have you, Helen, or die a-tryin'. [*She turns and looks at him; he continues quickly,*] Nothin' *underhand* though—nothin' underhand.

HELEN. [*With a scornful toss of her head.*] I should hope not. [*There is a note of defiance in her voice.*]

[UNCLE NAT *enters through the door, right.*]

UNCLE NAT. Helen— [*She runs to him and he says in a tense whisper.*] Sam's out there by the wood pile. He's got the money an'—

HELEN. [*Joyously.*] Got the hundred dollars? Where did he get it?

UNCLE NAT. [*Evading the question.*] He wants to see you— [HELEN *starts to go past him out the door. He stops her.*] Not thet way. Slip out through the woodhouse. [HELEN *runs out through the woodhouse door, left.*]

BLAKE. [*Suspecting something, starts to go to the window as* HELEN *crosses outside.*] What's the matter? Anything wrong?

[UNCLE NAT *stands between* BLAKE *and the window, picks up an apron and shakes it in his face.*]

UNCLE NAT. Helen's speckled pullet's fell inter the rain barrel.

BLAKE. Oh! I hope she ain't drowned. [*Trying to see through the window.*]

UNCLE NAT. No, she ain't drownded, but she's awful wet. [ANN *comes down the stairs, all freshened up, followed by* PERLEY.]

ANN [*Speaking as she comes down.*] Well, be we all ready, Perley?

PERLEY. Yes'm. [*Puts the potatoes on the table.*]

ANN. Well, let's have 'em in, Nathan'l.

UNCLE NAT. All right. You put the turkey on the table, an' I'll hev 'em in in three shakes of a lamb's tail.
[UNCLE NAT *goes into the sitting room. As he is supposed to open the sitting room door, a loud laugh is heard.*]
[ANN *puts the turkey on the table.*]

UNCLE NAT. [*Outside.*] Come, dinner's all sot, an' fetch three or four chairs with you.

ANN. [*For the first time seeing* BLAKE, *who has been standing at the window, his hands behind his back.*] Good afternoon, Mr. Blake. I was 'feared you couldn't git here, yeh're such a busy man.

BLAKE. [*Coming down to the table.*] I'd drop business any time to eat one o' *your* dinners, Mrs. Berry.

ANN. Well, I d'know whether the turkey sp'iled or not. Nathan'l's so fussy; I say, so fussy.
[*All the guests enter, laughing and chatting.* CAPTAIN BEN, *the* DOCTOR *and* MARTIN *carrying chairs.* UNCLE NAT *is also carrying a chair, and is laughing heartily at some remark that has just been made. The guests stand around expectantly, waiting for* ANN *to seat them.* MARTIN *goes to the head of the table and begins to carve the turkey. The children come on leading the twins, in the same manner as they went off.*]

CAPTAIN BEN. [*As he enters.*] It's the pootiest kind of a trip this time o' year.

MARTIN. How long'll you be gone this time?

CAPTAIN BEN. 'Bout six weeks to two months.

UNCLE NAT. When d'ye sail, Cap'n Ben?

CAPTAIN BEN. T'night—fust o' the tide.

UNCLE NAT. I've a durn good notion t' go with yeh. D'yeh want any more hands?

CAPTAIN BEN. Yep, come on, Nathan'l. I'll give you a berth, ten dollars an' found.

ANN. Oh, fer pity's sake, don't take him till I get these dishes washed.

MARTIN. Where'll yeh set us, Ma?

ANN. [*Who has been standing at the upper end of the table on* MARTIN'S *right, recollecting herself.*] Oh! Mr. Blake— [*He does not answer. She calls again.*] Mr. Blake!

BLAKE. [*Who has been at the window lost in thought, his arms folded behind him, his head bent.*] Eh? Oh, I beg pardon.

[*As* ANN *indicates each place, the guest acknowledges it with a little bow preparatory to taking his or her seat.*]

ANN. [*Indicating* BLAKE'S *place at her right.*] Set there please. I suppose I'd ought to make a speech—Mis' Nye— [*Indicates her place at* MARTIN'S *left, at the upper end of the table.*]—to thank yeh all—Doctor—[*Indicates his place left of* MRS. NYE.]—for yer pooty presents—Mis' Leonard— [*Indicates her place left of the* DOCTOR.]—but I never made a speech except once—Cap'n Ben—[*Indicates his place left of* MRS. LEONARD.]—'n thet was twenty-five years ago—Mis' Andrews—[*Indicates her place right of* BLAKE.]—an' then all I said was "yes"— [*All laugh. She shouts.*] Squire— Squire— [*He takes his place next to his wife.*] I tell Martin thet ef I do live with him twenty-five years longer—the children 'll hev t'wait—

BOB. [*Stamping his foot.*] Oh Gosh! I wish you'd never hev any company—we allus hev t' wait! [*Goes off left, leading* SIS LEONARD *by the hand, followed by* MARY *leading* BOB LEONARD. UNCLE NAT *half follows them off, motioning them to be quiet.*]

ANN. —it'll only be 'count of the presents. [*All laugh.*] Well, set by.

[*All busy themselves at the table, and do not see* HELEN, *who enters, right, crying. She comes to* UNCLE NAT, *who draws her to the centre of the stage.*]

HELEN. [*Softly.*] He *is* going to-night, Uncle Nat.

UNCLE NAT. [*Tensely and quietly, soothing her.*] There, don't let 'em see you cryin'. It'll all come right some day. You wait on the table. [*Turning to* ANN *and covering up his concern for* HELEN *with a cheery manner.*] Where be yeh a-goin' to put me, Ma?

[*By this time everybody is seated.*]

ANN. [*Pointing.*] Oh, you're down at the foot o' the class. [*All laugh.*]

UNCLE NAT. Allus was at the foot of the class— [*Laughs, and sits down.*]

[MILLIE *enters through the door, right, with her apron full of clam shells.*]

MILLIE. [*Dropping the shells on the floor.*] Where's my place, Mama?

MRS. NYE. Bless the darlin'!

CAPTAIN BEN. [*Gets up and offers his chair with mock ceremony.*] Set right down here, I'll wait.

MRS ANDREWS. [*Nudging the* SQUIRE.] Look at thet child.

SQUIRE ANDREWS. Yes—I will—

[*The above exclamations are simultaneous, and all are laughing.*]

ANN. My blossom! Come to Ma, precious.

[MILLIE *goes to her;* ANN *takes her on her lap, wipes her face and hands with a napkin, and puts her in her high chair which* PERLEY *has brought to the table.*]

[MARTIN *has gone on carving.* BLAKE *has tucked his napkin in his neck, diamond wise, and spread the ends all over his chest. The* DOCTOR *and* MRS. LEONARD *have placed their napkins in their laps.* MRS. NYE *has laid hers beside her place.* MRS. ANDREWS *fastens the* SQUIRE'S *napkin around his neck.* UNCLE NAT *sticks his in the breast of his vest like a handkerchief. All are laughing and chatting, then suddenly* MARTIN *taps on the table with the handle of his knife. They all pause instantly, and there is silence as they bow their heads in prayer. This must be done in a perfunctory manner, but in all seriousness.*]

MARTIN. [*Quickly.*] Now sing out what kind uv a j'int yeh'll hev.

[*The* SQUIRE *remains with his head on the table,* UNCLE NAT *shakes him.*]

UNCLE NAT. Squire, Squire! [*The* SQUIRE *looks up and places his hand to his ear.*] Meetin's out.

MRS. ANDREWS. I'll hev secon' j'int, an' the Squire 'll hev a bit o' the breast. [MRS. ANDREWS *has the* SQUIRE'S *plate.*]

SQUIRE ANDREWS. [*Puts his hand to his ear.*] Hey?—What?

MRS. ANDREWS. I said you'd hev a bit o' the breast.

MRS. NYE. I'll hev a wing.

CAPTAIN BEN. [*Heartily.*] Gimme anything so's it's turkey.

BLAKE. I've no particular choice.

UNCLE NAT. [*After all the others have spoken.*] Neither hev I. I'll hev the part that went over the fence last, ef nob'dy else *wants* it.

[MARTIN *helps rapidly.* ANN *serves the cranberry sauce.* PERLEY *and* HELEN *pass the vegetables, bread, and butter. They all eat heartily.*]

CAPTAIN BEN. [*With his mouth full.*] Now thet's what I call turkey.

UNCLE NAT. Thet's what we cooked her fer, Cap'n Ben. Ann, don't be so stingy with yer ol' cranberry sass. [*Passes his plate.*]

ANN. [*As she helps* UNCLE NAT *to cranberry sauce.*] Well, yeh can pass up again. There's plenty more in the sass dish.

UNCLE NAT. I only said that to be polite.

MARTIN. Now, folks, don't be bashful. It costs jes' the same whether yeh eat 'r not.
[*All laugh, except the* SQUIRE, *who is busy eating.*]

[JOEL GATES *appears in the doorway, carrying* UNCLE NAT'S *gun, with* MANDY *beside him. He stands there and cranes his neck to look over at the table, his eyes gloating over the food. No one notices him. They are all intent upon their food.*]

UNCLE NAT. I don't believe the Squire heard a word of it. Squire, did you hear what Martin said?

SQUIRE ANDREWS. [*With his hand back of his ear.*] Eh?

UNCLE NAT. He said it costs jes' the same whether yeh eat or not.

SQUIRE ANDREWS. Oh, we'll eat a lot.

UNCLE NAT. No, no— Not lot.

GATES. [*Still standing at the doorway, ingratiatingly.*] How d' do?

UNCLE NAT. [*Looking up and seeing him for the first time.*] Hello, Joel!

MARTIN. [*With hearty hospitality.*] Hello, Joel—jes' in time. Set by an' hev some dinner with us.
[*All the guests greet* GATES.]

GATES. [*Steps over the threshold, glowing at the invitation, followed by* MANDY.] I didn't know yeh hed comp'ny.

ANN. Perley, set 'm a chair; I say, a chair. [PERLEY *starts to get a chair for him.*]

GATES. [*Protestingly, to* PERLEY.] No! No! [*Apologetically, to all the guests.*] I ain't fit to set down with comp'ny, I ben workin' round the barn. I jes' fetched back yer gun, Nathan'l.

HELEN. I'll take her, Mr. Gates.

GATES. [*As he hands her the gun.*] Be careful, Hel'n, she's ludded.
[HELEN *sets the gun in the corner by the sink.*]

UNCLE NAT. [*Casually.*] Did yeh manage to kill thet there fox, Joel?

GATES. I found out 't wa'n't a fox. [*Very much interested in the turkey and the guests' enjoyment of it.*]

UNCLE NAT. Thet so. What was it?

GATES. 'Twas a skunk.
[*A murmur of amusement goes around the table.* GATES *starts to go.*]

MARTIN. Set down an' hev some turkey.

GATES. [*Deprecatingly, looking at the table longingly.*] No, I'm too s'iled. Ef I'd 'a' knowed you was hevin' turkey—I mean comp'ny, I'd 'a' cleaned myself up a bit.

UNCLE NAT. [*While eating.*] Now thet yeh be here, let Ma fix some on a plate to take hum with yeh.

ANN. Yes. Here, Martin, give him this, you can fix yerself some more. [*Holds* MARTIN's *plate;* MARTIN *fills it.*]

UNCLE NAT. [*To the child.*] Mandy, you come here an' git a piece of Ma Berry's pie.

GATES. [*To the child, who hesitates and looks up at him inquiringly*] Go 'n git it, ef yeh want to.
[MANDY *goes to* UNCLE NAT, *who gives her a huge piece of pie. She returns to her father, holding the pie with both hands, her face in a glow of wonder.*]

ANN. [*Giving* HELEN *a plate piled high with food.*] Helen, pass this to Mr. Gates.

GATES. [*As* HELEN *gives him the plate.*] Thank yeh, thank yeh. I'll jes' step inter the woodhouse an' eat it, then I kin hand the plate back.

MARTIN. No, set down there, ef yeh won't come to the table. Hel'n, give 'im a chair.

[HELEN *places a chair, centre. Her manner is very gentle and kind.*]

GATES. *Thank* yeh.

[HELEN *gets* MILLIE'S *small rocking-chair for* MANDY. *She sits down in it, and slowly rocks to and fro, and for the first time a look of childish joy appears on her face.*]

[GATES *settles himself in the chair carefully, with his knees drawn together and his toes resting on a rung, so as to make a table of his lap. With his shoulders hunched, he attacks the overflowing plate and becomes absorbed in the food. He eats as if he had been saving himself for this meal, and feeds the child generously with dainty morsels.*]

[*Meantime, the talk at the table continues.*]

DOCTOR. Oh! By the way, Mr. Blake, did you buy the Swazy place?

BLAKE. Yes.

CAPTAIN BEN. L'see, how many acres is there in thet place?

BLAKE. Eighty odd.

MARTIN. What'd yeh hev to pay fer it, if it's a fair question?

BLAKE. Paid enough fer it—they knew I had to hev it.

UNCLE NAT. They ain't givin' land away nowadays, be they, Mr. Blake?

DOCTOR. [*To* PERLEY.] Will you give me another cup of tea, please? [*She takes his cup and fills it from the teapot on the stove.*] I'd like to sell you that ma'sh of mine, Mr. Blake.

BLAKE. How much shore front hev yeh got there?

DOCTOR. Sixty-seven rod.

BLAKE. What'll yeh take fer it?

DOCTOR. Well, I'm asking twenty-five hundred dollars for it.

BLAKE. Good Heavens! You hev sot it up. I'll give yeh a thousand fer it, half cash.

DOCTOR. The Squire's offered me more than *that* for it.

BLAKE. [*Astonished.*] The Squire! What's he want with it?

SQUIRE ANDREWS. [*Hearing this.*] Thet's my business. You don't s'pose you're goin' to be the only one to git rich out'n the boom, do yeh?

BLAKE. I *started* it.

SQUIRE ANDREWS. Columbus discovered Americky, but he don't *own* it. [*All laugh. The* SQUIRE *looks round the table, well satisfied.*]

UNCLE NAT. [*Laughing uproariously, to the* SQUIRE *on his left.*] Squire, thet's the best thing yeh ever said in yer life —I say thet's the best— [*Pauses, as he realises the* SQUIRE *is paying no attention, but is busily eating.*] Yeh didn't know yeh said it, did yeh? [*The* SQUIRE *still pays no attention.* UNCLE NAT *turns to the rest of the company.*] He didn't hear himself say it. [*All laugh.*]

CAPTAIN BEN. So the Squire's got the fever too, eh?

SQUIRE ANDREWS. Yes, an' got it bad—see— [*Pulls out an oil paper map of his farm, laid off in lots, unfolds it and shows it to the company.*]

BLAKE. By George, he's got the start of all of us.

GATES. [*Picking gingerly on a drumstick.*] Mr. Blake, I'd like t' sell yeh thet seven acre o' mine. I got a great view there. Yeh kin see fer fifty mile round, ef yer eyesight's good enough.

BLAKE. What d'yeh want fer it?

GATES. [*Very importantly.*] Well, it's sort o' got round thet I sot a price. I told Gabe Kilpatrick, and he says I'd ought to git ten 'r fifteen thousand dollars fer it. [*All laugh.*] Gabe

says it'd make a great buildin' site fer Vanderbilt 'r Rocken-
feeder 'r any o' them far-seein' fellers. [*All laugh.*]

ANN. Oh, Martin, thet man thet was here to see yeh yesterday was here agin to-day—who is he?

MARTIN. [*Speaking slowly and unwillingly.*] His name's
Beardsley.

UNCLE NAT. [*Cheerfully and unsuspiciously.*] What is he,
Martin?

MARTIN. [*Ponderously.*] Surveyor!

UNCLE NAT. *Surveyor?*

MARTIN. Surveyor for this 'ere new geruntee land an' im-
prov'ment company.

CAPTAIN BEN. Martin, will yeh gimme jes' a leetle taste
more o' thet stuffin'? [*Passes his plate,* MARTIN *helps him.*]

ANN. [*For the first time a little uneasy.*] What's he want
here, Martin?

MARTIN. [*As if forced to a stand, defiantly.*] He's goin' to
survey the farm.

ANN. [*Gulping down her food.*] Survey it! What fer? I say,
what fer?

MARTIN. [*In desperation.*] I'm goin' to cut it up into buildin'
lots, ef yeh must know. [*The guests stop eating.*]
[ANN *is quite overcome at this news. She swiftly moves her
chair out from the table, and stares at* MARTIN *in consterna-
tion.*]

MARTIN. [*With forced change of tone.*] Hev another wing,
Mis' Nye.

MRS. NYE. [*Soothingly.*] Hain't et what I got on my plate
yit, Martin.
[*A damper now falls on the party.*]

ANN. [*Passionately.*] Martin Berry, you ain't a-goin' to sell
the farm, be yeh? I say, be yeh?

MARTIN. [*Stubbornly.*] You heerd what I said, didn't yeh?

ANN. Yes—I heerd yeh, but I can't *believe* yeh.

MARTIN. It's *mine*, ain't it?

ANN. [*Brokenly.*] Yes, I s'pose 'tis.

MARTIN. Well, hain't I got a right to do what I like with my own?

ANN. I d'know's you got any right to turn me an' the children out o' house 'n hum.

[GATES *gently rises and gives his empty plate to* HELEN, *a look of apprehension on his face. He tiptoes from the room through the door, right, followed by* MANDY.]
[UNCLE NAT *gets up and places his chair in a corner, left, and crosses to right centre.*]

MARTIN. Thet's sentiment—I ain't a-goin' to turn yeh out o' nothin'. I'm a-goin' to move yeh all up to Bangor—I'm a-goin' to git rich.

ANN. [*Rising and folding her arms, her head in the air, proudly and defiantly.*] You won't move *me* up to Bangor, not ef you git as rich as Methuselum.

MARTIN. I'll leave it to Mr. Blake ef I—

BLAKE. I must say I think Martin's scheme's a—

ANN. [*Still with spirit, but with a break in her voice.*] I don't allow's Mr. Blake's got any right to jedge atween you an' me in this: I say, in this.

MARTIN. [*Rising, and striking his fist on the table, angrily.*] Look a-here! I'm goin' to git rich in spite o' yeh. Doctor, will yeh hev another piece o' the breast? I ain't a-goin' to be browbeat.

DOCTOR. No, thank you.

MARTIN. [*In a great temper by this time.*] Fust Nathan'l tries it, an' then you must set up a—

UNCLE NAT. [*Very tensely, but quietly.*] I hain't never browbeat yeh, Martin—I only ast yeh to leave me thet little piece up yonder.

MARTIN. I won't leave yeh nothin'! I'm durned ef I don't sell the hull thing, humstead, graveyard an' every dum— [YOUNG NAT *enters through the door, right, out of breath and greatly agitated.*]

YOUNG NAT. Mr. Blake— Mr. Blake— Mr. Blake— [*Breathes fast.*] You're wanted up at the store. [*All are listening.*] There's been a package o' money took out o' the safe.

BLAKE. [*Swinging around in his chair so as to face* YOUNG NAT, *and resting his arms on the back as he talks.*] A package o' money! What sort of a package?

YOUNG NAT. A hundred dollar package.
[HELEN, *who is standing a little above right centre, listens intently.*]

BLAKE. Who's been in the store today, thet yeh know of?

YOUNG NAT. [*Breathlessly.*] Well, there was Mis' Peasley's hired girl, but she didn't take it. Joe Bennett—Dan Nourse— Sam Warren— [*Draws out* SAM WARREN'S *name significantly.*]

BLAKE. [*Quickly.*] Sam Warren! By George! [*Hitting the back of his chair with his hand.*] He stole it.

HELEN. [*With suppressed anger and shame.*] Oh, Mr. Blake!

BLAKE. [*To* UNCLE NAT, *with a significant look.*] Thet's the speckled pullet thet fell into the rain barrel! [*To the others.*] He hed to hev a hundred dollars to go out West with. [*All the guests except* CAPTAIN BEN *nod their heads as if to say* "That's so, that's bad."] He tried to borry it o' me. I wouldn't lend it to him, an' so he *stole* it. [*The guests all nod* "That's it."]

HELEN. [*Coming down swiftly to right centre, quietly but determinedly.*] You lie!

MARTIN. [*Who is still at the head of the table.*] Helen! [*A slight pause.*] How dast you call Mr. Blake a liar?

HELEN. [*Her voice quivering with indignation.*] How *dare* he call Dr. Warren a thief?

BLAKE. [*A little angrily.*] He *is* a—

HELEN. [*Fiercely.*] You're a—

MARTIN. [*In a low tense tone, approaching her angrily with his hand clenched and partly lifted.*] Helen, if you say that agin, I swear I'll—
[ANN *turns around with her back to the table, and starts crying into her apron.*]

UNCLE NAT. [*Who has been standing with his fingers to his lips, trembling, fearful of* MARTIN'S *anger, goes between them and lays his hand on* MARTIN'S *shoulder.*] Martin! Don't do nothin' thet yeh'll be sorry fer all the days o' yer life.
[*All the guests have risen, rather embarrassed, but fascinated by this scene, and are standing at their places around the table.* MRS. ANDREWS *explains to the* SQUIRE *through the ear trumpet.*]

MARTIN. [*Shaking* UNCLE NAT'S *hand off.*] Take yer hand off'n me. I tell yeh I won't be browbeat by you, an' I won't hev *her* [*With an angry gesture towards* HELEN] insult my friends.

HELEN. [*Her voice trembling with unshed tears of rage, her face flushed with angry excitement.*] He insulted *me*, and if Sam Warren doesn't *thrash* him before night, it'll be because I can't make him do it, that's all.
[HELEN, *during this scene, shows she is the modern girl, and has the temper inherited from her father.* MRS. BERRY *is the old-fashioned, submissive wife, awed and frightened at* HELEN'S *daring to oppose her father.*]

BLAKE. [*Losing his temper.*] He'll be in the lockup before

night, if I can put him there. [*Picks up his hat and cane from the table by the window.*]

MARTIN. [*Turning and picking up the gun from the corner by the sink, and rushing over to* BLAKE *with it.*] That's the thing to do. Git a warrant fer him an' ef he raises his hand to yeh—you—*shoot*—him.

[UNCLE NAT *has been standing at one side, his kind old face white and drawn with anguish. He now comes forward and interposes.*]

UNCLE NAT. Hol' on, Martin! Uncle Sam'l 's mine—an' she wa'n't never made fer *murderin'* folks. [*Quietly, but with authority, he takes the gun and puts it back in the corner by the sink.*]

BLAKE. [*Shaking his cane, a very heavy one, threateningly.*] This'll do me!

HELEN. [*Dominating the whole situation, in a low voice quivering with contempt, to* BLAKE.] Oh! You *coward!* [*Turning to her father.*] Father, Sam's going away to-day. [*With tremendous authority.*] You'd better let him go if you know when you're well off.

MARTIN. [*Taking her tone, tauntingly.*] You'd better not interfere if you know when *you're* well off. I s'pose you'd like to go with him?

HELEN. [*Throwing her head proudly in the air.*] Yes—I would.

MARTIN. [*Beside himself.*] By God! If I lay my hands on him, I'll kill him.

HELEN. If you dare to lay a finger on him, I'll— [*Springs towards* MARTIN *as she speaks, with hands clenched.* UNCLE NAT *catches her and puts his hand over her mouth. The tension is broken, and* HELEN *bursts into tears, her head resting on* UNCLE NAT'S *breast.*]

[*The guests now quietly leave the room, one by one, by the door left.* MRS. NYE *takes* MILLIE'S *hand and follows the others.*]

[PERLEY, *during all this, has gone on clearing away the table as if nothing had happened, only occasionally glancing in the direction of* HELEN *and* MARTIN. *She now goes into the woodhouse, taking the platter with the turkey on it, as if to have her dinner there.*]

MARTIN. [*Crossing to the door, right, as he speaks.*] You'll find out that I've got something to say about what you'll do and what you won't do! Who you'll marry and who you won't marry! [*He starts to go out.* YOUNG NAT *blocks his way, and he pushes him roughly outside.*] Come along, Mr. Blake! [BLAKE *passes out ahead of* MARTIN, *who turns and gives a last fierce fling at* HELEN.] You're not of age yet, my lady. I'll show Sam Warren thet ef my grandfathers *was* monkeys, they wa'n't thieves. [*He goes out.*]

[*As* HELEN *hears their receding footsteps, she runs to the window, and watches them out of sight. She is in a bitter, angry mood, and tears fill her eyes.*]

[UNCLE NAT *sinks wearily and despondently into a chair, left centre.*]

[ANN *is still standing with her back to the audience, crying into her apron. She is dazed and broken.*]

UNCLE NAT. Well, Ann, it seems es ef our turkey'd come to a sort of an ontimely *end*, hain't she?

[HELEN *leaves the window, takes a cup and saucer from the table, goes to the stove, pours out a cup of tea and comes down stage, slowly and listlessly, and seats herself left of the table. She mechanically reaches well across the table for the milk and sugar, stirs the tea, sips it, and nibbles a crust of bread.*]

ANN. [*Turning, her voice tremulous with tears.*] Oh, Nathan'l, I'm so 'shamed. I'll never look a neighbor in the face agin. Twenty-five years married, an' nothin' like this ever happened afore. [*Begins to cry.*] To think o' the dinner all sp'iled after me cookin' myself hoarse over it. [*Starts towards the sitting room door.*] It's enough to provoke a saint out of Heaven; I say, a saint out of Heaven. [*She goes off into the sitting room.*]

UNCLE NAT. [*In a quick decisive voice.*] Well, Helen, I guess Sam'd better git right away from here jes' 's quick 's he kin.

HELEN. [*Frightened, quickly, in an awed whisper.*] Do you think he took the money, Uncle Nat?

UNCLE NAT. [*Rising and going centre.*] 'Tain't thet, but there'll be trouble ef him an' Martin comes together. [*He takes off his coat, doubles it up and throws it in a chair, and begins to clear the table, first gathering the napkins, then the knives and forks, as he talks.*]

HELEN. He *has* got a hundred dollars, y'know.

UNCLE NAT. [*Continuing with his work at the table.*] I know thet. [*Reluctantly.*] I let him hev the biggest part of it myself.

HELEN. [*Amazed.*] You?

UNCLE NAT. It's the money me 'n Martin's ben a-savin' up to buy a tombstun fer Mother.

HELEN. [*Rising, and striking the table with her fist.*] Then he shan't stir—one—single—step. [*Determined, her eyes flashing.*]

UNCLE NAT. [*Dropping the knives and forks he has in his hand, and leaning over the table, appealingly.*] I beg of yeh, Nell—git him away from here. There'll be murder ef yeh don't! [*Crosses to the right with two chairs.*]

HELEN. I don't *care*. They *shan't* call him a thief.

UNCLE NAT. [*Stops and turns.*] Now—now— Haven't they called 'im everything they could lay their tongues to a'ready? Don't yeh see thet I dasn't tell Martin I let Sam hev thet money? [*Puts the chairs down and goes back to the table.*] Don't yeh see thet it won't do fer Martin an' *me* to come together? [*Taps the table with his forefinger.*] Things hes gone too fur now.

HELEN. That's so—he's got to go. He's got to pay that money back.

UNCLE NAT. [*Under the stress of deep conflict and emotion, half turns away from the table with the napkins in his hands; then he turns around again and drops the napkins back on the table.*] Yes, but he's jes' as pig-headed as any of the rest of us, an' if he knowed the money was Martin's he wouldn't tech a cent of it, not with a forty-foot pole. He'd want to stay right here an' fight it out—I'm 'feared. [*Picks up a chair and goes towards right centre with it.*]

HELEN. [*With quick decision.*] He mustn't do that. I'd go with him if it weren't for Mother.

UNCLE NAT. [*Putting down the chair and, turning around amazed and awed, whispers quickly*] Would yeh, Nell? [*He comes back to the table.*]

HELEN. [*Bitterly.*] This'll never be a home to me any more.

UNCLE NAT. [*Taking another chair and going to the window.*] It'll never be a hum to anybody any more, Nell. It's goin' to be all cut up into buildin' lots anyway.

[*By this time* HELEN *has worked her way round to the foot of the table. She now goes to* UNCLE NAT *and says*]

HELEN. If it weren't for Mother, I wouldn't stay here another minute. [*Appealingly.*] Would you blame me, Uncle Nat?

UNCLE NAT. [*Down left, goes to her and they meet centre. He says tenderly*] How could I blame yeh, Helen? Things'll never be the same here agin, an' Sam'd be all upsot out there athout you—an' you'd never be satisfied here athout him. [*With gentle insinuation.*] Now would yeh? He might get

goin' to the dogs out there, an' then yeh'd worry—an' blame
yerself—an'— [*Persuasively.*] I d'know—seems to me—'s
ef—

HELEN. [*Taking fire from his suggestion, is all eagerness
and determination.*] How can we get away? They'd see us
on the train.

UNCLE NAT. [*Considering.*] Oh, you mustn't go by no train.
I'll drive yeh over as far as Ellsworth, an'—

[*At this moment,* CAPTAIN BEN *passes the window.* UNCLE
NAT *glances up and sees him, over his shoulder. He is struck
by a sudden idea, and goes towards the window and calls.*]

UNCLE NAT. Oh, Cap'n Ben!— Cap'n Ben! [*As* UNCLE NAT
calls, CAPTAIN BEN *turns and stands leaning on the window-
sill, looking into the room.*] When did yeh say yeh was
a-goin' t' sail?

CAPTAIN BEN. 'Bout an hour'r so—ef it don't come on to
blow—looks kinder as ef we *might* git a sou'easter afore
mornin'. [*Turns and starts to go, scanning the sky.*]

UNCLE NAT. [*Stopping him again in a voice of hushed anxiety.*] Cap'n Ben! [CAPTAIN BEN *again pauses, and looks at*
UNCLE NAT.] Helen an' Sam 's ben a-thinkin' o' takin' a
trip down the coast fer quite a spell— [*Looks and nods at
him significantly.*] Would you mind droppin' 'em at St. Andrews's 'r somewheres along there?

CAPTAIN BEN. [*Taken aback for a moment, then, comprehending the situation, answers with bluff heartiness.*] No,
plenty o' room an' plenty o' grub aboard.

UNCLE NAT. Kin they go aboard now an' be stowed away
somewheres?

CAPTAIN BEN. Yes, I guess so. Nell, yeh kin come right along
with me now in my buggy. [*He leaves the window and continues off, right.*]

[*During this scene,* HELEN *has been standing tense as*

she begins to realise the significance of UNCLE NAT'S *talk with* CAPTAIN BEN. *Now she turns and darts towards the pegs beside the woodhouse door, where hang her jacket and tam-o'-shanter. She pulls the cap quickly on her head, thrusts her arms into the sleeves of her jacket, and dashes swiftly to the door, right.* UNCLE NAT *checks her flight.*]

UNCLE NAT. Helen!—Helen!

HELEN. [*Stopping.*] What is it, Uncle Nat?

[*There is a moment's pause as they both stand looking at each other. Then* HELEN *comes slowly back.*]

UNCLE NAT. [*Significantly, taking a plain little silver ring off his finger.*] Thet's my mother's weddin' ring. You give it to Sam, an' tell 'im to use it the fust chance he gits. [*He takes her hand, puts the ring into it, and folds her fingers around it.*] Now run along. Cap'n Ben's a-waitin'. [*He pushes her gently towards the door, and goes quickly to the table as though to hide his emotion.*]

[HELEN *walks slowly to the door, looking at the ring. She stops, and a sudden sense of loss seizes her. She turns, and, with a cry, goes back to* UNCLE NAT.]

HELEN. Oh, Uncle Nat, I don't believe I *can* leave you and Mother—not even for him. [*Flings herself into his arms and bursts into tears.*]

UNCLE NAT. [*Folding her in his arms, his voice shaking with tears.*] There now, don't talk l'k thet—Don't yeh start me a-cryin', 'cause ef yeh do, I'm afeared I won't let yeh go. [*As he talks, he turns and moves with her very slowly towards the door. His tone is the soothing one he would use to a child.*] Now, see here. To-night's my watch at the light, an' when you an' Sam an' Cap'n Ben an' all on yeh is a-sailin' down the harbor, a-singin' an' a-laughin' an' enj'yin' yer-selves—jes' as yeh git to the light, you look over there an' sez you to Sam, sez you— There's ol' Uncle Nat's eye, sez you— He's a-winkin' an' a-blinkin' an' a-thinkin' of us, sez you.

HELEN. Good-bye, Uncle Nat.

UNCLE NAT. No! We ain't a-goin' t' say good-bye; we're jes' a-goin' to say good afternoon, thet's all! [*Tries to laugh.*] P'r'aps I'll come out there and see yeh one o' these days.

HELEN. [*Who has been comforted by* UNCLE NAT'S *words, laughs at him almost joyously through her tears.*] Oh!— Will you, Uncle Nat?

UNCLE NAT. [*His face taking on a look of longing, with something of renunciation.*] I said—p'r'aps— [*A pause.*] In thet there palace o' yourn yeh used to talk s'much about when yeh was little. Remember when yeh was little how yeh used to say thet when yeh growed up, yeh'd marry a prince an' live in a gol' palace, an' I was to come an' see yeh, an' yeh was to dress me all up in silks, an' satins, an' di'monds, an' velvets—

[*He half laughs, half cries, kisses her, almost pushes her out of the door, closes the door and bursts into tears, leaning his two arms on the door and burying his face in them.*]

CURTAIN

ACT THIRD

SCENE I

"Havin' an Understandin' "

INTERIOR *of Berry Lighthouse.*

SCENE: *The room is octagonal in shape, with walls of white-washed stone, and its chief feature is an iron stairway leading to the tower above. This stairway starts well down left, then makes a turn, and extends up and across the back wall. There are small windows at intervals along the stairway. Beneath the stairs, about centre, is a small, high, barred window, through which a terrific storm is seen raging. At intervals waves dash against the window.*

The entrance to the lighthouse is through a door on the right; it is made of heavy planks, and has a large latch and a heavy, old-fashioned lock. (NOTE: This door must be framed and set so as to slam with force.)

The whole room has an oily look and smell. On a shelf to the right of the window, about eighteen inches from the floor, is an oil barrel with a brass cock; beside it are some oil-cans and a brass gallon measure for filling the lighthouse lamps. There is a brass pan on the floor beneath the barrel to catch the drip. Beside it is a wooden bucket. There is a shears for trimming the lamps on the floor at the foot of the stairway, and near it lies a coil of life-saving rope. A ship's glass, a sou'wester, an oilskin coat and a pair of oilskin overalls hang on pegs on the wall, left. Leaning against the wall are oars and a boat hook. Several unlighted lanterns are standing about the floor.

The light from above shines down on the room.

At the rise of the curtain rain is heard falling in torrents out-

*side. The wind howls, lightning flashes and thunder crashes
at intervals.*

UNCLE NAT *is discovered down left sweeping the floor. He
has the dirt in a little heap and is getting it into a shovel with
a broom. His actions are mechanical and his manner is preoccupied. He has on his working clothes and his trousers are
tucked into high boots.*

MARTIN *enters hurriedly from the right. He wears oilskins
and carries a lighted lantern. He is pale and excited. As he
opens the door, the rain, wind and thunder can be heard
outside. He slams the door behind him, puts the lantern on
the floor, right, and stands a picture of excited anger.*

MARTIN. [*Standing down right.*] Helen's gone!

UNCLE NAT. [*Who has looked up over his shoulder as* MAR-
TIN *entered, and then immediately resumed his work, quietly
says*] Y—e—s.

MARTIN. Along with Sam Warren. [UNCLE NAT *looks up,
concludes not to speak and continues his work.*] Did you
know she was a-goin'?

UNCLE NAT. [*Without looking up.*] Yeh.

MARTIN. Why didn't yeh tell me?

UNCLE NAT. [*Has got all the dirt on the shovel by this
time; now he empties it into the bucket, right, sweeping off
the shovel so that no dust will remain on it. He speaks as he
does this.*] 'Cause yeh didn't desarve to be told!

MARTIN. [*Striking a clenched fist against his open palm.*]
I'm her father, ain't I?

UNCLE NAT. [*Dryly as he hangs the shovel against the wall.*]
Yeh didn't act's ef yeh was, today.

MARTIN. [*Who is still standing down right.*] Then yeh blame
me?

UNCLE NAT. [*Quietly.*] Well, I ain't a-goin' to lie about it,
Martin. [*He hangs up the broom.*]

MARTIN. An' yeh uphold her?

UNCLE NAT. Yeh didn't know your own child, Martin, thet's all. Ef yeh hed yeh'd 'a' knowed thet yeh might jest's well 'a' stuck thet there gaft— [*Points to the boat hook.*]—inter her heart as to hev said what yeh did 'bout Sam Warren. [*He knocks on the oil barrel to see how much it contains.*]

MARTIN. [*With concentrated bitterness.*] He's a thief.

UNCLE NAT. Tut! Tut! Tut! He ain't. An' you know it jes' as well 's I do. [*He takes up the pan from beneath the barrel, pours the drippings into an oil-can, wipes the pan with a bunch of waste, then wipes the cock of the barrel.*] Yeh unly said it 'cos yeh was crazy, crazier'n a loon. I knowed she wouldn't stay here long after thet. Yeh see, she ain't me, Martin—she's young, an'— [*Slight pause.*]

MARTIN. Where's Tim?

UNCLE NAT. Tim went to Ells'orth this evenin', hain't got back yit.

MARTIN. How'd they go?

UNCLE NAT. 'Long o' the mail. [*Crosses to the window, wipes the pane and peers out at the storm.*]

MARTIN. I said how'd *they* go?

UNCLE NAT. Oh! Cap'n Ben took 'em in the "Liddy Ann."

MARTIN. [*Still standing right.*] What time'd they start?

UNCLE NAT. [*Up centre near the window.*] Fust o' the ebb.

MARTIN. [*Slowly and with hate.*] I hope they sink afore ever they pass the light.

UNCLE NAT. [*Quietly, turning and looking at* MARTIN.] I wouldn't say thet if I was you, Martin— [*There is a brilliant flash of lightning followed by a loud crash of thunder.* UNCLE NAT *nods towards the window, indicating the storm, and adds*] You mought git yer wish.

MARTIN. [*As before.*] I mean ev'ry word I say. She's *disgraced* me.

UNCLE NAT. [*Never losing his tone of patient gentleness.*] You've disgraced yourself, Martin, I guess. [*He is wiping the things on the bench with the waste.*]

MARTIN. [*Slowly, through his teeth.*] Be they married?

UNCLE NAT. No!

MARTIN. [*With a sneer.*] Humph!

UNCLE NAT. Not—yit.

MARTIN. [*Bitterly.*] An' never will be.

UNCLE NAT. [*With quiet confidence; he is down left.*] Oh yes, they will. [*Thunder and lightning.*] Ef they ever live to git to any place. Helen ain't a-goin' to forgit thet she's got a mother an' sisters—an'—

MARTIN. [*Going to him left, and laughing derisively.*] You're tryin' to make me believe 'twas me that made her go—d'ye think I'm blind? She went 'cause she hed to go to hide suthin' wuss from her mother 'n me; she went 'cause she couldn't 'a' held up 'r head much longer here—she's—

UNCLE NAT. [*Dropping his work and turning on him and for the first time showing deep feeling.*] Martin, don't yeh dare say it! Fer ef yeh do, I swear I'll strangle yeh right where yeh stand. [*The light from the tower grows dim.*]

[*Note: This must be worked very gradually.*]

MARTIN. [*Stubbornly standing his ground.*] It's true an' you know it. Thet's why yeh hurried 'em away.

UNCLE NAT. [*Making a movement as though to spring at* MARTIN'S *throat, shrieks hoarsely*] Martin, you've got to take thet back! [*The light in the tower flickers and goes almost out. There is the distant sound of a ship's gun.*]

UNCLE NAT. [*With a sudden change of manner, in a quick, startled voice, as he glances up at the light.*] Good land, what's the matter with the light? [*He crosses down right, and picks up the lighted lantern which* MARTIN *placed there on his entrance, speaking as he does so.*] Tim's fergot to trim thet lamp, sure's you're born. [*Lantern in hand, he turns to go up the stairs. At the same moment* MARTIN *seizes the boat hook, and stands in front of the stairs, barring* UNCLE NAT'S *way.*]

MARTIN. [*Hoarsely, but determined.*] Yeh shan't go up them stairs.

UNCLE NAT. [*Paralyzed with horror.*] Martin!

[*The ship's gun is heard again; it is nearer this time.*]

MARTIN. [*In cold and measured tones.*] I say yeh shan't go up them stairs.

[*Again the gun sounds outside.*]

UNCLE NAT. [*Almost beside himself.*] Why, Martin!—Thet's the "Liddy Ann"! [*The gun is heard once more.*] Thet's her gun!

MARTIN. [*Stolid, quiet, intense.*] I know it.

UNCLE NAT. [*With a cry of protest and unbelief.*] She'll go to pieces on the reef!

MARTIN. [*Grimly.*] Let her go.

UNCLE NAT. [*Half crazed.*] Yes—but—Helen'll go with 'er! [*He starts for the stairs.*]

MARTIN. [*Stopping him.*] Keep away, Nathan'l. I tell yeh thet light ain't a-goin' to be lit.

UNCLE NAT. [*Frantically pleading, his voice broken with emotion.*] Martin, f'r God's sake, list'n to *me!*

MARTIN. [*Doggedly.*] I won't listen to nothin'.

UNCLE NAT. [*Walking firmly over to him, speaking as he does so.*] You've *got* to listen. [MARTIN *makes an angry movement.*] I say—you've got to listen! We've got to hev an understandin' right here and now. [MARTIN *submits sullenly, and* UNCLE NAT *continues to talk in hurried, nerv-*

ous tones, pacing up and down the space between MARTIN *and the door, like a caged lion, rolling and unrolling the sleeves of his red flannel shirt.*] I've ben playin' secon' fiddle to you long enough, Martin Berry, ever sence yeh was born. When yeh was a baby I walked the floor with yeh, an' sung yeh t' sleep night after night. At school I fit yer battles fer yeh, an' once I saved yer life.
[*The gun is heard outside.*]

MARTIN. Yeh needn't throw thet in my face.

UNCLE NAT. I hain't a-throwin' it in yer face. I only want yeh not to forgit to remember it, thet's all. [*He goes to the window and peers out.*]

MARTIN. [*Doggedly.*] I know all about thet, I tell yeh.

UNCLE NAT. Do yeh? Well, then I'll tell yeh somethin' yeh didn't know. [*Walks over and deliberately faces him, and says emphatically*] Did yeh ever know thet I might 'a' married your wife Ann?

MARTIN. [*Raising the boat hook, making a step towards him, white with rage, almost shrieks*] W—h—a—t?

UNCLE NAT. [*Hurried, tense and almost hysterical.*] Hol' on—I ain't through yit. I thought more o' her than ever a miser did o' money. But when I see thet you liked her too —I jes' went off t' the war—an' I let yeh hev her! [*Taps* MARTIN'S *chest with his forefinger.*] An' thet's sumpthin' yeh didn't know all about—wa'n't it, Martin Berry? [*The gun is heard outside.*] But thet's neither here nor there—her child is out there—my child by rights! [*With sudden sublime conviction, almost heaven-inspired.*] Martin, thet light hez got to be lit! [*With an angry snarl.*] I give yeh the mother, but I'm damned ef I'm a-goin' to let yeh murder the child! Come away from them stairs, Martin—come away from them stairs, I say!

[UNCLE NAT *seizes* MARTIN, *and the two men have a quick struggle. Then* UNCLE NAT *with almost superhuman strength throws* MARTIN *the whole length of the room.* MARTIN *is dazed; he reels and staggers like a drunken man towards the door by which he entered, and blindly gropes his way out into the storm.*]

UNCLE NAT *seizes the lantern and starts to crawl up the stairs. It is hard work to climb them, the excitement has been too much for him. He gets up a few steps, then slips down again; he crawls up again on hands and knees, and once more slips down. He makes still another effort, falters, staggers, and, with a heartbreaking cry, falls and rolls down the stairs.*]

UNCLE NAT. God help me! I hain't got the strength!

[*The thunder crashes, the sea roars, the lightning flashes.*]
[*The stage darkens as the light above goes completely out.*]

END OF SCENE I

ACT THIRD

SCENE II

"The 'Liddy Ann' in a Sou'easter"

EXTERIOR *of Berry Lighthouse.*

(*NOTE: The storm noises are well worked up before the scene opens. The stage is completely dark, as is the front of the theatre.*)

SCENE: *An expanse of wild, storm-tossed waves, with the lighthouse, a dark, shadowy bulk, rising from the rocky coast on the left. The rain is pouring in torrents, the thunder roars, the lightning flashes. The boom of a ship's gun is heard above the din of the storm, and in the darkness, the "Liddy Ann," sloop-rigged and under reefed jib, makes her way slowly through the heavy seas, from right to left. She is off her course and perilously near the rocks. At intervals her gun booms and she sends up distress signals. The figures of* CAPTAIN BEN, DAVE BURGESS, GABE KILPATRICK, *and* BILL HODGEKINS, *as well as* SAM *and* HELEN, *can be dimly discerned on board. The shouts of* CAPTAIN BEN *giving orders, and the replies of the crew are drowned by the noise of the storm.*

For a few moments the "Liddy Ann" tosses helplessly in the darkness. Then a tiny light appears in the lowest window of the lighthouse. For a second it wavers, then slowly it rises from window to window, as UNCLE NAT *climbs the stairs to the tower. In another moment the light in the tower blazes forth, showing the "Liddy Ann" her course. A shout of relief goes up from those on the boat, and as the "Liddy Ann" makes her way safely past the rocks*

THE CURTAIN DESCENDS

88

ACT FOURTH

"ME AN' THE CHILDREN"

THE *scene is the same as in Act Second. It is fifteen months later.*

SCENE: *Snow is falling heavily outside. The wind is howling; a little drift of snow can be seen on the window sash. A fire burns briskly in the stove and everything has the appearance of the day's work being over. The leaves of the table are folded, and a red checked cloth covers the table on which is a lighted lamp. The tea kettle is singing on the fire.* UNCLE NAT'S *gun is in its place in the corner by the sink, and his old army coat and cap are hanging on the pegs under the stairs, as in Act Second. There is a large rocking-chair up right, and a small one stands above the table, left. At the rise of the curtain,* YOUNG NAT *is seated reading a book at the upper end of the table; he now wears long trousers instead of knickerbockers. From time to time he turns a page but instantly resumes his position to preserve the idea that he is very intent on the story before him. His elbows are resting on the table at either side of the book and his head is supported by both hands.*

MARTIN *is seated on a chair, which is tilted back against the wall below the door, right. On his knees lies a blueprint map of his farm, which has been surveyed and laid off in lots. He is very dejected and in deep thought. Without realizing it he is grieving over the absence of his daughter, filled with bitter remorse for having driven her out of her home.*

ANN *is sitting at the right of the table, mending stockings. She wears a warm-colored woolen dress, with a white embroidered collar, and a crisp white apron.*

UNCLE NAT *and* PERLEY *are preparing the children for*

bed. UNCLE NAT *is seated, centre, and* PERLEY *stands beside him.* UNCLE NAT *is just finishing buttoning up* MILLIE'S *nightdress, while* PERLEY *is helping* MARY.

The children all have nightdresses and worsted slippers on, and their clothes are lying in little heaps, one in front of each child, as though they had just stepped out of them. MILLIE'S *hair is in curl papers.* MARY'S *hair is braided and tied. The children's nightdresses are made of Canton flannel, with legs and arms, covering them from the neck to the ankles, and they button at the back,* MARY'S *and* BOB'S *straight up and down, and* MILLIE'S *with a little fall behind to let down.*

UNCLE NAT, PERLEY *and the children are having a great deal of fun as the curtain goes up.*

YOUNG NAT. [*Looking up from his book, as though continuing a conversation.*] I tell yeh there ain't no Santy Claus! It's y'r father and mother!

MILLIE. They is too a Santy Claus, ain't they, Uncle Nat?

UNCLE NAT. Of course there is. See here, Nat, you jest read your book. When a boy gits too big to know there ain't no Santy Claus, he ought to know enough to keep his thumb out'n the Christmas puddin'.

[YOUNG NAT *laughs and resumes his reading.*]

MILLIE. Did yeh ever see him, Uncle Nat?

UNCLE NAT. See'm? Yes, sir, I seen him—lots o' times.

BOB. [*Smiling.*] When was it, Uncle Nat? [*The children surround* UNCLE NAT *scenting a story.*]

UNCLE NAT. It was a g-r-e-a-t many years ago, when I was a little boy, not near so big's as you be, Bob.

MILLIE. Was you ever as big as Bob?

UNCLE NAT. Yes, sir, an' bigger. I was as big as you be once, an' once I was as little as Mis' Pearce's new baby.

[*The* CHILDREN *all laugh.*]

MILLIE. An' didn't have no more hair on yer head?

UNCLE NAT. [*Chuckling.*] I hain't got much more now. [*The* CHILDREN *all laugh.*]

ANN. [*Looking up from her mending.*] Now young uns, hang up yer stockin's an' go to bed, I say go to bed. [*The* CHILDREN, *all excitement, prepare to hang up their stockings.*]

BOB. I'm goin' to hang up my pants.

UNCLE NAT. You give me a piece of string an' I'll tie up one leg an' you tie up t'other, an' thet way we'll get done quicker. [BOB *ties up one leg,* UNCLE NAT *the other.*]

MILLIE. [*Watching enviously.*] I wish I wore pants.

UNCLE NAT. Do yeh, Millie? Well yeh may yit afore yeh die. Don't you git discouraged. Things is comin' your way mighty fast. I tell you what you do. You give me yer petticoat and I'll tie up the skirt and make as good a bag as Bob's pants. That'll beat yer stockin's.

[*The* CHILDREN *all agree to this enthusiastically.*]

ANN. [*While* UNCLE NAT *is busy tying* MILLIE's *petticoat.*] Mary, ain't you goin' to hang up yourn?

MARY. Yes, mother. [*With a smile.*] But I'm afeared I won't get anything.

[*The* CHILDREN *remove some towels which have been hanging on a line at the back of the stove, to make room for their stockings.*]

UNCLE NAT. Now come on, git some pins. Bob, you get some clothespins. [*They rush to* ANN, *who gives them pins.*] We'll hang Millie in the middle—jes' like a fiddle. Gimme a couple o' them pins, Mary. Bob, you go over there—[*Hanging* BOB's *knickerbockers on the line right.*] You got the clothespins, Bob? [BOB *rushes into the woodhouse, and comes back with two clothespins.* UNCLE NAT *fastens his knickerbockers to*

the line with them.] Mary, where'll you go?—oh, over here—
[*He hangs* MARY's *stocking, left.*[

[*During this scene* PERLEY *has lighted a candle and stands
waiting to show the children to bed.* ANN *watches* UNCLE
NAT *and the children with amused interest.*]

UNCLE NAT. Nat, ain't you goin' to hang up?

YOUNG NAT. Naw! 'Cause I know there ain't no Santy Claus.

MILLIE. [*Crossing to him and almost crying.*] They is too,
Nat Berry—you won't go to Heaven ef you say thet.

UNCLE NAT. He won't go to Heaven at all ef he don't say
his prayers. Come now, gether up yer duds an' be off to bed.

[*The* CHILDREN *all pick up their clothes and shoes.* MARY
and BOB *say "Good night" and kiss their* UNCLE NAT, *then
their father, who is moody, and their mother last. She kisses
them tenderly. They go upstairs.* PERLEY *stands at the foot
of the stairs lighting them up.*]

MILLIE. [*To* UNCLE NAT *who picks her up in his arms,
clothes and all.*] I wish you'd sleep with me to-night, Uncle
Nat.

UNCLE NAT. Oh! My suz! I couldn't git inter *your* bed—be
yeh skeered?

MILLIE. Jes' a 'ittle teeny might. [*Hides her head in his
neck.*]

UNCLE NAT. No, yeh ain't nuther. Yeh jes' want t' git me to
try to git my long legs inter thet trundle bed o' yourn, [*Puts
her down.*] and then kick me out on the floor like yeh did
las' Sunday mornin'. But yeh ain't a-goin' to do it to-morry
mornin'. [*Spanks her playfully.*] Go 'long with yeh, yeh little
hypocrite.

MILLIE. [*Goes over and stands by her father demurely, with
her clothes under her arm.*] Good night, Papa. [MARTIN *picks
her up by her elbows, takes her in his arms, and kisses her,
quite tenderly, and unconsciously lets the map fall to the*

floor, where it lies unobserved. Then he sets MILLIE *down and becomes once more lost in his thoughts.*]

[MILLIE *moves a few steps away from* MARTIN, *then turns and looks at him and says softly and shyly*] I wish you a Merry Kiss'mus.

[MARTIN *makes no response, and* MILLIE *turns to* UNCLE NAT *lingeringly, as though loth to go to bed.*] I wish it was mornin' so's I could see what's in my petticoat.

UNCLE NAT. [*Dogmatically.*] Oh! Yeh do—do yeh? Tell yeh what yeh do, Millie. Yeh go to bed an' sleep till mornin' and then t'will be mornin' in the mornin'.

MILLIE. [*Going over to her mother.*] Good night, Mama. [*Kisses her.*]

ANN. Good night, I say good night. [*Bends over and kisses her tenderly.*]

MILLIE. [*Full of Old Nick.*] Good night, Uncle Nat. [*Going to him.*]

UNCLE NAT. Good night.

MILLIE. Sleep tight.

UNCLE NAT. Go t' bed, yeh little baggage yeh! Be yeh going to bed 'r not? [*Shoos her away.*]

MILLIE. [*Goes to the foot of stairs, and stops suddenly.*] Oh! Uncle Nat?

UNCLE NAT. What is it?

MILLIE. [*In a mysterious whisper.*] Look what's behind yeh!

UNCLE NAT. [*Entering into her play.*] Oh, I'm skeered to look—what is it?

MILLIE. [*In the same manner.*] Santy Claus!

UNCLE NAT. [*Pretending to be frightened, jumps.*] Where? [MILLIE *laughs.*] Ain't yeh 'shamed to skeer me like thet— I've a good mind to— [*He runs after her, she runs and laughs.*]

MILLIE. Yeh can't ketch me! [*Laughs and runs around the table.* BOB *and* MARY *appear at the top of the stairs laughing and say* "*Run, Millie, quick, Millie!*" UNCLE NAT *pretends he can't catch* MILLIE.]

UNCLE NAT. [*At last catching* MILLIE *by the waist of her nightdress at the back, and carrying her as he would a carpet bag. She laughs very heartily all through the scene.*] Now, my young lady. I've got yeh and I'll see whether yeh'll go to bed or not! [*Carries her upstairs triumphantly, followed by* PERLEY *with the candle. He is heard talking all the way up the stairs;* MILLIE *is laughing.*] I bet I'll put yeh to bed—or I'll know the reason why. [UNCLE NAT, PERLEY *and the children go off through the door at the top of the stairs, and their voices die away in the distance.*]

ANN. [*Calling after them.*] I swan, Nathan'l, you're wuss 'n the young uns—I say wuss 'n the young uns! [*Gets up and goes to the window and looks out at the storm.*] Mussy on me, what a night! I pity anybody thet's got to be out on sech a night as this. [*She turns from the window, and notices* MARTIN, *who sits brooding.*] Martin, ain't you well—I say ain't you well?

MARTIN. [*Gloomily, not crossly.*] Oh yes. I s'pose I'm well enough.

ANN. [*Crosses to him and smooths his hair.*] Yeh worry too much—'tain't a mite o' use to worry. I wish you'd take some o' thet pikrey—I know it'd do you good—I say I know it'd do you good.

MARTIN. I d'want n-o—pik-rey. Pik-rey won't do me no good.

ANN. [*Goes back to the table and resumes her work.*] Thet's jes' what Cap'n Ben Hutchins said last spring. But Liddy Ann managed to git some on't inter his vittels right along athout his knowin' of it an' it cured him. He was mad's a hornet when he found it out. I've half a mind to try it—I say to try it.

MARTIN. [*In the same manner.*] Don't you put no pikrey inter my vittels if you know when you're well off.

ANN. [*Gently, with placid confidence and assurance.*] Well, Martin, jes' as soon as you sell a few o' them lots yeh got laid off,—yeh said yeh was goin' to sell a couple a hundred of 'em in the spring, didn't yeh? I say didn't yeh? [*Absorbed in her mending.*]

MARTIN. [*As if evading the question.*] I said I *hoped* I'd sell some on 'em in the spring.

ANN. [*Gently.*] Well I sh'd hope so, now thet you've cut the farm all up inter griddle cakes. Well soon's yeh do—I'm goin' to hev yeh go up t' Boston an' see a *reel* doctor. Not but what Dr. Leonard's good enough, but now thet we're goin' to git rich, we kin afford a little better one. You ain't right an' I know it—I say, an' I know it. [*There is a tremendous burst of laughter from upstairs. Then* UNCLE NAT *comes flying down, followed by all the clothes, shoes etc. the children had carried up. He half falls, and lands sitting on the bottom step. The children all appear at the top of the stairs with* PERLEY, *laughing.* MARTIN *jumps.* ANN *gives a scream and rises.*] Mussy on me—I tho't t'was an earthquake! I say an earthquake! What in time's the matter with yeh?

UNCLE NAT. [*Looking up with an apologetic air.*] Me'n the children hevin' a little fun, thet's all.

ANN. I should think yeh was. [*She crosses over to the stairs and calls up to the children.*] Ef I come up there 'th my slipper I'll give you suthin' to cut up about. Go to bed this minute, every man jack o' yeh, an' don't let me hear another word out o' yeh this night. [*As* ANN *speaks there is a dead silence and the children all sneak away on tiptoe.*] Perley, come and git these duds. I say git these duds. [PERLEY *comes*

*down and gathers up the clothes and goes off with them up-
stairs.* ANN *sits down to her darning again, and for the first
time observes* YOUNG NAT.] Nat Berry, ben't you goin' to
bed to-night?

YOUNG NAT. [*Absorbed in his book; without looking up.*]
Jes's soon's I finish this chapter. The Black Ranger's got
the girl in his power an' Walter Danforth's on his trail.

ANN. Le'see. [*She seizes the book and becomes absorbed in
it.* YOUNG NAT *thrums on the table; he is impatient, but polite; finally he falls into a reverie over what he has been
reading.*]

[*During the talk between* YOUNG NAT *and his mother,* UNCLE
NAT *slowly rises from the stairs. Now he goes up stage and
peers out of the window, speaking as he does so.*]

UNCLE NAT. By George—we'll hev sleighin' to-morry an' *no*
mistake, ef this keeps on! [*He comes down stage and addresses the rest of the speech directly to* MARTIN *who pays
no attention to him.* UNCLE NAT *takes a chair and sits a
little to the right of centre. He lifts his left leg with his
hands to cross it over his right, but a rheumatic twinge stops
him. He tries a second time, and succeeds in crossing his
legs; his hands are clasped over his knee. His half-furtive
glances at* MARTIN, *now and then, are full of affection and
sympathy. The desire to engage his brother's attention is
the persistent note of his mood, and* MARTIN'S *rebuffs only
act as a stimulus to his efforts. Now he looks expectantly at*
MARTIN, *who continues to ignore him. Then he becomes interested in his shoe as he detects a broken place in it. He
examines it carefully, and runs his finger over it. There is a
slight pause and again he resumes his efforts to break down
his brother's sullen resentment. There is an intimate tone in
his voice as he remarks:*] I hain't seen sech a storm—not
sence I d'know when. Not sence thet *big* snowstorm we had
'way back in '59. [*He looks at* MARTIN'S *blank face as if for
confirmation, but there is no response.*] Thet *was* a snowstorm! Couldn't see no fences n'r nothin'. Mail didn't git

along here fer more'n a week. [*He looks at* MARTIN *as before. The same forbidding mask meets his inviting smile. He shakes his foot meditatively as if to gain sympathy from it; then he gives a long sigh.*] Ol' Sam Hutchins was a-haulin' wood, an' got snowed in, an' when they dug him out he was friz stiffer'n a poker, a-settin' right on his lud. [*A pause. He steals a quick, inquiring glance at his brother's immobile face, then with the manner of one who find himself in pleasant company, he remarks with fine unction:*] I kinder like to see snow on Christmas. It kinder—I d'know—seems kinder sorter more Christmassier—somehow. [*He gives another glance at the unresponsive* MARTIN, *then he rises. He leans heavily on his right foot, then he moves the foot up and down, his shoe creaking loudly as he does so. He goes up to the window and looks out once more at the storm.*] Phew! Ain't she a-comin' down! The ol' woman up in the sky's pluckin' her geese tonight fur all she's worth an' no mistake. [*He comes down, sees the map* MARTIN *has dropped, and picks it up. He handles it as though it were something precious. He looks at it a moment, and then bends his eyes upon his brother in a fine pride, as having in this map achieved a rare and wonderful thing. Then he seats himself in the same chair as before and looks over the map.*] Treemont Str—eet. [*Tracing the map with his forefinger.*] Corn—hill Str—eet. [*With a glance of pride at* MARTIN.] Wash—in'—ton Str—eet. [*There is a long pause, then* UNCLE NAT *glances about the room.*] 'Y George, Washin'ton Street's a-goin' to run right straight through the kitchen here, ain't she? [*He looks at* MARTIN, *who, for the first time meets* UNCLE NAT'S *eye, and shifts uneasily in his chair.*] Haw—thorne Av—en—oo. [*He traces the map with his forefinger.* MARTIN *casts impatient furtive glances at him from under his eyebrows; then he gets up and goes towards* UNCLE NAT.] Hawthorne Avenoo begins at the Northeast end o' the ol' barn an' runs due east to—

MARTIN. [*Quietly taking the map from him, folding it up*

and putting it in the breast pocket of his coat.] Ef you hain't got nuthin' better t' do than to set there a-devilin' me, I'd advise you to go to bed. [*He returns to his chair and lapses into his former mood.*]

[UNCLE NAT *and* ANN *exchange glances of wonderment and pleasure at the thought of* MARTIN'S *having spoken to* UNCLE NAT. *It is a big moment for them.* ANN *catches her breath and a look of surprise and delight crosses her face. She starts to speak, but* UNCLE NAT *motions her to be quiet by putting his right hand over his lips and waving his left hand at her for additional emphasis. Then he rises and takes a few steps towards* MARTIN. *His face is illumined and quivers with joy, he speaks feelingly.*]

UNCLE NAT. Martin—thet's the fust word you've spoke to me in over fifteen months. [MARTIN *remains stolid and silent.* UNCLE NAT *continues half sadly, half jokingly*] Don't you think I've wore black fer you long enough? [*Wistfully*] Say, Martin, let's you and me shake hands and wish each other Merry Christmas to-morry, jes' like we used to—when we was boys together—will yeh?

MARTIN. I don't care nuthin' 'bout Christmas—one day's good's another t' me.

UNCLE NAT. [*Gently.*] 'Twa'n't allus so.

MARTIN. Well it's so now. Merry Christmas—Humph! I'd like t'know what I've got to be merry about.

UNCLE NAT. Yeh've got *me*—ef yeh'll hev me—

MARTIN. [*Significantly.*] Humph!

UNCLE NAT. You've got Ann. [MARTIN *looks up.* UNCLE NAT *continues quickly as if he should not have said that*] You've got the children.

MARTIN. [*Half-bitterly.*] Yes, till they git big enough to be some help, then they'll clear out an' leave me as their sister did.

UNCLE NAT. [*Very gently.*] Now—now—now— Helen didn't

clear out an' leave *you*. She never'd 'a' gone ef you hadn't 'a'
—said what yeh said about—

MARTIN. [*Murmurs almost inaudibly.*] There now.

UNCLE NAT. [*Finishing the sentence under his breath.*]—Sam
Warren.

MARTIN. I don't want to git inter no argument 'th you to-
night! I know what I done an' I know what *she* done.

UNCLE NAT. Yeh never will let me tell yeh nothin'.

MARTIN. I don't want to *know* nothin'—

UNCLE NAT. [*With a quizzical smile.*] Well—yeh come pooty
nigh a-knowin' of it. I never see a man s' fond o' huggin' a
sore thumb 's you be. [*With a complete change of tone.*] Will
yeh help me to fill the children's stockin's?

MARTIN. [*Half-softening.*] I hain't got nothin' to put in 'em.

UNCLE NAT. Well, I hain't got much, but what I hev got 's
a-goin' in. Come, Ma, let's you and me play Santa Claus, then
I'll go to bed. [ANN *makes no reply.* UNCLE NAT *sees that
she is absorbed in her book, chuckles, and decides to leave
her alone. He passes* YOUNG NAT, *flicking him on the shoulder with his handkerchief as he does so and says,*] Nat, come
out in the woodhouse and lend 's a hand here, will yeh?

[UNCLE NAT *goes off into the woodhouse.* YOUNG NAT *gives
his mother an impatient look, then shrugs his shoulders resignedly and follows* UNCLE NAT *off. They return almost immediately, carrying between them a large wood-basket con-
taining a lot of bundles, which they place down centre.* UNCLE
NAT *sits in the same chair as before,* YOUNG NAT *kneels at
his left and they begin to undo the presents. There are dolls,
slates, picture books, big candy canes, a sleigh, a pair of
skates, mittens, comforters, and any quantity of cheap toys,
also a new dress pattern. As the things begin to reveal themselves,* MARTIN *is interested in spite of himself.*]

YOUNG NAT. [*With a note of triumph in his voice*] I *told* yeh
't was yer father an' mother all the time.

UNCLE NAT. [*Continuing with his work.*] Did yeh? Well, yeh didn't know's much as yeh thought yeh did, old smarty. It ain't yer father an' mother *this* time—it's yer Uncle Nat, by George! [*They both laugh.*]

MARTIN. I hope yeh hain't been a-runnin' yerself in debt agin fer them children.

UNCLE NAT. No, I hain't run in debt this time. I paid spot cash *this time.* Thet's how I got such good bargains. [*Shows a harlequin with a string to make it jump.*] Jes' look at thet now fer five cents. [*Pulls the string and laughs.*] It's wuth more'n thet to see Milly pull the string jes' once. [*Chuckling.*]

MARTIN. I didn't know yeh had any money by yeh.

UNCLE NAT. I hadn't. I got Blake t' cash my pension warrant. [*He says this without making any boast of it.*].

MARTIN. An' spent the hull on't on the young uns as usual, I s'pose.

UNCLE NAT. [*Still busy with the things; in a matter-of-fact tone.*] Yep!

MARTIN. *Eight dollars* on sech foolishness—it's wicked.

UNCLE NAT. [*For the first time stopping his work and looking up.*] Say, what d'yeh s'pose I stood up to be shot at fer thirteen dollars a month fer, ef it wa'n't t' hev a little fun on my income? Think I'm a-carryin' around this bullet in my shoulder all these years f'r nuthin'? Not much, Johnny Roach! [*Goes back to his work.*]

MARTIN. [*Gently.*] Yeh might 'a' bought yerself an overcut—

UNCLE NAT. Overcut—such weather as this? [*Holding up a candy cane.*] Not while candy canes is a-sellin' b'low cost. What's the matter with the one I've got?

MARTIN. Thet ol' army cut? It's patched from one end to t'other.

UNCLE NAT. Thet makes it all the warmer. [*With humor.*]

'Sides, yeh mustn't never despise a man jes' 'cause he wears a ragged cut.

ANN. [*Slamming the book shut with a sense of supreme satisfaction.*] There! Ef ever a mean, contemptible houn' got his jest deserts thet Black Ranger got his'n—I say thet Black Ranger got his'n. Walter Danforth jes'—

YOUNG NAT. [*With loud protest.*] Oh, *Mother*, don't tell! I want to read it myself. [*Goes back to the table, sits down and resumes reading.*]

ANN. I swan ef I didn't forgit it was Christmas Eve—an' all about the stockin's. Nat Berry—don't you ever bring another one o' them books inside these doors when I've got work to do. [*Jumps up and begins helping* UNCLE NAT.] Ain't thet a pooty dolly—I say a pooty dolly!

[*They now proceed to fill the children's clothes, and hang things on the outside of them. There must be enough stuff to pack them. At the same time footsteps are heard on the porch outside, there is a stamping of feet as if to knock off the snow, and* BLAKE *enters. The snow drifts in as he opens the door and the wind howls. He is covered with snow and well muffled up.* MARTIN *who has been half interested in the business of the Christmas presents, rises.* ANN *and* UNCLE NAT *stop in their work.* YOUNG NAT *looks up from his reading.* UNCLE NAT *takes the empty basket, and puts it back in the woodhouse.*]

BLAKE. Too blizzardy to stop to knock. By George, what a night! I hain't seen such a storm since I dunno when. [*He is about to shake the snow from his clothing when* ANN *stops him.*]

ANN. Don't shake it off on my clean floor, Mr. Blake. Nathan'l, git a broom.

[UNCLE NAT *gets the broom, takes* BLAKE *up stage and sweeps the snow from his clothes, as the dialogue continues.*]
[PERLEY *comes downstairs with the lighted candle, and puts*

it on the table. Then she crosses over to help with the presents.]

BLAKE. Didn't think I'd ever git here—by George. The snow's waist deep— [*To* UNCLE NAT.] Thank yeh, thet'll do I guess.

UNCLE NAT. [*Hanging up the broom.*] Set down by the fire an' warm yerself. [*He places a chair for* BLAKE.] Ef yer feet are cold stick 'em in the oven an' toast 'em a bit.

BLAKE. I'll thaw out my back first. [*Stands in front of the stove with his coat tails drawn apart and warms his back.* UNCLE NAT *and* ANN *resume their work.* PERLEY *helping them.* BLAKE *observes them a moment in silence.*] Well, y're at it I see. [*He watches them with a tinge of sadness in his face.*]

UNCLE NAT. Yep! Christmas only comes oncet a year, y'know, in this family.

ANN. [*Displaying the dress pattern.*] Thet's a-goin' to make Millie an awful pooty dress. Nathan'l, what was thet a yard?

UNCLE NAT. I d'know—I never ask no prices.

ANN. [*Contemplating the dress pattern.*] Won't Millie be proud o' thet! I'll have it made up jes' 's stylish 's kin be. [*Puts it in* MILLIE'S *skirt, or beneath it.*] I say jes' 's stylish 's kin be.

UNCLE NAT. I heerd yeh—I *heerd* yeh—

BLAKE. By George, Martin, I'd give all I'm wuth in the world to hev jes' *one* stockin' a-hangin' in my chimney corner to-night.

ANN. You'd ought t' got married long ago, Mr. Blake.

BLAKE. I never saw but one girl wuth *hevin'* and she wouldn't hev *me*. [*Sighing.*] I'll never git married now.

ANN. It must be kinder lunsome athout no children nor nothin', specially at Christmas. I say at Christmas.

BLAKE. I never noticed how lunsome it was till I see you

a-fillin' them stockin's. I've ben s' busy all my life makin'
money I hain't hed time to git lunsome. Now I'm gittin' old,
I begin to see thet p'r'aps I might— [*He shakes off his retro-
spective mood.*] Oh, Martin! [*He sets a chair down stage in
front of* MARTIN, *sits astride it, and leans his hands on the
back. They talk in low tones while* ANN, PERLEY *and* UNCLE
NAT *continue their work.* BLAKE'S *tone now is tense and low.*]
Did you hear about the Land Company's bustin'?

MARTIN. [*Alarmed.*] Bustin'? What? When? How? [*He
starts to rise.* BLAKE *motions him back in his chair and hushes
him.*]

BLAKE. [*As if discharging a disagreeable duty.*] Sh! Yes sir,
busted cleaner'n a whistle. Opposition fellers done it. They've
bought up Lemoine, an' thrown it on the Boston market way
down. Got a lot of Boston big bugs goin' to build there soon's
the weather breaks.

MARTIN. Then *your* boom's over?

BLAKE. Yes, for five years anyway. [*Apologetically.*] Folks
ain't a-goin' to come here when they can go to Lemoine for
the same money'r less.

MARTIN. [*With finality.*] An' I'm ruined.

BLAKE. [*Really sorry.*] Looks thet way—now—I'm sorry to
say.

MARTIN. [*Slowly.*] With my farm mortgaged to you for
fifteen hundred dollars, an' the money spent in cuttin' it up
inter buildin' lots. [BLAKE *drums on the back of the chair
with his fingers.* MARTIN *rises as if to spring at him and says
between his teeth but in a low tone.*] Damn you—I—

BLAKE. [*Quieting him in the same way as before.*] Hol' on.
[*Points to* ANN *and* UNCLE NAT.] Yeh don't want them t'
know, do yeh?

MARTIN. [*Sinking back in his chair and covering his face
with his hands.*] No, not to-night, don't tell 'em to-night.

[HELEN *and* SAM *appear at the window.* HELEN *has a baby
in her arms.* UNCLE NAT *looks up, sees them, gives a start.*]

UNCLE NAT. Oh! My! [*They cross the window and disappear.*]

ANN. What in time is the matter with you?

[BLAKE *looks up,* MARTIN *does not stir.*]

UNCLE NAT. A tech of rheumatiz I guess. [*Rubs his shoulder.*]

ANN. La! You sot my heart right in my mouth.

[BLAKE *resumes his former attitude.* UNCLE NAT *whispers in* ANN's *ear. She starts to scream, and he claps his hand over her mouth then he motions her towards the woodhouse door.* ANN *runs out.* PERLEY *comes over to* UNCLE NAT *to find out what is the matter. He whispers to her also, she gives a little scream and he claps his hand over her mouth and cautions her to be quiet.* UNCLE NAT *goes out through the woodhouse door, followed by* PERLEY. *All this is unobserved by* BLAKE *and* MARTIN.]

BLAKE. [*In an undertone to* MARTIN; *this can just be heard by the audience.*] Don't worry, Martin, mebbe things'll come out all right.

[MARTIN *shakes his head without looking up.*]

BLAKE. All yeh've got to do is to keep up the interest—y'know.

MARTIN. [*Without looking up.*] Interest—how'm I goin' t' pay interest an' the farm all cut up?

BLAKE. I know, it's goin' to be a tough job. You'll hev to begin all over agin—seed down the avenoos—cut down the shade trees—an' plow up the hotel site.

[*Enter* UNCLE NAT *from the woodhouse, carrying a baby, and followed by* ANN. MARTIN *and* BLAKE *are so absorbed in their talk that they do not see them.*]

MARTIN. I wish you'd ben struck dumb afore ever you come here to set us all by the ears with y'r blame land scheme—I hain't had a minute's peace sence you fust put it inter my head.

BLAKE. [*Good-naturedly.*] Thet's right, blame me. *Blame me.*

MARTIN. [*Flaming up in bitterness.*] Who else *should* I blame? Ef it hadn't 'a' ben fer you, I'd 'a' ben satisfied as I was. [UNCLE NAT *comes to centre and* ANN *takes the baby, takes the shawl from around it and hands it back to* UNCLE NAT, *who comes slowly down centre.*] Helen'd never left hum ef it hadn't 'a' ben fer you— [*Raising his head aloft.*] I wish I was dead. I'm ashamed to look my wife an' children in the face. [*Just at this moment he sees* UNCLE NAT *who has been drawing near, the baby in his arms.* MARTIN *rises, and pauses, startled.*] What's thet—?

UNCLE NAT. [*Beaming, his voice almost choking with joy.*] Kinder sorter looks like a baby—don't it—?

MARTIN. [*Puzzled.*] Whose is it?

UNCLE NAT. [*Looking down at the baby and rocking it back and forth in his arms.*] I d'know's I jes' know!

MARTIN. [*Looks all round the room.*] Where'd it come from?

UNCLE NAT. I got it—out on the doorstep jes' now.

MARTIN. Well, put it right straight back on the doorstep—I ain't the poor-master.

UNCLE NAT. This baby ain't lookin' fer no poorhouse—this baby's goin' to stay right here.

MARTIN. There's too many babies here now.

UNCLE NAT. No there ain't nuther. Yeh can't hev too many babies in a home. [*He crosses and sits in chair centre, and rocks the baby in his arms.*]

BLAKE. [*Hungrily, coming forward.*] Give it to me. By George, I'll take it!

ANN. [*Coming down to* MARTIN, *and speaking gently, her voice full of tears.*] Martin, won't yeh guess whose baby this is?

MARTIN. I ain't a-guessin' babies.

ANN. [*Twining her arms around his neck.*] Guess this one, jes' fer me, Martin. Jes' as a sort of a Christmas present.

MARTIN. [*Looks at her earnestly, then says softly.*] Tain't —Nell's—?

ANN. [*Drops her eyes to the floor, afraid of how he will take her answer.*] Yes—It's poor Nell's.

MARTIN. [*In a fierce loud whisper.*] Poor Nell's? Yeh don't mean to say thet he didn't marry her?

[UNCLE NAT *draws the baby close to his breast as if to shield it from even that thought.*]

ANN. Oh yes, Martin, he married her.

MARTIN. [*Misinterpreting her words and her action, aghast, slowly, in a loud whisper.*] You don't mean to say she's *dead?*

ANN. No, Martin, she ain't dead.

MARTIN. [*After a pause.*] Where is she?

ANN. [*Points to the woodhouse.*] Out there.

[MARTIN *looks from* ANN *to* UNCLE NAT, *and back to* ANN. *Then he walks slowly up stage towards the woodhouse. At the door he pauses, hesitates, and finally says,*]

MARTIN. Nathan'l—be keerful—don't drop that baby. [*He goes slowly out through the woodhouse door.*]

[UNCLE NAT, *still seated, continues to rock the baby back and forth.* ANN *looks down into the baby's face.* BLAKE *goes to the stove and stands with his back to it, and his coat tails parted behind him, absorbed in thought.*]

UNCLE NAT. [*As* MARTIN *goes out, with quiet, sly humor.*] I've held you many a time an' I never dropped *you.* [*Pause.*] Well, Ma, I s'pose you're awful proud 'cause yeh're a gran'-mother. [*Reflectively.*] Seems only the day 'fore yist'day sence Nell was a baby herself.

[*The woodhouse door opens and* MARTIN *enters slowly lead-*

ing HELEN *by the hand. She looks dazed, but very happy to be back in her home. They are followed by* SAM, *now a bearded handsome man who appears to be perfectly happy and gratified that* HELEN'S *wish to bring her baby home has been fulfilled.* SAM *has returned from the West a prosperous, successful man; they are both well dressed and have an air of achievement.* PERLEY *follows* SAM *into the room, her face beaming with joy. There is a long pause; everybody's eyes are on* MARTIN *and* HELEN. *He leads her proudly and slowly down the stage before he speaks.*]

MARTIN. Nell—my girl—I'm glad to see yeh back, thet's all I got to say.

[*It is with difficulty that* MARTIN *can get these words out. Tears are in his eyes and voice. He kisses her.* BLAKE *has been standing spellbound, and now he blows his nose to hide his emotion.* HELEN *creeps into her father's embrace, puts her arms around his neck and looks pleadingly first at him and then at* SAM, *as though to say "Father, haven't you got a word for Sam?"* MARTIN'S *gaze follows hers and he sees* SAM. HELEN *draws away a little and* MARTIN *moves towards* SAM. ANN *goes to* HELEN *and puts her arms about her; both women are tense, expectantly waiting to see what* MARTIN *will do.*]

MARTIN. [*Making a big effort to conquer his pride.*] Sam, I don't b'lieve I acted jes's a father ought to hev acted towards Nell, an' I didn't treat you quite right I know—I— [*Hesitantly stretches out his hand which* SAM *takes in a hearty grasp, and the two men shake hands.*]
[ANN *and* HELEN, *in great relief, embrace each other joyously.*]

SAM. [*In a big warmhearted manner.*] Oh! That's all right, Mr. Berry! You didn't quite understand me, that's all.

MARTIN. [*Introspectively.*] Thet must 'a' ben it, I didn't understand yeh. [*Then with a complete change of manner* MARTIN *turns briskly to* UNCLE NAT *who is still seated in the chair nursing the baby, and in an almost boyish manner, says to him with an air of ownership]* Give me thet baby!

[*During this scene,* HELEN *and* SAM *go up left centre to* YOUNG NAT *and greet him affectionately. He proudly displays his long trousers. Then they turn to* PERLEY *who stands above the table and greet her warmly. She helps* HELEN *off with her things, also takes* SAM'S *hat and coat, and hangs them up on the pegs beside the woodhouse door.*]

UNCLE NAT. [*Imperturbably.*] No sir, this baby goes right straight back on the door step where it come from—

MARTIN. Give me thet baby I tell yeh—

UNCLE NAT. [*Rocking the baby in his arms.*] No sir! there's too many babies here now. This ain't no poorhouse.

MARTIN. You give me thet baby.

UNCLE NAT. [*Getting up and handing him the baby.*] All right—take y'r ol' baby—I'm durned ef I don't hev a baby o' my own one o' these days—yeh see ef I don't—an' then I'm durned ef I'll lend her to any of yeh— [*He goes up stage.*]

[*During the next scene,* ANN *goes up stage, pokes the fire, and puts the kettle which is on the back of the stove, in one of the front holes, where it at once begins to sing; she bustles about, gets the teapot and makes some tea.* MARTIN *is standing centre, holding the baby in his arms, with* SAM *on one side and* HELEN *on the other.*]

MARTIN. [*Looking down at the baby.*] How old is it?

HELEN. Three months last Sunday.

MARTIN. Thet so? [*Looking down at it and smiling proudly.*] It's a pooty baby. [*A pause.*] What is it?

SAM. [*Proudly.*] Boy!

MARTIN. Thet so? [*Glancing up.*] H-h-hev—yeh—named him yit?

HELEN. Sam calls him Martin.

MARTIN. Thet so! [*Calls to* UNCLE NAT, *full of pride.*] Nathan'l, he's a boy an' his name's Martin.

UNCLE NAT. Oh! Good Lord! I knowed all 'bout thet long ago. [*Sits in the rocking-chair.*]

MARTIN. Thet so—I thought I was tellin' yeh news.

UNCLE NAT. Yeh wa'n't tellin' me no news, was he, Nell?

HELEN. No, indeed.

MARTIN. Gimme that rockin'-chair.

UNCLE NAT. [*Getting up from the rocking-chair and placing it in the middle of the stage.*] Give him the rockin'-chair— he's a grandfather. He owns the *house* now—

[MARTIN *seats himself in the rocking-chair with the baby on his knee.* UNCLE NAT *sits in the chair down right formerly occupied by* MARTIN.]

ANN. [*Bringing the pot of tea and cups and saucers over to the table.*] Here, Hel'n, you an' Sam drink this cup o' tea.

[HELEN *and* SAM *sit down at the table,* SAM *at the upper end and* HELEN *on his right.* YOUNG NAT *is seated on the left of the table. During the preceding scene,* BLAKE *has been hovering on the outskirts of the group, forgotten for the moment by all, profoundly moved at what is taking place. He now musters up his courage to speak to* SAM.]

BLAKE. Dr. Warren! Oh, Dr. Warren!

SAM. [*Rises and goes to him.*] Hello, Mr. Blake. Helen, here's Mr. Blake.

HELEN. [*Bows pleasantly.*] Why, how do you do, Mr. Blake?

BLAKE. Oh, I'm feeling pretty good for an old man. [*Turning to* SAM.] Dr. Warren, I'm awfully ashamed of the part I had in drivin' you away. It was small potatoes an' few in a hill.

SAM. [*With the same hearty manner in which he spoke to* MARTIN.] Oh, that's all right, Mr. Blake. You folks around here didn't understand fellows like me, that's all.

BLAKE. Well, I'm ashamed of it all the same. [*He crosses to* HELEN.] Helen—I mean Mrs. Warren—will you shake hands with me?

HELEN. Why certainly, Mr. Blake. [*They shake hands.*] Oh, by the way, Mr. Blake, did you ever find out who stole your hundred dollars that time?

[*All listen.*]

BLAKE. [*Ashamed.*] Well to tell the truth it never *was* stole.

ALL. What!

HELEN. [*Amazed.*] Never was stolen?

BLAKE. No! We found it stuck away in the back part o' the safe—among a lot of papers.

YOUNG NAT. [*Rising and standing left below the table, half grinning and half ashamed, with a sort of bravado.*] That was some o' *my* work. I hid it there.

HELEN. You—?

ANN. You—what fer—I say what fer?

YOUNG NAT. [*Half crying.*] I wanted to git even with Sam Warren fer pullin' my ear—I heerd him ask Mr. Blake fer a hundred dollars an' I hid the package. I was sorry the minute I done it and I'd 'a' told long ago only I was afraid of a lickin'.

ANN. Well, I swan to goodness ef you ain't wuss'n the Black Ranger—I say wuss'n the Black Ranger! G' long up to bed this minute an' not a doughnut nor a mouthful o' pie do you git fer a week—I say fer a week!

YOUNG NAT. [*Picking up his book, and taking the candle which* PERLEY *hands him, crying.*] I won't stay here after to-morry—you see if I do—I'll go out West an' be a cowboy 'r somethin'—you see if I don't! [*He stamps upstairs in a rage.*]

ANN. [*Calling after him.*] Gimme thet book—I say gimme thet book!

YOUNG NAT. [*At the top of the stairs, throws the book which almost strikes* PERLEY.] Take yer ol' book! I don't want it! [*He tramps off, banging the door.*]

ANN. Perley—put thet book in the fire. [PERLEY *picks up the book, starts to the stove with it, opens it, becomes absorbed in it, backs to the small rocking-chair above the table, sits down and reads it.*] Martin Berry, be you a-goin' to let thet boy go out West an' be a cowboy or somethin'—I say or somethin'? [*Her voice rises in an angry shriek.*]

UNCLE NAT. [*Who is still seated down right.*] You set him to milkin' ol' Brindle to-morry—she'll knock all the cowboy out'n him.

[*They all laugh.*]

BLAKE. Meanness is like a kickin' gun, ain't it? A feller never knows when it's goin' to knock him over.

MARTIN. [*Curiously.*] Ef it's a fair question, Sam, where did yeh git the hundred dollars yeh went away with?

SAM. [*Pointing to* UNCLE NAT.] Didn't he ever tell you?

UNCLE NAT. I let him hev ninety-two dollars an' eight cents of it.

MARTIN. [*Surprised.*] Where'd *you* get it?

UNCLE NAT. I borrowed the ninety-two dollars. Borrowed it off'n you an' me an' Mother. I knowed Mother wouldn't mind waitin' a month or two longer an'—it's all paid back long ago, Martin. It's in the ol' bean pot in the pantry there. [*To* BLAKE.] Mr. Blake, thet was the speckled pullet thet fell into the rain barrel thet time.

BLAKE. Well, I don't know as it's goin' to do any good to stand here callin' ourselves hard names. Martin, I wish you'd let me hold thet baby jes' a minute.

[SAM *leans over to* HELEN *as if to say "Don't let him, he' might drop it."*]

MARTIN. No, *sir*—

ANN. Be keerful, you ain't used to handlin' babies, Mr. Blake, I say babies.

BLAKE. I suppose I could learn, same's the rest of yeh, if I had a chance, couldn't I? [*He takes the baby carefully in his arms, and looks lovingly at it.*] Mrs. Warren, I hope you won't bias me with the Junior here—I feel's if me an' the Junior was goin' to be great cronies. [*Leans over the baby.*] Look here, if they're mean to you here, you jes' come up to Blake's an' yeh can hev all the candy an' apples an' crackers yeh can lug off.

UNCLE NAT. [*With concern.*] See here, Blake, you mustn't go to feedin' thet baby on green apples up to thet store—

BLAKE. [*To* HELEN, *a little wistfully.*] I suppose I can come over an' see him once in a while?

HELEN. Certainly!

BLAKE. Thank yeh. [*He looks at her.* ANN *comes and takes the baby. A knock is heard at the door, right.*]

ANN. Come in—I say, come in.

[*Enter* GATES *and* MANDY, *both muffled up to their chins in worn, ragged garments, and covered with snow.* MANDY'S *eyes instantly fall on the presents hanging by the stove, and throughout the scene she continues to stare wistfully at them.*]

GATES. [*Speaking as he enters.*] How d'do? [*He sees* HELEN *and* SAM, *and his tone changes to one of surprise.*] Why, how' d'do? I'd no idee you'd got back. Ef I'd 'a' knowed thet, I'd ben over afore— [*He sees* ANN *with the baby in her arms.*] What's thet?

ANN. A baby—what'd yeh suppose 'twas? [*She crosses down left and seats herself in a low chair by the sitting room door, rocking the baby on her knees.* UNCLE NAT *goes back to his work with the presents.*]

GATES. [*Confusedly.*] I wa'n't supposin' nothin.' I hadn't

heerd any rumours afloat 'bout your havin'— [*The mistake dawns upon the characters who look from one to the other and burst into a laugh, not sudden, but gradual.* GATES *is nonplussed.*] Uh—whose is it?

HELEN. Mine.

GATES. *Yourn?* Well, who'd ever 'a' thought o' *your* havin' a baby? I tell yeh what, Nathan'l, thet West *is* a growin' country an' *no* mistake! [*To* ANN.] I jes' come over to see ef I could leave Mandy here a spell to-morry—I got a job over t' Pearce's thet's *got* to be done to-morry, an' they got measles over there an' I'm skeered to take'r with me—

ANN. What'n the name o' common sense'd yeh want to fetch'r out such a night's this fur? D'yeh want to kill'r—I say kill'r?

GATES. Kill'r? Gosh, I guess *not.* [*He pats* MANDY *lovingly.*] She wouldn't stay t'hum.

ANN. Lunsome I guess, I say lunsome.

GATES. I guess'o—she's allus lunsome. Seems lunsomer Christmasses than any other time.

ANN. Let'r stay here now. She can sleep with the children, I say with the children.

GATES. Want to, Mandy? [*She looks up at him, he leans down to her and she whispers in his ear. With an apologetic smile,*] Says she'd ruther sleep with me.

ANN. Well, she mustn't be lunsome to-morry—she must come over an' spend this Christmas with us—

UNCLE NAT. [*Coming down from the stove where he has been working with the presents, with a doll which he gives to* MANDY.] Here's a dolly fer yeh, Mandy. This's goin' t'be the jolliest Christmas we've had fer many a year.

MARTIN. [*Suddenly remembering.*] An' the last one we'll ever hev in this ol' house.

SAM. The last—I hope not.

HELEN. [*At the same time.*] Why, father, what do you mean?

[UNCLE NAT *looks at* MARTIN *in amazement.*]

MARTIN. My durn land boom's busted.

ANN. [*Looking over at him full of sympathy.*] An' thet's what's been a-worryin' of yeh! Poor Martin, I say poor Martin!

[ALL *the faces change; all are silent for a moment.*]

GATES. [*To* BLAKE.] Is thet *so?*

BLAKE. [*Earnestly and sympathetically.*] That's 'bout so.

GATES. Then yeh ain't a-goin' t'build thet there Opperry House?

BLAKE. Well—no—not right off—I guess.

GATES. Sorry. I'd like t'seen thet Opperry House. Them plans was beautiful. Knocks me out'n a job too— [*Chuckles.*] I guess I got 'bout th' unly farm in the county thet hain't ben surveyed 'r cut up fer sumpthin' 'r other.

[UNCLE NAT *places a chair for him, right centre.* GATES *sits with* MANDY *standing between his knees.* UNCLE NAT *goes back to his work.*]

MARTIN. Hel'n, I'm poorer'n I was the day I come into the world. Blake owns Shore Acres now—or will by spring when his mortgage comes due.

SAM. How much is it mortgaged for, Mr. Berry?

BLAKE. All it's wuth.

ANN. Fifteen hundred dollars!

MARTIN. It'd take me ten years to lift it.

GATES. [*Shakes his head.*] Yeh couldn't do it in ten year. [*Reflectively.*] No sir,—fifteen hundred dollars!

[*During the above scene* SAM *has been talking to* HELEN *in a whisper, unheard by the audience.*]

SAM. Nell, what d'you say if we mortgage our home and lend the money to your father?

HELEN. [*Delighted.*] Of course—that's the thing to do—

SAM. We may lose it—

HELEN. No we won't—and if we do we're young—we'll get another.

SAM. Shall I tell him—?

HELEN. Yes.

SAM. All right, here goes. [*Aloud.*] Father—I mean Mr. Berry—we can help you *some*. We can reduce the principal a little and keep up the interest for you. Nell and I have scraped a little home together out there. We'd hate to lose it, but we'll borrow what we can on it and—

MARTIN. [*Deeply moved.*] No—you shan't do thet—let the ol' place go—

SAM. Come out West with us and make a fresh start.

HELEN. [*Eagerly.*] Oh yes, father—do!

MARTIN. No, I'm 'feared I hain't got spunk enough. I'll stay here. Mother'n the children an' Nathan'l can go ef they've a mind to—

ANN. [*Her voice breaking.*] Martin Berry, I didn't marry yeh to leave yeh. I'll stay right here with yeh. We'll live in the lighthouse ef we hev to, I say ef we hev to.

UNCLE NAT. [*In a gentle drawl.*] Well, ef you think yeh're a-goin' to get red o' *me*—yeh're mighty much mistaken. Mother allus told me to watch out fer yeh, an' now by George thet yeh're gettin' into yer secon' childhood, I'm a-goin' to do it—

SAM. Mr. Blake won't foreclose—will you, Mr. Blake?

BLAKE. [*Regretfully.*] I'm sorry, but it's out o' my hands. I'm as bad off as Martin is. I've bought, and mortgaged and borrowed on everything I had— I can't realize fifty cents on the dollar. I'm simply land poor. Interest a-eatin' me up, principal a-comin' due,—I don't know which way to turn. My lawyers advise me to make an assignment the first o' the year. Well, I guess I'll be a-joggin' along hum—

UNCLE NAT. What's yer hurry, Mr. Blake?

BLAKE. [*With a big sigh.*] Well—it's a-gettin' late—an' I don't feel jes' right somehow— [*He gets into his coat and hat,* UNCLE NAT *helping him.*]

HELEN. Better let Sam prescribe for you, Mr. Blake.

BLAKE. [*Glancing at her and then at the baby, says gently.*] He has—that's what ails me I guess.

SAM. I can fetch you around all right, Mr. Blake.

BLAKE. [*Hunting in his coat pockets for his gloves, and laughing in an effort to assume his old, cheery manner.*] What with, sugar shot? No, by George, I hain't got t' thet yet— [*He pulls out his gloves, and with them a letter postmarked and stamped, and addressed to* NATHANIEL BERRY.] Oh, Nathan'l, here's a letter come for you this evenin'. It's postmarked Washington, D. C. Weather bein' so bad I thought I'd bring it over.

UNCLE NAT. [*Taking letter, mildly surprised and interested.*] Much obleeged, but I dunno who'd write me from Washin'-ton.

ANN. The Pres'dent mebbe, wishin' yeh a Merry Christmas.

GATES. Yes! The Pres'dent ginerally wishes everybody a Merry Christmas—specially ef it's a-comin' on election time.

UNCLE NAT. [*Turning the letter over and over.*] Nell, would you mind a-readin' this? Your eyes is younger'n mine. [*Gives her the letter.*]

HELEN. [*Opens the letter and reads it aloud. The letter is written on a letter sheet with a small printed heading, such as is used by attorneys at law, not a commercial letterhead.*]

"Washington, D. C., December 18, 1892. Nathaniel Berry Esquire, Berry, Maine. Sir: Dr. Samuel Warren of Trinidad, Colorado, some months ago commissioned us to present your claim to back pension. We are pleased to inform you that our efforts on your behalf have been successful and that your claim amounting to $1,768.92 has been finally allowed. We have this day written Dr. Warren. Awaiting your further pleasure, we are, Very truly yours, Higgins and Wells, Attorneys at law."
Oh! Uncle Nat!

[*There is a general murmur of amazement.*]

UNCLE NAT. [*Who is standing beside* HELEN.] Well, I won't tech it. I d'want no back pension, an' I don't want nothin' to do with no durn lawyers. A pension grabber's next thing to a bounty jumper, an' I'll be jiggered ef I tech it.

ANN. [*Still sitting down left with the baby.*] Why not? I say why not?

UNCLE NAT. 'Cause I never fit fer no back pension. I fit— 'Cause— [*He catches* ANN's *eye and stops.* ANN *looks at him significantly, and then at* MARTIN, *who sits, the picture of dejection.* UNCLE NAT *glances around at the others, and reads the same implication in all their eyes. He wavers and finishes lamely.*] 'Cause I fit.

ANN. Yeh airned it—didn't yeh? I say yeh airned it?

SAM. You know there's a good deal of difference between earning a pension and grabbing a pension.

GATES. Oh! My—yes—heaps. Seems to me—ef I was you— [*No one pays any attention to* GATES *and his voice trails off into silence.*]

UNCLE NAT. Thet's so—I didn't think o' thet. Le's see— [*His face is illumined with a rarely beautiful smile.*] To-morry's Christmas, ain't it? Ma, I hain't made you a *reel* Christmas present—not sence the day you was married, hev I?

ANN. [*Smiling at him.*] Thet wa'n't Christmas.

UNCLE NAT. [*Chuckling.*] Jes' as good—wa'n't it? I'll tell yeh what I'll do—ef Martin'll make the place over to you —I'll take the back pension.

MARTIN. [*Broken and greatly touched by* UNCLE NAT'S *generosity.*] I'd know as I've got a right to say either yes or no. I'll do whatever you and Mother wants I should. I hain't got a word to say.

UNCLE NAT. [*Going to* MARTIN *and clapping him on the back.*] Yeh don't need to say another word, Martin, not another blessed word. [*Turning to* HELEN.] Helen, git me ol' Uncle Sam'l. Say, Martin, Uncle Sam'l's the gal thet won the pension, an' she's the feller thet ought to hev it. [HELEN *brings the gun down to* UNCLE NAT, *who is standing centre. He takes it, and speaks to it affectionately, half crying, half laughing.*] Well, ol' gal, yeh've got yer deserts at last. Yeh not only saved the Union, but, by Gosh, yeh've saved this hull family! [*Still holding the gun,* UNCLE NAT *starts to go through the Manual of Arms, while* GATES *watches him and imitates him.*] Attention! [*He comes stiffly to attention.* GATES *does the same.*] Shoulder-r-r Arms! [*He brings the gun to his shoulder.* GATES *pretends to do the same thing.*] Carr-r-r-y Arms! Pre-e-sent Arms!

[*As* UNCLE NAT *starts to present arms, the gun goes off suddenly. It must be loaded so as to make a great smoke and not too much noise. There is a movement of general excitement and panic.* HELEN'S *first thought is for her baby, and she rushes over to* ANN *and takes it in her arms.* GATES *picks up* MANDY, *heels in the air, and head down, and rushes to the door, right, as if to save her anyway. He stands frantically pawing the door in the attempt to find the latch and escape with* MANDY *out of harm's way, giving frightened little gasps as he does so. As the smoke clears away, the others all gather around* UNCLE NAT *who explains that the explosion was an accident. They are all excitedly talking and laughing, and completely oblivious of* GATES, *who, as the*

panic dies down, comes to his senses, and turns his atten-
tion to MANDY. *She is completely enveloped in her wraps*
and he has some difficulty in getting her right side up. When
he finally discovers her feet, he sets her on the ground, frees
her head from its wrappings, smooths her hair, feels her
body to assure himself that no bones are broken, kisses her
and croons over her. UNCLE NAT, *still holding the gun, comes*
down to him, and starts to explain, but, at his approach
GATES *has another attack of fright, and seizing* MANDY, *he*
starts to back towards the door, waving UNCLE NAT *away.*]

UNCLE NAT. [*Laughing.*] That's the fust time Uncle Sam'l
ever kicked me!

GATES. [*Putting his fingers in his ears.*] Gosh, that deefened
me! [*Then, as if to test his hearing, he cries,*] Oh! Oh! Oh!

[*Everyone laughs. They have all recovered their spirits as*
readily as they became depressed.]

BLAKE. [*Who has got to the door by this time.*] Well, good
night. [*He goes out.*]

GATES. [*Who is still nervous.*] I go your way a piece, Mr.
Blake. [*He hurries after* BLAKE, *dragging* MANDY *with him.*
UNCLE NAT *shows them out, closes the door and locks it after*
them.]

ALL. [*Calling after them.*] Good night, good night.

ANN. Come now, it's bedtime, I say bedtime.

[*There is a general movement.* UNCLE NAT *puts the gun*
away, then he turns and begins the task of locking up for the
night, plodding slowly and methodically about the room.
PERLEY *lights a candle, and goes upstairs and off.* ANN *lights*
a candle which she leaves on the table for UNCLE NAT, *and*
picks up the lamp. She and HELEN *move towards the door*
down left.]

HELEN. Yes—I'm pretty tired. Shall we sleep in my old
room?

ANN. O'course.

HELEN. [*As she goes off left.*] Are all the children well?

ANN. [*Following* HELEN *off.*] You'd 'a' thought so if you'd seen'm trainin' around here this evenin'— [*Outside.*] with Nathan'l.

[SAM *and* MARTIN *come down left, following* ANN *and* HELEN. MARTIN *has his arm around* SAM's *shoulders.*]

MARTIN. So you're a-doin' well out there, eh Sam?

SAM. First rate. That's the country for a young man.

MARTIN. I s'pose 'tis. Chicago must be a great city.

SAM. A wonderful city. Why don't you come out for the World's Fair? [*He goes off through the door lower left.* MARTIN *pauses at the door, turns, and looks at* UNCLE NAT.]

MARTIN. [*In a low voice.*] Nathan'l. [UNCLE NAT *looks up.*] Yeh never told Ann about that night in the lighthouse—did yeh?

UNCLE NAT. [*Coming down a few steps towards him; in a deep whisper.*] I never told her nothin'.

MARTIN. [*After a pause.*] She'd ought to 'a' had you. 'Twan't jes' right somehow— [*He goes slowly off, lower left, closing the door.*]

[UNCLE NAT *stands looking after* MARTIN, *his face lighted up by an inner glow of peace and happiness. His thoughts are reflected in his face, but not a word is spoken. The scene is played in absolute silence.*]

[*He sinks into the rocking-chair close by with a sigh of content and satisfaction. He settles himself comfortably, with his chin resting in his right hand as he thinks.*]

UNCLE NAT. [*He thinks this.*] Well, everythin's all right again. [*He nods his head approvingly.*] I wonder how long Nell 'n' Sam's a-goin' to stay? A month 'r two anyway. [*Then a soft, tender smile creeps slowly into his face at the thought of the baby.*] Bless thet baby! I wonder what the young uns'll say in the mornin'? It'll be better'n a circus here when Millie sees thet baby. [*He chuckles softly at the thought. Then suddenly he scans the door, wondering if he locked it. He rises slowly, easing himself on the arms of the chair, and plods to the door; he tries the lock, then tucks the doormat snugly against the sill to keep the snow from drifting in. Then he goes to the window, rubs the pane to clear the frost from it and peers out.*] Gracious! What a night! [*He stoops down, and looks up to find the lighthouse beacon. He nods his head.*] Ol' Berry's all right— Tim's there. [*As he turns from the window, shrugging his shoulders and shivering a little,*] Snow'll be ten foot deep in the mornin'. [*He goes to the stove and sets the kettle back, lifts one of the lids and looks at the fire. A thought strikes him.*] By George, it's a-goin' to be pooty hard work to git the ol' farm inter shape agin! [*He shuts the damper.*] Well, hard work never skeered me— [*He goes to the woodhouse door and fastens the bolt. Coming down to the table he picks up the candle which* ANN *left there for him and starts to go up the stairs. At the foot he pauses, then he moves down to the door, softly pushes it open and stands there for a moment looking off. He smiles to himself as he thinks,*] I wonder what the young uns'll say in the mornin'? [*For a moment he is lost in thought; his right arm slowly relaxes. Then he turns and starts to climb slowly up the stairs, his heavy footfalls echoing through the empty room. The wind howls outside; the sharp snow tinkles rhythmically upon the window-pane. The stage darkens slightly. He reaches the top of the stairs and goes off, closing the door after him. The stage is left in darkness except for the firelight flickering through the chinks of the stove. The cuckoo clock strikes twelve and the curtain slowly descends.*]

THE END OF THE PLAY

SAG HARBOR

"AN OLD STORY."

A Play in Four Acts

By

JAMES A. HERNE

CHARACTERS

WILLIAM TURNER, *formerly of Islip, Long Island, now Sag Harbor agent for the steamer, "Antelope."*

BEN TURNER, *his son, a boat builder.*

FRANK TURNER, *Ben's younger brother, seaman in U. S. N.*

CAP'N DAN MARBLE, *owner of the sloop "Kacy"; scallops in her winters, sails company in her summers.*

FREEMAN WHITMARSH, *house, sign and ornamental painter and glazier. Leads the choir.*

GEORGE SALTER, *Ben's right-hand man.*

HOSEA STEVENS, *bar keeper at the Nassau House.*

JIM ADAMS
ED MILLS } *Ship carpenters.*

TWO MAN-O'WARS-MEN.

MRS. JOHN RUSSELL, *a widow.*

ELIZABETH ANNE TURNER, *William's maiden sister.*

MARTHA REESE, *an orphan.*

JANE CAULDWELL, *of Bridgehampton, a music teacher.*

FRANCES TOWD, *née Seely, of Water Mill.*

MISS BAILEY, *of Gloversville, N. Y.*

SUSAN MURPHY, *the hired girl.*

THE BABY.

A group of villagers.

ACT I.   May, 1895.
          "A little old country shipyard."

ACT II. The next afternoon.
          The interior of Ben Turner's shop.

ACT III. April, 1897.
          The living room of the Turner home.

ACT IV. The next day. "Easter Sunday."
          Same as Act III.

PLACE—Sag Harbor, Long Island.

SAG HARBOR

ACT FIRST

May, *1895*.

"A little old country shipyard."

SCENE: *A corner of the shipyard looking towards Shelter Island, with a view of Gardiner's Bay beyond. At back, on the right, is a view of North Haven, on the left is the village of Sag Harbor.*

The yard is a picturesque place, and is littered with saw' horses, timber, shipbuilder's tools, chips and rope. In the centre, well on the scene, is the stern of a forty-foot sloop on the ways. Her hull is painted black, with a white trim, and the words, "KACY, SAG HARBOR, N. Y." are painted in white letters on her stern.

BEN'S *shop, with the door open, runs up and down stage on the left. There is an entrance left, above the shop, leading off through the yard to the Turner home. An entrance on the right leads off through the yard to the main street. A steam yacht, one or two sloop yachts and some dories and working boats, are lying at anchor in the harbor beyond the yard. It is a warm afternoon in early May, and the atmosphere of the scene is one of lazy content. As the action progresses, the sun sets, and when the act finishes, it is twilight. At the rise of the curtain,* CAP'N DAN MARBLE *and* ELIZABETH ANNE *are seated on an old spar which lies across the yard from left to right. They are playing cat's cradle.* ELIZABETH *has the string on her hands, and* CAP'N DAN *is preparing to take it off. They are both absorbed in their game.*

[CAP'N DAN *is a hale, hearty man in his late fifties. His face is tanned and wrinkled, and his hair is iron-grey. He wears short grey side whiskers, cut close. He is dressed in his last*

127

year's sailing-master's blue suit. His manner is cheery and genial and, in his scenes with ELIZABETH, *a little wistful. He has a quaint and ready humour.*]

[ELIZABETH ANNE *is a sweet wholesome-looking woman of the New England type, about forty-five. Everything about her is simple, but well-kept and dainty. Her gingham dress is immaculate, her hair has a fine sheen.*]

[*Enter from behind the "Kacy" up left,* GEORGE SALTER, *in working dress. He has a writing pad and a pencil, and has been making notes of the work to be done on the boat.*]

GEORGE. [*Coming up right centre, carelessly.*] You two cat's cradlin' again?

CAP'N DAN. Yep—that's the only cradle we're ever likely to need, I guess.

GEORGE. [*Carelessly.*] Oh! I hope not.

CAP'N DAN. I hope not, but it looks that way, George.

GEORGE. [*Looking over his memoranda.*] Well, I guess I've got everythin'.

CAP'N DAN. Good. What have you got?

GEORGE. [*Reading.*] "Caulk her thoroughly."

CAP'N DAN. First class oakum. Fill her seams with red lead.

GEORGE. [*Nods and reads.*] "Give her bottom two coats— raise her water line."

CAP'N DAN. Three inches aft, to nothin' for'ard.

GEORGE. [*Nods and reads.*] "New topmast—"

CAP'N DAN. Eighteen inches longer than the old one. Tops'l never stood on the old one, it was allus too short. [GEORGE *nods.*]

GEORGE. [*Reading.*] "Riggin' all to be set up and served over new."

CAP'N DAN. Yes yes. Have Preston do that. [GEORGE *nods.*]

And see 't he puts on thin canvas and tars it before he serves it—an' asphalts the servin' and splices all the deadeyes an' sets 'em up tighter.

GEORGE. [*Nods and reads.*] "Raise floor four inches."

CAP'N DAN. Yes. It's too low. That is, when she gets into a sea, the water blows right through the sealin'. Can't keep no carpets dry.

GEORGE. [*Going centre.*] You'll paint her yourself, I suppose?

CAP'N DAN. Yes yes, I want to save all the pennies I can. Freeman'll do the gilt work.

GEORGE. All right. [*He goes into the shop, left.*]

CAP'N DAN. [*Calling after him.*] When can I have her?

GEORGE. [*Outside.*] Oh, inside of ten days, I guess.

ELIZABETH. Pretty extravagant this spring, ain't yeh?

CAP'N DAN. D'know's I *am*—d'know *as* I am; got to spend money to make money.

[FREEMAN WHITMARSH *enters from the right. He is a tall lank, gawky man in his early thirties, with a long nose, angular features, and unkempt red hair. He is slow in all his movements, and is in the habit of speaking through his closed teeth. He is dressed in a painter's white suit—overalls, jumper and cap, all of which are well daubed with paint of various colours.*]

FREEMAN. [*Referring to the boat, but without making a gesture of any sort, and in a tone that might indicate a woman or anything else.*] Got the old girl hauled out, I see.

ELIZABETH. [*Haughtily.*] Got what old girl hauled out, Freeman Whitmarsh?

FREEMAN. [*Carelessly.*] The "Kacy."

ELIZABETH. Oh! I beg your pardon.

CAP'N DAN. Yes.

FREEMAN. Quit scallopin' early, didn't yeh?

CAP'N DAN. Weather got so hot all of a suddint.

FREEMAN. Got many shells?

CAP'N DAN. 'Bout four thousand bushel. I hain't measured 'em, but I should say that's 'bout what they is of 'em.

FREEMAN. [*At left.*] What'll they fetch this year?

CAP'N DAN. Three to five cents, there 'r thereabouts.

FREEMAN. Did yeh hear that Annie Truesdell's married?

CAP'N DAN. [*With a broad grin.*] No-o-o?

FREEMAN. Yes, married yisterday.

CAP'N DAN. Who'd she marry?

FREEMAN. That New York pants drummer. The fellah that had that mammoth pants sale here last winter.

CAP'N DAN. Yes yes!

FREEMAN. She's goin' to live with his folks in New York.

CAP'N DAN. See—what's his name agin?

FREEMAN. Morris Cohen.

CAP'N DAN. Nice lookin' fellah. *Jew,* ain't he?

FREEMAN. [*Ingenuously.*] I think he is. [*He goes into the shop.* CAP'N DAN *and* ELIZABETH *continue their game.*]

ELIZABETH. [*Smiling fondly at him.*] Take it under—stupid.

CAP'N DAN. What's the difference?

ELIZABETH. The difference between the right way and the wrong way. [*He has the string by this time.*] Now, hold still.

CAP'N DAN. Say, 'Lizbeth, you and I have been courtin' in this innocuous desuetude sort of way nigh on to fifteen year.

ELIZABETH. [*Placidly.*] I've enjoyed it, haven't you?

CAP'N DAN. [*Tentatively.*] Yes yes! [*With gentle insinua-*

tion.] But we don't seem to get any closer together. [*She has the string now.*]

ELIZABETH. [*Laughing.*] We've got so's one chair does for both Sunday evenings.

CAP'N DAN. [*Smiling.*] You know blame well what I mean. [*He takes the string from her hands.*]

ELIZABETH. [*Surveying the string, and trying to avoid answering directly.*] This *is* a hard one. [*She hesitates about taking it off.*]

CAP'N DAN. I'm not gettin' any younger—an' you're—

ELIZABETH. [*Interrupting dryly.*] Don't finish it. I know exactly what you are going to say.

CAP'N DAN. [*Smiling.*] What now?

ELIZABETH. You were going to say, I'm getting to be an old maid. [*She takes the string off his hands.*]

CAP'N DAN. [*Laughing.*] I wa'n't neither. I was goin' to say you've got your full growth— [*He gives her a sly teasing smile, then he returns to the attack.*] I don't see any sense in waitin' till we get as old as Methuselah. [*He takes the string off.*]

ELIZABETH. [*With mild reproof.*] There, don't bring up that old reprobate.

CAP'N DAN. [*Pleadingly.*] If we're goin' to get married at all—

ELIZABETH. [*She has the string on her hands by this time.*] Well, Dan'l—[*Her hands are straight out before her now, with the cat's cradle on them. He puts his arm around her.*] Take your arm away.

CAP'N DAN. I won't do it.

ELIZABETH. [*Pretending anger.*] Oh, you coward, you know my hands are tied!

CAP'N DAN. Well, I'm glad of it. [*He tries to kiss her.*]

ELIZABETH. [*With mild severity.*] Dan'l Marble, you're chewing tobacco again!

CAP'N DAN. [*Taking away his arm and moving away a little, guiltily.*] No. Just put a little in the hollow of my tooth. 'Twas achin'. [*He takes the string off her hands.*]

ELIZABETH. [*Concerned.*] Be they your new ones?

CAP'N DAN. Yep. Brand new set—eight dollars!

ELIZABETH. [*Puzzled.*] I don't see why they should ache.

CAP'N DAN. Nor I, but they do.

ELIZABETH. Didn't he warrant 'em?

CAP'N DAN. Yes.

ELIZABETH. Sing'lar! See, what was I talking about?

CAP'N DAN. About you and me and old Methuselah.

ELIZABETH. Oh yes! [*With gentle gravity.*] Well, you and I are not children, Dan'l. We're not ashamed or afraid to tell each other the truth. I've told you my reasons for not wanting to get married.

CAP'N DAN. [*In discouraged protest.*] Yes, I know—but—a house without no children or nothin'—wouldn't be no home at all.

ELIZABETH. *I* know that, as well as *you* do.

CAP'N DAN. [*With eager pleading.*] 'Lizbeth, I'll give you my bank book—I'll give you every shillin' I earn, 'cept of course, a fellah's got to have a little change in his pocket. Sometimes over there at Jim Adams's they'll be a-chuckin' dice for segars—or—

ELIZABETH. [*Innocently.*] Oh yes, of course, I d'want you should go around sponging off people.

CAP'N DAN. [*With wistful longing.*] But I *do* want a *home.*

ELIZABETH. [*With quiet finality.*] I won't live in a house alone with a man.

CAP'N DAN. You wouldn't be livin' alone with no man—I'd be your husband.

ELIZABETH. You'd be a man all the same.

CAP'N DAN. [*Slowly.*] Yep, I s'pose I *would*. But yeh hadn't ought to lay that up against a fellah. [*He rises and goes a little towards the right.*]

ELIZABETH. [*With casual expectancy.*] Coming over this evening?

CAP'N DAN. Don't know *as* I be—don't know *but* I be. [*He puts the cord they have been playing with in his pocket, and takes out a woman's handkerchief. He gazes at it as though mystified.*] Oh! [*Then, with pretended innocence, he says,*] This yours?

ELIZABETH. Yes, one of my Sunday ones. [*She rises, smiling.*] How'd it get into your pocket?

CAP'N DAN. [*Smiling at her.*] Must 'a' had legs. [*He holds it out to her, she takes it.*] I found it there Thursday evenin' after I got home.

[ELIZABETH *snaps the handkerchief at him, and he tries to catch it. All this flirtation must be played by them as ingenuously as if they were two young people; there must be no kittenish old maid business about it.*]

CAP'N DAN. If I git it agin, I'll keep it.

ELIZABETH. *Will* you?

CAP'N DAN. Yes, I *will*. [*He snatches at the handkerchief, she puts it behind her and laughs.*]

ELIZABETH. Yeh didn't do it, smarty! [*She turns and goes up left a few steps.*]
[CAP'N DAN *takes a yellow package of "Velvets" out of his*

pocket, opens it, puts one in his mouth and puts the pack-age back into his pocket. ELIZABETH *watches him.*]

ELIZABETH. W-e-l-l! Of a-l-l—the *s-t-i-n-g-y*—

CAP'N DAN. [*With a teasing laugh.*] I'm afraid they'd make your teeth ache, ain't you?

ELIZABETH. No, I'm not. If there's anything I *am* proud of, it's my teeth.

CAP'N DAN. [*Going to her right.*] And y'r hair. [*Tenderly.*] And y'r eyes—you've got reg'lar seal's eyes, 'Lizbeth. [*He takes out the candy box and opens it as though to give her a piece.*] Open your mouth and shut your eyes. [*She does so. He attempts to kiss her, and she fools him by opening her eyes and moving a little away.*]

ELIZABETH. [*Laughing.*] Catch a weasel asleep!

CAP'N DAN. [*Following her and laughing, as he holds out a piece of candy.*] Here! [*As she hesitates.*] Honest now! Open your mouth. [*She does so, and he puts a candy into her mouth. She closes her teeth on it and laughs. He gives her the package of candy.*] Here, take this and go home. 'Y George, I won't do nothin' all day if you stay here. I wish you had a wart on the end of your nose, or somethin', so I wouldn't be so fond of you.

ELIZABETH. [*Taking the candy as she goes.*] Come over this evening, and I'll read you some more of "Puddin'head Wilson." [*She goes off left, above the shop.*]

CAP'N DAN. [*Following her up and waving to her, calls after her cheerfully,*] Yes yes, we ought to finish it by New Year's. [*He looks after her in profound admiration, then he mechanically wets one thumb and makes an imprint of it on his other hand.*]

[FREEMAN WHITMARSH *enters from the shop, left. He has a putty knife and a lump of putty in his left hand, which he works as he walks. A painter's duster is sticking out of his hip pocket, and a diamond out of his jumper pocket. He*

SAG HARBOR. ACT I. READING FROM LEFT TO RIGHT THE ACTORS ARE: MARION ABBOTT, JAMES A. HERNE, AND CHARLES PITT

carries a medium-sized pane of window glass and a square under his right arm. He occasionally wipes the putty knife backward and forward on his overalls.]

FREEMAN. [*As he crosses, right.*] Say, seen anything o' my partner?

[FRANCES TOWD *is heard off left, singing "There is a happy land," in a high unmusical voice.*]

CAP'N DAN. Who is he?

FREEMAN. She ain't a *he*—she's a *she*—Frances Towd of Water Mill. [*He nods his head in the direction of the song.*] That's her.

[FRANCES TOWD *enters from behind the shop, singing as she enters, "With a wreath of orange blossoms on her snow-white brow." She is a small and unattractive-looking woman of middle age, with insignificant features and straggling sandy hair. She has on one of* FREEMAN'S *caps and one of his jumpers. She wears over her calico dress a large apron made of sacking which covers her breast in front and forms a complete skirt. She is well daubed with paint. In her left hand she carries a pot of white paint and a paint brush. Over her right shoulder she carries a painter's stepladder.*]

FRANCES. [*To* FREEMAN, *in a loud voice.*] Say, what yeh want I should do with these 'ere 'coutrements? [*Sniffs.*]

FREEMAN. [*Correcting her patronisingly.*] They're not 'coutrements—they're tools. You're not in the army. You're in a profession. [*In a tone of command.*] Put 'em in the shop and get that pot of chrome yellah I mixed this mornin', and bring a clean brush.

FRANCES. [*Obediently, sniffing.*] Yes sir. [*She starts for the shop, then turns.*] Am I—[*Sniffs.*]—goin' up on to the scaffold?

FREEMAN. Of course. [*She sniffs and goes off into the shop, left.* FREEMAN *turns to* CAP'N DAN.] Gosh, she says scaffold as if it was the gallows!

CAP'N DAN. [*Who has been regarding* FRANCES *curiously, now goes up to the shop and looks after her in astonishment.*] Say, what did you say her name was?

FREEMAN. [*At right.*] *Was* Seely, afore she married. She's a widder. Two boys.

CAP'N DAN. [*Coming centre to* FREEMAN, *in a lower voice.*] Got a cold in her head, hain't she?

FREEMAN. No—habit. [*Confidentially.*] That's one of the things I don't like about her. Both the boys have got it, too.

CAP'N DAN. [*Very much interested.*] Think you'll—

FREEMAN. [*Complacently.*] D'know—Mother hasn't been dead a year yet. [*With a deprecating yet rather fatuous smile.*] There's so many of 'em wants me! She's got money. She's offered me seventy-five dollars and a set o' double harnesses for a half-interest in the business.

CAP'N DAN. Is she a painter?

FREEMAN. [*Dubiously.*] Well, she's taken *some* lessons. This is her first day with me.

[FRANCES *enters from the shop with a pot of chrome yellow paint and a clean brush.*]

FREEMAN. Cap'n Marble, shake hands with Mis' Towd. [FRANCES *crosses to centre, and they shake hands.*]

CAP'N DAN. [*Rather doubtfully. This woman is a new figure to him.*] How d'do? You're the first *woman* painter I ever see.

FRANCES. [*In a matter-of-fact tone, sniffing.*] Oh, bless you, women are going into everything nowadays. Architects, doctors, lawyers, barbers—they *vote* out West. [*Sniffs.*]

CAP'N DAN. *I* think a woman's place is to hum.

FRANCES. [*Sniffs.*] You must have knew my husband—Joe Towd—harnessmaker over there. [*She nods in the direction of Water Mill.*]

CAP'N DAN. [*Who is not sure about it.*] Y-e-s—I seldom get so far as Water Mill.

FRANCES. [*In the casual tone she would use in referring to a dog or a pocketbook, sniffing.*] I lost him about a year ago.

CAP'N DAN. How'd you come to do that?

FRANCES. Typhus fever. [*Sniffs.*]

CAP'N DAN. Got a cold, haven't you?

FRANCES. [*With a bland smile.*] No! Why? [*She takes out a folded freshly-ironed handkerchief, feels in her pockets for another, then says:*] Humph! That's funny! [*To* FREE-MAN.] Did you see my handkerchief? [*She looks about to see if she has dropped it.*]

FREEMAN. [*Indicating the one she is holding.*] You've got it in y'r hand.

FRANCES. That's my *shower.* I allus carry a shower and a blower. I've lost my blower. I kind of hate to use my shower. [*She blows her nose with the handkerchief.*]

FREEMAN. Well, this ain't paintin'.

FRANCES. [*Sniffs, and says as she starts to go off, left,*] If I have to do much outside work, I'll wear bloomers, I guess.

[*She goes off above the shop.* CAP'N DAN *follows her up and looks after her.*]

FREEMAN. [*Calling after her.*] Reg'lar overalls is what you want. [*To* CAP'N DAN, *as he crosses right.*] Say, did you tell Ben what I told you?

CAP'N DAN. [*Coming down right centre.*] No, not yet, I will, first chance I get. Where are you goin'?

FREEMAN. To set a light o' glass into Baldwin's office window.

CAP'N DAN. [*Interested.*] I didn't know he had one out.

FREEMAN. Well, he has; Jennin's boy knocked it out with a baseball.

CAP'N DAN. Pu'pose?

FREEMAN. [*Going.*] D'know.

CAP'N DAN. See—who'll have to pay for that?

FREEMAN. Baldwin'll pay me. I guess Jennin's 'll have to settle with him. [*He goes off, right, singing "Oh the poor workhouse boy."*]

CAP'N DAN. [*Watches* FREEMAN *off. He takes up the tune and hums it as he contemplates his boat:*]

> "Oh! the poor workhouse boy,
> Oh! the poor workhouse boy,
> Fatherless—motherless—
> Sisterless—brotherless—"

[*While he is singing,* BEN TURNER *enters left, above the shop. He is a fine, tall, handsome fellow about forty. His face is smooth-shaven, and he is dressed in working clothes, wears a cap, and has a gold watch and chain. He carries a bunch of letters in his hand as though he had just come from the post office, and he opens them and runs through them as he talks.* BEN *is a cheery, prosperous, big-hearted man.*]

BEN. [*Coming left centre.*] Hello, Cap!

CAP'N DAN. Hello, Ben. Did yeh ever hear Freeman sing that?

BEN. [*Busy with his letters.*] Oh, yes.

CAP'N DAN. [*Coming right centre.*] Didn't it make yeh cry?

BEN. No, I d'know's it did.

CAP'N DAN. Gosh! [*Singing.*]

> "Fatherless—motherless—
> Sisterless—brotherless—"

I forget if he was auntless and uncleless or not! Gosh! It's too touchin' for me! Can you imagine a more forlorn spectacle than that little boy a-settin' on the workhouse stoop—

Fatherless—motherless—
Sisterless—brotherless—

Reminds me for all the world of Martha Reese, the day her mother died.

BEN. [*Interested for the first time, looks up and says sympathetically,*] Does, some, doesn't it?

CAP'N DAN. Yes, yes. She was just such another—fatherless —motherless—sisterless—brotherless! An' they'd 'a' sent *her* to the a'mshouse if it hadn't been for you.

BEN. [*Seating himself on a nail keg, left.*] Not while you were around, I guess, Cap.

CAP'N DAN. W-w-well, you got there first.

BEN. I got there first—that's all.

CAP'N DAN. [*Smiling.*] That's enough. I can see you now, luggin' her home here, just like a big Newfoundland dog that had found a stray kitten or somethin'. [*Laughs.*]

BEN. [*Lovingly, in tender reminiscence.*] She was a beautiful baby.

CAP'N DAN. Yes, yes. But do you know, I think all babies are beautiful. An' to think of her comin' from such stock. Ol' Jim Reese—

BEN. [*Pityingly.*] Rum got the best of him. [*He picks up a shaving and plays with it while he talks.*] I always pity a man that rum gets the best of.

CAP'N DAN. [*Seating himself on the spar.*] Yes, but they was naturally shiftless. He never done no work, and Lizzie was always readin' novels. She wa'n't bad, she was simple-minded. She'd give you anythin' she had. When the cholery carried Jim off an' everybody else said "Good reddance," she sat down an' grieved herself to death after him in less'n a week.

BEN. Pathetic, wasn't it?

CAP'N DAN. Pathetic? It was funny.

[*Enter* MRS. RUSSELL, *right.* BEN *and* CAP'N DAN *rise. She is a beautiful old lady of seventy-five, a sweet-spirited, cheery woman, in love with life, the world and everybody in it. She is dressed for walking in a brown silk dress, simply but tastefully made, a bonnet, a silk shawl or mantilla, and lace half-mitts. She carries a silk bag on her arm, and a parasol. She wears gold spectacles, and has a long slender gold chain around her neck, to which is attached a man's old-fashioned gold watch.*]

MRS. RUSSELL. [*As she crosses to the centre, in a slow gentle voice, and with great sweetness of manner*] Good evenin', Mr. Turner, Good evenin', Cap'n Dan'l.

BEN. [*Taking off his cap.*] Good evening, Mrs. Russell.

CAP'N DAN. [*Touching his cap.*] Good evenin'.

[*They both speak at once. Both men treat the old lady with great courtesy.*]

MRS. RUSSELL. [*Smiling.*] I always like to come through the yard. I love the smell of the chips and the tar and all. My father was a boat builder, y' know, Silas Terrell. [*Smiles.*] That was before you all came here from Islip.

BEN. Yes, his yard was right over yonder.

MRS. RUSSELL. Yes, where Baldwin's coalyard is now. We all burnt wood in those days. Islip must be a pretty place. It's got such a pretty name. [*Smiles.*]

CAP'N DAN. [*Enthusiastically.*] It's a *beautiful* place!

MRS. RUSSELL. [*Smiling.*] I guess any place you're born in is beautiful, don't you? My husband, Cap'n John, y' know, [*They nod affirmatively*]—he came from Marblehead, Mas-

sachusetts. He thought there was no place like it. [*Smiles.*]
Sin'glar, so few *great* men are born in the cities. [*Nods as if
answering her own question.*] Places change so. I was thinkin' as I came along how the Harbor has changed. It used to
be one of the *busiest* little places when I was a girl— My!
CAP'N DAN. That was in its whalin' days.

MRS. RUSSELL. Yes, those were its best days, I guess. My!
It was a famous harbor in those days. I've seen a fleet of
s-e-v-e-n-t-y whalers lyin' out there, [*Points to the bay*]
—at once. My husband's ship was one of 'em. He was
cap'n of a whaler for oh, so many years—Cap'n John was,
y' know. [*They nod. She smiles.*] It was a grand sight, to
see seventy of 'em sail out— My! You never went whalin',
did you, Cap'n Dan'l?

CAP'N DAN. No'm—scallopin' an' bunker fishin' mostly. Ed
Cornin', Ben Heath and some more of us caught three off
Amagansett winter afore last. We see 'em blow off there
an'— [*Laughs*]—everybody in sight, I guess, put off after
'em. [*Ingenuously, delighted with himself.*] We drove 'em
right in onto the beach. Gosh! It was excitin'! They come
from all over, some clear from Greenport, to see 'em.

MRS. RUSSELL. [*In gentle disparagement.*] They wa'n't real
whales, I guess.

CAP'N DAN. Oh, no'm! Just everyday, 'round-here whales.

MRS. RUSSELL. It's a great sight to see 'em catch a big sperm
whale.

BEN. Must be.

MRS. RUSSELL. Some of 'em a hundred and fifty feet long.

CAP'N DAN. My, my!

MRS. RUSSELL. I went with my husband several voyages. It
was lonesome here without him. Yeh see, I had no children.
Never had but one baby, my daughter, Mrs. Doctor Reynolds,
y' know. [*They nod, she smiles.*] I tell the Doctor I had to
go to sea to get her. [*Laughs.*] In whalin' everything de-

pends on the harpooner, y' know. If the iron don't strike vital, there's very apt to be trouble. I've seen 'em tow boats for miles and the men have all they could do to keep the lines from settin' the boats afire.

CAP'N DAN. Hev to keep bailin' water onto 'em, don't they?

MRS. RUSSELL. Yes. And then again I've seen a bull struck with six irons at once, and start off like lightnin', and all of a sudden dart back and send two or three boats twenty feet into the air.

CAP'N DAN. He's generally struck vital when he does that, ain't he?

MRS. RUSSELL. Generally, not always. [*Smiles.*] Cap'n John and I have seen some marvellous sights, and we had a good many happy years together. [*Smiles.*] But, like a good many others, he went to sea one voyage too many. [*Smiles, and nods at her own thoughts.*] Yes, I love Sag Harbor. I was born here—I married Cap'n John here, and I guess I'll be buried here now. I'm proud of the Harbor, but somehow it isn't the same—that is, to me. [*To* BEN.] Elizabeth Anne's at home, isn't she?

CAP'N DAN. [*With an air of ownership.*] Yes, yes.

MRS. RUSSELL. I'll drop in a minute. Good evenin' all. [*She goes off, left.*]

BEN *and* CAP'N DAN. [*Together.*] Good evening.

BEN. [*After she goes.*] What a cheery old lady!

CAP'N DAN. [*Sitting on the spar.*] Old! Young lady. She'll never be old, Ben.

BEN. [*Reflectively.*] Seafaring's risky, isn't it?

CAP'N DAN. Nothin's so risky's a horse. I know where I am on a boat, but I don't want nothin' to do with horses. [*He lights his pipe.*]

BEN. [*On the keg, left.*] Frank'll be home tonight. Did you know it?

CAP'N DAN. Yes, Ed Hawkins' boy got home this mornin'.

BEN. I wish I could persuade Frank to stay home.

CAP'N DAN. Yes yes. There's no money in goin' to sea nowadays. That is, not for wages.

BEN. If he'd only settle down and marry one of the nice girls around here.

CAP'N DAN. [*Significantly.*] Ben, did you ever think of it yourself?

BEN. Think of what?

CAP'N DAN. Gittin' married!

BEN. [*Half affirmatively.*] N-o-o. Have you?

CAP'N DAN. I won't answer such a dumned silly question. [*Smiling.*] You know blamed well I have. We'd have been married too, long ago, if it hadn't 'a' been for the book o' Genesis.

BEN. [*Puzzled.*] What's the book of Genesis got to do with it?

CAP'N DAN. [*Ingenuously.*] Scared her. [BEN *is puzzled.* CAP'N DAN *explains further.*] All them begats. [BEN *still looks puzzled. Then* CAP'N DAN, *in a half-undertone, as if partly to himself, continues with disgust:*] Isaac begat Jacob, an' Jacob begat Enos—an' Enos was eight hundred and ninety-seven year old an' he begat—

BEN. [*With a smile of comprehension.*] Ah, I see!

CAP'N DAN. [*Puffing on his pipe.*] Ben, do you know folks is beginnin' to call you "The dog in the manger"?

BEN. [*Smiling.*] What about?

CAP'N DAN. Martha. [*He picks up a piece of wood and begins to whittle it.* BEN *looks at him a little consciously, as if thinking to himself "Does he know I love her?"* CAP'N DAN *continues:*] They say you won't marry her yourself an'— you won't let anybody else.

BEN. Where did you hear all this?

CAP'N DAN. I didn't hear it. Freeman Whitmarsh heard it over to the church. Him an' me got to talkin' t'other day—

BEN. *Got* to talking— [*Laughs and rises.*] You're *always* talking—you two! You know everybody's business.

CAP'N DAN. [*Laughs.*] Somebody's got to know it! And Freeman hears lots o' things you and me never'd hear—account of leadin' the choir, y' know.

BEN. [*Good-naturedly, as he goes towards the shop.*] They're always backbiting some one over at that church.

CAP'N DAN. [*Still seated.*] They wa'n't backbitin' you—

BEN. [*Astonished.*] Me? [*He turns back to* CAP'N DAN.]

CAP'N DAN. They was discussin' of you—

BEN. [*Serious for the first time.*] What did they say?

CAP'N DAN. [*Rises, and gives a little embarrassed laugh.*] Well, Ma Travers says it don't look well for Martha to be livin' here with you, even if you have got a superannuated father and an embi*cile* aunt. [*Laughs.*]

BEN. [*Uneasily.*] Oh! My—this's too bad.

CAP'N DAN. An' Em Budd says if ever a girl sot her cap for a fellah, Martha has for you; an' Ida Williams says, she's only waitin' for leap year to come 'round again, so's she can ask you herself.

BEN. [*At left centre.*] Ida Williams! [*With disgust.*] I wouldn't marry her if she were the last—

CAP'N DAN. No—no—! Said that Martha was waitin'. [*Confidentially.*] Say, be you and Martha engaged?

BEN. [*Staggered for a moment.*] Engaged? [*Recovers himself.*] Yes—minding our own business.

CAP'N DAN. I told Freeman that if you was, I'd be sure to know it. *They* said you was.

BEN. [*Half pleased; the idea fascinates him.*] How do they know?

CAP'N DAN. [*Laughs.*] Freeman says the way Martha acts, he guesses. Sort o' owns you.

BEN. [*Laughing.*] Well, she can just own anything she wants to own around these diggings.

CAP'N DAN. [*Smiling.*] She knows that, I guess.

BEN. [*Wistfully, dismissing the thought.*] She's nothing but a child. I'm old enough to be her father.

CAP'N DAN. That's nothin'. Look at me. [*Confidentially.*] Say, I'm ten years older than 'Lisbeth.

BEN. [*Laughing.*] How many?

CAP'N DAN. [*Laughing.*] Fifteen. But that's not the reason she won't marry me. Look at them Genesis fellahs—some of 'em was three thousand—

BEN. Well, I'm not a Genesis fellow—

CAP'N DAN. Did you ever sound Martha on the marryin' question?

BEN. [*With assumed carelessness.*] Naw!

CAP'N DAN. Well, you ought to.

BEN. [*Again allowing the idea to take possession of him.*] Why?

CAP'N DAN. [*Oracularly.*] Well, Freeman says so. Freeman says she's got to the age when all girls expect somebody to ask 'em to have 'em, and he guesses she'd rather you'd ask her than anyone else. And I guess I guess so, too.

BEN. [*Impressed in spite of himself.*] When did you come to that conclusion?

CAP'N DAN. Oh, 'steen years ago. I can see after four o'clock ef my grandfather was Dutch.

BEN. [*Walks up and down at the left, and says after reflec-*

tion.] Pshaw! I don't suppose she's ever given me a thought in that way. It's all gossip.

CAP'N DAN. P'r'aps not. [*Mysteriously.*] Did you ever see what she's got on the end of that ribbon she wears around her neck?

BEN. No.

CAP'N DAN. [*Nodding wisely.*] Ask her to show you some day.

BEN. It's none of my business.

CAP'N DAN. [*With affected indifference.*] N-o-o—I d'know's it is.

BEN. [*Struggling with his curiosity, goes to* CAP'N DAN.] Do you know?

CAP'N DAN. [*Very importantly.*] Yes.

BEN. What?

CAP'N DAN. A po'trait.

BEN. Oh, her mother's!

CAP'N DAN. No.

BEN. Her father's?

CAP'N DAN. Well—sorter.

BEN. Old Jim?

CAP'N DAN. [*With a happy confident smile, as though imparting the most delightful news.*] Old Ben.

BEN. [*Stunned.*] Me?

CAP'N DAN. I thought it wa'n't none o' your business?

BEN. [*Incredulous. He is deeply moved.*] She hasn't got my picture.

CAP'N DAN. Then I'm a liar.

BEN. [*Trying to speak in a matter-of-fact way, but he can*

hardly keep the joy out of his voice.] How do you know it's me?

CAP'N DAN. Well, to tell you the truth, Freeman surmised it fust off—then I saw it.

BEN. When?

CAP'N DAN. This afternoon.

BEN. Where?

CAP'N DAN. Over to the post office.

BEN. [*Innocently.*] What were *you* doing at the post office?

CAP'N DAN. [*Looking at him rather indignantly.*] I got a right into the post office, hain't I?

BEN. You never get a letter.

CAP'N DAN. I know it, but I go there once in a while. I like to see 'em git 'em. Well, she got one and was a-readin' it. She didn't see me. I was goin' up behind her to play "Who is it?", y' know— [*He makes the motion of putting his hands over his eyes*]—when she took the picture out of her bosom. I looked over her shoulder, and I see it was you.

BEN. Are you sure?

CAP'N DAN. [*Impatiently.*] Now, don't catechise me. It's you —only younger. You're in a sailor suit, same as yeh are in 'Lizbeth's album.

BEN. [*Astonished and delighted.*] Oh my! That was taken over twenty years ago. I wonder if she's had that copied.

CAP'N DAN. [*Who shares* BEN'S *pleasure.*] By jinks! I'll ask Freeman. That's it! That shows you! Freeman says that when a girl gets so she wears a fellah's picture in her bosom, it's next thing to the fellah himself.

BEN. [*With sudden decision.*] By George! I'll talk to her about it.

CAP'N DAN. [*Laughing.*] She'll do all the talkin' if you give her a chance, I guess.

BEN. And if it's all true, I'll make you a present of a gold watch.

CAP'N DAN. I don't want no gold watch. [*Laughs.*] I've got a watch—cylinder escapement, the one Joshua used to start the sun a-goin' with. [*He takes out his watch, glances at it, and a look of amazement comes over his face.*] By Jinks! She's stopped.

[BEN *laughs,* CAP'N DAN *joins him.* CAP'N DAN *crosses to the right, and seats himself on the spar, right centre.*]

[MARTHA REESE *enters left, above the shop. She is a pretty girl of about twenty, with a sweet ingenuous manner; just now she is bubbling over with happiness. She is dressed in a very simple but dainty summer frock, and has a locket hanging by a ribbon about her neck. She speaks as she enters, at the same time taking a letter from her pocket.*]

MARTHA. Hello boys!

BEN. [*Turns and goes to her at once, overjoyed at seeing her.*] Hello!

MARTHA. [*Looking at him naïvely, and holding out the letter.*] I've got a letter from somebody you know. [*She is centre, with* BEN *on her left and* CAP'N DAN *on her right.*]

BEN. [*Cheerily.*] Frank?

MARTHA. [*Laughing joyously.*] Yes. How'd you know?

BEN. Guessed it. He'll be home tonight or in the morning.

MARTHA. Aren't you glad? [*Laughs.*] I'm wild. [*She squeezes herself up with girlish glee. Then she says naïvely:*] He's been away five years.

BEN. Five years.

MARTHA. [*Counting on her fingers.*] Eighteen—and five— twenty-three. [*With joy.*] Why, he's a man. [*Seriously.*] I wonder if he's got a moustache.

CAP'N DAN. [*Still seated on the spar, dryly.*] If he has, 'Lisbeth'll shear him. She won't allow no moustaches around the house; they're so sloppy at table.

[*They all laugh.*]

MARTHA. [*To* BEN.] How old was I when he went away?

CAP'N DAN. Gosh! You! You were—[*Laughs*]—runnin' around here barefooted.

BEN. You were a child, Martha, fifteen.

MARTHA. [*Ingenuously.*] Have I changed very much?

CAP'N DAN. Oh my! I should say—

BEN. [*Taking her hand, lovingly.*] You're a woman now. [*He holds her hand for a moment, then drops it a little consciously.*]

MARTHA. [*Naïvely.*] D'you think he'll know me?

CAP'N DAN. N-a-w! I'll introduce you.

[*They all laugh.*]

MARTHA. Thank you, I'll introduce myself. [*She sits down beside* CAP'N DAN.] I wonder if he's much different.

CAP'N DAN. I don't guess he could carry you on his back now, could he, Martha?

MARTHA. [*Laughing.*] I don't guess I'd let him.

CAP'N DAN. You used to have great ol' times, you and he and Janey Cauldwell.

MARTHA. [*Laughs.*] I guess we did.

BEN. What a beautiful girl Janey's got to be.

CAP'N DAN. Say, Ben—

MARTHA. And just as good as she is beautiful. Dear old Janey! I don't see enough of her since she moved to Bridgehampton.

CAP'N DAN. Remember the Sunday he was carryin' you both

across the creek? [*Laughs.*] Yeh had your clothes all tucked up.

MARTHA. We were playing Paul and Virginia. He was playing he had two Virginias.

[*They all laugh.*]

CAP'N DAN. Well he had when he started. He Virginia'd you over all right, but he dropped Janey into the creek. I always thought he done that on purpose.

MARTHA. We got even with him.

BEN. [*Laughing.*] The day he was in swimming?

MARTHA. Um'm!

CAP'N DAN. [*Laughing.*] Yes, yes—and he had to come home in a barrel!

MARTHA. Um'm!

[*They all laugh.*]

CAP'N DAN. That was her doin's. Of all the little divils, Janey Cauldwell was the worst. What you two couldn't think of, she could. I used to call her the triplet. [*He rises.*] Ah well, those were great days, as Mrs. Russell says.

[MARTHA *laughs and goes up stage to the left, opens her letter and reads it, smiling to herself.*

CAP'N DAN. [*Crossing over to* BEN, *says to him in a low voice.*] Now's your chance.

BEN. [*Anxiously.*] Think so?

CAP'N DAN. Yes, if I was you I'd talk to her right now.

BEN. [*In the same manner.*] Would you?

CAP'N DAN. Yes, yes. It'll tickle her to death to have yeh ask her right out here.

[FREEMAN *is heard off right, singing, "When other lips and other hearts." They all listen.*]

CAP'N DAN. Here comes Freeman, I'll ask him. [*He crosses to the right,* BEN *follows him a few steps and stands centre, by the spar.* MARTHA *remains up left.*]

[FREEMAN *enters, right, and continues across the yard towards the exit above the shop. He is singing as he goes "In such a sc-e-ene some recollection be-e-e."*]

CAP'N DAN. [*Calls to him.*] Got 'r sot?

FREEMAN. [*Without pausing.*] Yes. [*Sings.*] "Of days that hev as happy ben"— Good evenin', Marthy.

MARTHA [*Pleasantly.*] Good day, Mr. Whitmarsh.

FREEMAN. [*Pauses for a moment and says without the slightest change of expression either in his face or in his voice, and with absolute seriousness*] Say, if you ain't married by the first of July—Mother'll be dead a year the first day o' July—I'll be open for propositions after that.

[MARTHA *smiles in amusement.* FREEMAN *starts to sing again.* CAP'N DAN *joins him.* FREEMAN *goes off left, above the shop, followed by* CAP'N DAN. *They can be heard away off in the distance, finishing the song, "Then you'll remember me."*]

BEN. [*Looking off after* FREEMAN *and* CAP'N DAN, *and smiling with amusement.*] I wonder who told those fellows they could sing?

MARTHA. They can—sing. [*Laughs.*]

BEN. [*Sitting on the spar, centre.*] Martha, come here and sit down. I want to have a talk with you.

MARTHA. [*Comes down and sits on the ground at* BEN's *feet, left centre.*] Do you? Isn't that funny! I came here to have a talk with you! [*Laughs.*] See how great minds assimilate!

BEN. [*Looking down at her and smiling tenderly.*] What's in your mind?

MARTHA. [*Looking up and laughing back at him.*] What's in yours?

BEN. Yankee! [*He laughs, then grows serious.*] Well—you, for one thing.

MARTHA. [*Lightly.*] Oh, that's nothing new. You're always in mine.

[*Throughout this scene,* MARTHA *shows the deep affection she feels for* BEN, *and the perfect trust she has in him.*]

BEN. [*Deeply moved, taking her hand.*] Am I?

MARTHA. [*Ingenuously.*] Of course.

BEN. [*With quiet earnestness.*] Do you love me?

MARTHA. [*Speaking with all her heart, but with no idea that* BEN *is putting another construction on her words.*] Do I? I worship you, Ben. How can I help it? I owe everything to you—all my happy childlife—

BEN. You have been happy, haven't you?

MARTHA. I guess I have. [*Bubbling over with happy memories.*] I tell you—there are very few girls—

BEN. [*Reflectively.*] I've been a sort of a good old father to you, haven't I?

MARTHA. [*Putting both her hands on his knee, and looking up at him with tender adoration.*] Oh, Ben, you've been more like a beautiful mother.

BEN. [*Deeply moved.*] Have I? [*She nods. He points to the ribbon on her neck.*] What you got on that ribbon?

MARTHA. [*Laughing a little consciously.*] A picture.

BEN. [*Smiling confidently, not doubting but that the locket contains his own picture.*] Portrait? [*She nods.*] Man—or—woman?

MARTHA. [*Still smiling.*] Neither—b-o-y.

BEN. [*Prolonging his pleasure in the little comedy.*] Do I know him?

MARTHA. [*Nodding.*] Um'm.

BEN. Let me see. [*He leans towards her as though to look at the locket, but she pulls away from him.*]

MARTHA. [*Laughing.*] N-n-n-n-nit!

BEN. Ah! You! Let's see—what was it I wanted to talk about?

MARTHA. [*Laughing.*] I forget.

BEN. Well, let's begin with Frank.

MARTHA. [*Pleased, settling herself comfortably.*] Yes, let's.

BEN. I want him to give up the sea, if he will.

MARTHA. [*Delighted.*] Do you? Oh he will—[*She checks herself a little consciously.*]—I guess.

BEN. I want him to go into business here with me.

MARTHA. Oh! [*Her heart is filled to overflowing with joy.*] That's just like you—nobody—but dear old Ben! Won't he be surprised!

BEN. He ought to settle down now and get married.

[MARTHA *plays this whole scene as if she were certain that* BEN *knew she and* FRANK *loved each other.*]

MARTHA. Yes, that's so. But who is he to marry?

BEN. Oh, any nice girl. [*Laughs.*] Let him alone, he'll find some one.

MARTHA. [*Shyly.*] Perhaps he will.

BEN. You'd like to see him married, wouldn't you?

MARTHA. [*Hesitates, a little embarrassed.*] Well—yes—I think I would.

BEN. [*With a change of tone, earnestly.*] Would you like to see me married?

MARTHA. Yes, Ben, I would. I'd like to see you married to a real good girl, who loved you.

BEN. As you do?

MARTHA. [*Frankly.*] Yes, as well as I do.

BEN. [*Who is absolutely sure now that she has loved him all along, laughs.*] Gosh! Wasn't I stupid not to have seen it before!

MARTHA. [*Puzzled, but joining in his laugh.*] Seen what?

BEN. [*Smiling down at her.*] Oh, but you can keep a secret. [*Wistfully.*] Y'know, I was always afraid to tell you—I thought I was too old for you.

MARTHA. [*Half realizing.*] Why—B-e-n!

BEN. [*Laughing and taking her hand.*] I wouldn't dare to tell you now, only we're so well acquainted. [*As if he were giving her the wish of her heart.*] Yes, Martha, it's all true —I love you. I love you, and I'm going to make you just as good a husband as I have a father—or [*laughs*]—mother— which was it? [*With great tenderness and feeling.*] Some fellahs do all their courting before marriage, I'll do all mine after. [MARTHA *is silent, dazed with the revelation of* BEN'S *love. He does not realize what his words mean to her, and he continues opening his heart to her.*] We've lived so long under one roof anyhow—just think, nearly twenty years. Gosh! I didn't think the day your mother hired me to take care of you—

MARTHA. [*Trying to keep back her tears.*] Hired you?

BEN. [*Laughing.*] Oh, you don't know anything about that. You weren't much bigger than a good sized ear of corn. One Saturday I was going fishing—she bribed me with bread and sugar to mind you for a couple of hours.

MARTHA. [*Who is crying silently, now makes an effort to smile.*] Is that the first time you ever saw me? [*As she speaks she nervously fingers the locket around her neck, and the ribbon with which it is tied becomes unfastened.*]

BEN. [*He is so lost in his own happiness that he does not realize the effect of his words upon* MARTHA.] Yes. I didn't think then that I'd be sitting here today, asking you to be my wife—did you?

MARTHA. [*Trying to control her sobs.*] N-n-no. I didn't know anything about it, y' know. [*She bursts into tears, and throws herself on* BEN'S *knees, shaken with emotion.*]

BEN. [*Gently, astonished.*] What are you crying about? Because I spoke of your mother?

MARTHA. No, I don't know— [*The locket falls to the ground without her being aware of it. She is hysterical now, but makes an effort to control herself.*] I suppose I wouldn't be a girl if I didn't cry. In some stories, the girls cry when they're happiest— [*She laughs, then continues anxiously,*] You don't want my answer now—do you—not just this minute? [*Laughs and cries.*] Y' know—

[BEN *cannot understand* MARTHA'S *attitude, and for the first time a feeling of doubt enters his mind. He speaks slowly and earnestly.*]

BEN. No-o-o. Only don't say no, if you can help it, will you?

MARTHA. I don't think I'm going to—but—I'd like to wait until Frank comes— [*Laughs and cries.*] What with his letter—and your—wanting—to marry me—I'm so excited—and—so—so—happy—that I— [*She bursts into tears and falls on his breast. He tries to comfort her. She pulls herself together, makes a pitiful effort to laugh, and rises.*] There, now, I'm not going to cry another single cry. I'm going home to get you a nice supper. You must be starved—you've had no dinner you know. I've got to take good care of you now, haven't I? [*She starts to go, then turns and says with great seriousness.*] Ben, I'm going to pray tonight as I've never prayed before, and tomorrow, perhaps, I'll give you my answer. [CAP'N DAN *is heard singing outside.*] Hurry in—I'll have something nice for you. Good-bye. [*She bursts into tears and runs off left, above the shop, without looking back.* BEN, *greatly disturbed, follows her up and looks after her.*]

[CAP'N DAN *enters, left, singing "An' the ship went down with all on board." He crosses to right centre as he says:*]

CAP'N DAN. Ben, I was thinkin' that while we're about it, we ought to burn the paint off of "Kacy" 's sides.

BEN. [*Still looking after* MARTHA, *speaks slowly.*] Say—does a girl always cry—when the man she loves asks her to marry him?

CAP'N DAN. [*Standing centre and regarding the boat, speaks offhandedly.*] D'know's she does, and d'know *as* she does. Freeman can tell you. Why?

BEN. [*Thoughtfully.*] She cried.

CAP'N DAN. [*Quickly, interested, going to him.*] Oh, ast her—did you?

BEN. Yes.

CAP'N DAN. Well?

BEN. [*As before.*] She cried.

CAP'N DAN. [*Confidently.*] Oh, that's all right. [*Laughs.*] I guess I'll take that gold watch. [*He sees the locket where it has fallen among the chips beside the spar, and picks it up.*] What'd you throw this away for?

BEN. [*Abstractedly.*] What?

CAP'N DAN. This fillimijig with y'r picture into it.

BEN. [*Crosses to* CAP'N DAN, *centre.*] She must have dropped it. I saw her kiss it. Give it to me. I'll give it to her.

CAP'N DAN. [*Chuckling with delight now that he has settled the whole thing.*] Wait until I have another peep at yeh. Let's see if you're as han'some in a frame as you are out of it. [*He opens the locket and looks at the picture. The smile leaves his face, giving way to a look of horrified dismay.*] G-o-s-h!

BEN. [*Startled.*] What's the matter?

[BEN *snatches the locket from* CAP'N DAN, *and is about to look at it, but* CAP'N DAN *grasps his hand and prevents him from doing so.*]

CAP'N DAN. [*Pleadingly, in a voice trembling with emotion.*] Don't look at it, Ben! For God's sake don't look at it! It's all a mistake! It's the dead image of you but it ain't you.

BEN. [*Not daring to look at the locket, hoarsely.*] Who is it? [*Slowly.*] I'll kill him.

CAP'N DAN. [*In a heartbroken voice.*] That's the worst of it, Ben—you can't. It's your brother Frank.

BEN. [*With an anguished groan.*] Oh!

CAP'N DAN. Don't say a word, Ben, I've done it this time. I haven't got a word to say. I'm knocked deef, dumb and blind. I've ruined you. [*He bursts into tears.*] Ruined the hull on yeh.

BEN. [*Preoccupied with his own thoughts, not heeding him, says sadly,*] I see now why she cried. Poor girl!

[*The whistle of a railroad train is heard off right.*]

CAP'N DAN. [*Frightened.*] That's the New York train. I hope he ain't on it.

BEN. [*Who has pulled himself together, makes an effort to be his old cheerful self.*] I hope he is. The sooner he comes now, the better.

CAP'N DAN. What'll yeh do?

BEN. Nothing. She's his—not mine. [*He looks down at the locket wistfully.*] I'd give a good deal if this was my picture, wouldn't you?

CAP'N DAN. [*Earnestly.*] Yes, I would, Ben.

BEN. But it ain't.

CAP'N DAN. I was goin' to say if I was you—I guess I've give advice enough for one day. [*With suppressed fury.*] The first time I lay my hands on Freeman Whitmarsh, I'll— [*He crosses right.*]

BEN. [*Making an effort to speak cheerfully, as he crosses left.*] Come in to supper with me; she said she'd have something nice for supper.

CAP'N DAN. [*Shaking his head.*] No—can't eat nothin'—I tell yeh things is pooty bad with me when I can't eat.

FRANK. [*He is heard talking off right, his voice vibrant with joyousness.*] All right, boys—I'll see you in the morning. I'm in a big hurry now.

[FRANK *runs on, right. He is a handsome, stalwart young fellow in his early twenties, cheery and with all the joy of youth. He wears a sailor's uniform. He is followed by* FREEMAN, *who carries his sailor's bag and a new grip, and by two shipmates, who are carrying their sailor's dunnage.* FREEMAN *puts down* FRANK'S *luggage, and stands smiling, enjoying the scene. The sailors stop for a moment, then go off right, as if to their own homes.* FRANK *runs to* BEN, *who is standing left centre, and the two brothers embrace heartily.*]

BEN. [*Earnestly.*] Frank, I never was so glad to see you in all my life as I am tonight.

FRANK [*Laughing happily.*] That's what you say every time I come home. [*To* CAP'N DAN.] Hello, Cap! [*He crosses and shakes hands with him.*]

CAP'N DAN. [*Vacantly.*] You're heavier than you was, ain't you?

FRANK. [*Lightly.*] Naturally. [*Crossing to* BEN, *left.*] Where's Sis—inside?

BEN. [*Putting his arm around* FRANK'S *neck.*] Yes, she sort of hoped you'd get here for supper. [*Starts to lead him off.*] She's got something nice for you, I guess.

FRANK. Good!

[BEN *goes off left above the shop.* FRANK *crosses to* FREEMAN *and starts to pick up his luggage.*]

FRANK. I'll take these things in, Freeman.

FREEMAN. I'll take 'em in.

FRANK. Thanks, all right. [*Crosses left.*] See you in the morning, Cap. [*He goes off left, above the shop.*]

FREEMAN. [*To* CAP'N DAN.] What was the matter with the lot of yeh—deef? Didn't yeh hear the train whistle? If it hadn't 'a' been for me, there wouldn't have been a soul to meet him. [*He picks up* FRANK'S *luggage and is about to follow him off, left, singing, " 'Tis the last rose of summer," when* CAP'N DAN *interposes and stops him.*]

CAP'N DAN. [*Savagely.*] Don't go in there. You've raised Hell, you have! [*Points toward the house, then says slowly.*] Drop that dunnage an' go hum. [FREEMAN *drops the luggage in amazement.*] And if yeh attempt to sing— [*He picks up a stone.*] I swear I'll brain you! [*Crying with rage and speaking in the tone he would use to a disobedient dog.*] G'hum—hum 'th yeh—hum with yeh I say. [*He stands, glaring threateningly at* FREEMAN.]

FREEMAN. [*Looks at* CAP'N DAN *in amazement, concludes he has gone suddenly mad, and says as though to himself,*] Must have been in his family. [*He sinks on the spar, centre.*]

CURTAIN

ACT SECOND

THE *next afternoon.*

The interior of BEN TURNER'S *shop.*

SCENE: *The shop is a large, bare place of rough, unpainted boards. At the back, centre, are double doors, opening out and into the yard. Through the doorway, part of the shipyard and the harbor can be seen, with a view of Shelter Island in the distance. There is another wide doorway, not so large as the centre one, on the upper left-hand side of the shop, through which can be seen part of* BEN'S *house and dooryard. Opposite this, on the right, is a smaller doorway. Below these doors, at right and left of the shop, are two carpenter's benches, complete for working. There are two windows set in the wall above each bench.*

Overhead, on beams, are pieces of timber and boards in various stages of manufacture, from which pieces have been cut. On the walls hang tools, and ship models. The floor is littered with chips, pieces of rigging, blocks and tools. On wooden horses, which run up and down the stage, right centre, is a partially finished topmast. Down left is the summerhouse of the "Kacy," white, with a yellow top.

At the rise of the curtain, GEORGE SALTER *is discovered at the upper end of the left-hand bench, seated on a high stool, drawing a pattern on a board.* JIM ADAMS, *a ship carpenter, is working on the topmast, right centre, and* ED MILLS, *another carpenter, is planing a fine piece of oak at the bench, right.*

[FREEMAN WHITMARSH *enters centre from the right. He has a new truck ball in his hand. His hands are pretty well daubed with black paint, and he has some on his overalls and jumper. He is accompanied by* CAP'N DAN, *in bedticking overalls and jumper, his hands and clothes also showing he has been using*

160

black paint. They each carry a pot of yellow paint and a brush. They are talking as they enter.]

FREEMAN. [*Going left, argumentatively.*] The top o' your house is yellah, your stripe and scroll work are yellah, and this—[*Indicating the ball in his hand*]—ought to be yellah.

CAP'N DAN. [*Who is right centre, very gravely, as if it were a matter of the greatest moment.*] I d'know but it had; I'd like it gilted, but—

FREEMAN. [*Seriously.*] It'd be out o' harmony. [*Lays the ball down on the bench, left.*] Well, le's get at this house. I can't give you but today. I never was so pushed's I be this spring.

[*They set to work painting the summerhouse.*[1]]

CAP'N DAN. [*Reluctantly.*] Yes, I guess yellah's the best.

[WILLIAM TURNER *enters from the house by the door on the left. He is a spry, wiry old man of seventy, with a round face, whose kindly expression is belied by his mildly querulous manner. He wears spectacles, and has a stubby, white beard, but his upper lip is clean-shaven. He is always tidy, and his blue overalls and jumper are spotless. His straw hat has seen several summers, but is not broken.* TURNER *is a simple soul, and the pride of his life is the "Antelope" and his connection with her.*]

TURNER. [*Coming down right centre.*] Say, George Salter, there's a lot of cordage and one truck or 'nuther come over from New London for you folks. Why didn't yeh come and get it?

[CAP'N DAN *and* FREEMAN *stop work to listen, smiling at each other in amusement.*]

GEORGE. [*Still at work at the bench, good-naturedly.*] Didn't know your steamer—ahem! had got in.

---

[1] *NOTE:* Freeman and Cap'n Dan must use some preparation that will stick to Cap'n Dan's clothes when he sits on the freshly painted cabin later on.

TURNER. Didn't yeh hear her whistle?

GEORGE. [*Pretending to be surprised.*] Was that her? I thought somebody had run over a hawg in the road.

[CAP'N DAN *and* FREEMAN *laugh. The men at work on the topmast and at the bench laugh also.*]

TURNER. [*Good-naturedly.*] If our steamboat ain't good enough for you, don't ship nothin' by her, that's all.

GEORGE. Oh, she's good enough, only a fellah never knows when the ol' tub's going to get in or go out.

[*All laugh except* TURNER, *who smiles good-naturedly at the gibe.*]

TURNER. [*As though reading from a time table, reprovingly.*] "Leaves New London daily, Sunday excepted, at nine A. M. every mornin'. Arrives Sag Harbor—"

GEORGE. [*Still at the bench, finishes for him.*] When she gets good and ready.   •

[*All laugh.*]

TURNER. [*As before.*] "Leaves Sag Harbor—"

GEORGE. Same schedule. For further particulars, enquire of William Turner, agent, Sag Harbor, N. Y.

TURNER. You send over and get y'r truck, or I'll be danged if I don't chuck it into the bay.

GEORGE [*Crossing to him, centre.*] I'll drive over with you now, Uncle Billy.

TURNER. I'll be danged if yeh do. I ain't goin' over there now.

GEORGE. [*Laughing.*] Well, when'll yeh be there?

TURNER. That's my business. When a man gets to be as old's I be, he don't want to keep a-runnin' over to that dock every five minutes in the day, for you nor nobody else.

GEORGE. Well, when can we get our stuff?

TURNER. When I'm there to give it to yeh, if yeh want it, and if yeh don't, yeh can leave it there, and I'll charge yeh storage, you're so danged smart. [*Chuckles.*] How's that for high, boys?

[*All laugh.*]

TURNER. I ought to charge yeh five cents for tellin' yeh it was there.

GEORGE. [*Putting his hand into his pocket as if to take out money.*] Have you got five cents in change, Uncle Billy?

TURNER. [*Who expects he is going to get a dime, puts his hand into his pocket in the same way.*] I guess I have.

GEORGE. Well, give it to me, and I'll owe yeh a dime.

TURNER. [*Squaring off.*] See here, if you poke fun at me—

[BEN *enters through the centre door from the left. He has lost his cheery manner, and wears a troubled look.* TURNER *turns to him and says half in fun and half in earnest,*]

TURNER. Say, Ben, I wish you'd discharge this foreman of yours and hire me.

BEN. [*Crossing to him, right, and putting his hand affectionately on the old man's shoulder.*] I'm afraid the "Antelope" folks can't spare you, Father.

TURNER. [*Anxiously.*] What's the matter, Ben, ain't you well?

BEN. [*Making an effort to speak in his usual cheery way.*] Yes, why?

[CAP'N DAN *and* FREEMAN *are observing* BEN *closely, while pretending to be busily at work.*]

TURNER. Yeh look's if yeh hadn't slep' well. Have yeh?

BEN. [*Evasively.*] Well, I didn't sleep as well as I generally do, it was so hot. [*To the others.*] Did you ever see it so hot this time o' year?

TURNER. Yeh stick too close to the shop. Yeh ought to take a trip across the Sound.

GEORGE. [*Teasingly.*] On the "Antelope?" [*He goes to the*

bench, right, and begins to sort over some pieces of lumber, measuring them with his pocket rule.]

TURNER. [*Looking around at him, quickly.*] Yes, on the "Antelope." [*To* BEN.] It'd do yeh lots of good. You're not yourself. 'Lizbeth says your bed wasn't slep' in at all last night.

BEN. Too hot, I tell you. [*Pats him on the shoulder.*] I'll sleep all right tonight.

TURNER. [*Sighing, with the pathetic affection of old age.*] I don't believe I'd last long if I was to lose you, Ben.

BEN. [*Laughing reassuringly.*] You're not going to lose me.

TURNER. [*In the same tone.*] There's a lot of cordage and truck come in for you this mornin'. Le's drive over and get it.

BEN. Yes, soon's I get Payne's boat into the water. [*To the men.*] Boys, let's get the "Gypsy" into the water, will yeh?

[*The two carpenters go off centre, to the right.*]

TURNER. [*At once assuming an official manner that is full of bustle and importance.*] I'll go and get the keys. [*He goes out of the door, upper left.*]

BEN. George, let's get that boat off the ways, will yeh? [*He goes out centre, to the right.*]

GEORGE. Yes, sir. [*He lays the lumber on the workbench, right, and follows* BEN *off, centre.*]

CAP'N DAN. [*Whose eyes have followed* BEN *off anxiously, turns to* FREEMAN *and says in a voice of tragic conviction,*] It's wearin' on him—it'll kill him. If it does, you'll never see me agin—leastways, you won't know me. I'll be in the Salvation Army.

FREEMAN. [*Gravely.*] I wouldn't do that. [*After reflection.*] He'll see some one else after awhile, don't yeh think?

CAP'N DAN. [*Shaking his head.*] I'm afraid not.

FREEMAN. Oh, yes, he will too. [*He rises and crosses, right.*] See what a shock I had a spell ago 'bout that Skinner girl.

CAP'N DAN. [*With great solemnity.*] The one 'at used to have fits?

FREEMAN. Yes. Everybody thought I was goin' into a decline.

CAP'N DAN. [*Rising also and following* FREEMAN *right, seriously.*] Didn't yeh take nothin'?

FREEMAN. No—nothin'. Et considerable green stuff, cereals, an' milk, an' all that.

[*They are about to go out through the centre doors, when* JANE CAULDWELL *enters through them from the left.* JANE *is a bright, cheery, beautiful girl of about* MARTHA's *age, with a great deal of poise and considerable common sense. She is charmingly, but simply, dressed, and carries a parasol and a roll of music.*]

JANE. [*Pausing centre, and extending her hand to* FREEMAN *with a great deal of formality.*] How do you do, Mr. Whitmarsh?

FREEMAN. [*At once all eagerness, rushing to her.*] Why, Miss Cauldwell! [*He offers her his hand, then noticing it is covered with paint, withdraws it quickly, saying apologetically:*] I'm sorry I can't shake hands with you.

JANE. [*Laughing; she never for a moment takes* FREEMAN *seriously.*] We'll take the will for the deed. [*She crosses to* CAP'N DAN.] How d'do, Captain?

CAP'N DAN. [*Cheerfully.*] How d'do? [*Laughs.*] I s'pose I dasn't call you Mischievous Janey, now?

JANE. [*Laughing, and looking about the shop, as though expecting to see some one.*] Oh, yes, you dare call me anything you like.

CAP'N DAN. Seen Frank yet?

JANE. [*Eagerly, almost unable to conceal her interest.*] No; I—that's what—I— How does he look?

CAP'N DAN. Oh, just as han'some as ever.

FREEMAN. [*Up centre, a little enviously.*] He's as fat as a seal.

JANE [*Horrified.*] Oh, my, he isn't—is he, Captain?

CAP'N DAN. [*Reassuringly.*] No, he's just right.

JANE. [*Smiling with relief.*] I thought not. I can't imagine him fat. I was giving a lesson, and I thought I'd run over. Martha at home?

CAP'N DAN. I guess so.

JANE. [*Going towards the door on the left, asks casually,*] Why haven't you been over, Mr. Whitmarsh?

FREEMAN. [*Who imagines that every girl who speaks to him is in love with him, says with a fatuous smile,*] Well, I am ashamed—but—well, Mother hasn't been dead quite a year yet—and I ain't callin' on anyone reg'lar yet.

JANE. [*Turning and looking back at him over her shoulder, says with gentle mockery,*] Tell that to the marines!

FREEMAN. [*Earnestly, assuring her.*] Oh, honest! I'm in second mournin' yet. [*Starting towards her.*] Now, after the first of July—

JANE. [*As she goes out, calls back laughing,*] Oh, my! That's a long time to wait. [*She goes off through the door, upper left.*]

CAP'N DAN. By Gosh! She's a han'some girl.

FREEMAN. [*Who stands right centre, looking after* JANE, *as though speaking his thoughts aloud,*] If Bridgehampton wasn't so far to go nights—

CAP'N DAN. [*Heartily.*] What's the matter with you? Hain't you got a wheel? Let's see the boys get that boat into the water. [*He goes off centre to the right.*]

FREEMAN. [*Half to himself.*] She *is* han'some. [*He follows* CAP'N DAN *off.*]

[MARTHA *enters through the side door at the right, followed by* FRANK. *They are in the midst of a serious conversation.* MARTHA *is greatly agitated and on the verge of tears, but makes an effort to control herself.* FRANK *is outwardly calm, but is inwardly consumed with a smouldering rage.*]

FRANK. [*As he follows* MARTHA *down centre.*] When did all this happen?

MARTHA. [*In a low hushed voice.*] Yesterday afternoon. I'd been to the post office and got your letter. I was so happy —I ran to tell him everything—you told me to.

FRANK. Well?

MARTHA. He began to talk. He took my breath away—at first I was sure he knew all about you and me—and all of a sudden he asked me to marry him. [*She goes down towards the bench, left.*]

FRANK. [*Reproachfully.*] Why didn't you tell him then that—

MARTHA. [*Turning to him.*] I hadn't the courage. You should have seen his face. He frightened me.

FRANK. [*Contemptuously.*] Humph! I'll tell him—in good, straight American. [*He sits on the topmast, right.*]

MARTHA. [*Anxiously.*] No, no, you mustn't. It would kill him.

FRANK. [*Bitterly.*] Kill him—is he any better than I am?

MARTHA. [*Going to him and putting her hand on his shoulder, gently.*] No—only different. You're young—you have so much. He has only me.

FRANK. [*Stubbornly, as though unwilling to admit the truth of her words.*] If he weren't blind, he'd see that you don't love him.

MARTHA. [*Frightened.*] Oh, Frank, that's the worst of it.

He believes I do. [*She kneels on the floor at* FRANK's *feet in the same attitude she assumed with* BEN *in Act First.*]

FRANK. [*Incredulously.*] What?

MARTHA. [*Crying.*] Yes, he's got that notion into his head, somehow. P'r'aps I've put it there. [*Reflectively.*] P'r'aps I've led him on. [*After a slight pause.*] Yes, come to think, I must have done so. We've been so intimate, y'know—why—he believes I've been waiting for him to ask me to be his wife.

FRANK. [*Scornfully.*] The fool!

MARTHA. [*With gentle reproof.*] Ah, no, no, no! I've been alone here with him—you've been away so much—and—and —don't you see, if—if—there had been no *you*— [*Winding her arms around his neck.*] It—it would all have been true. [*She cries.*]

FRANK. [*With mournful conviction.*] Martha, you don't love me any longer!

MARTHA. [*Putting her hand over his mouth.*] Frank, you mustn't say that.

FRANK. [*Reproachfully.*] You're going to throw me overboard—

MARTHA. Oh, don't say that! [*She rises and moves to centre, as though unwilling to face Frank.*]

FRANK. [*Rising.*] And marry my brother.

MARTHA. I must do that.

FRANK. [*Crossing to her.*] Why must you?

MARTHA. Because—well—because— [*She hesitates.*]

FRANK. [*Standing, right, beside* MARTHA, *asks sneeringly,*] Because—what?

MARTHA. He—he has done so much for me.

FRANK. [*Softening.*] What has he done that anyone wouldn't have done for you, Martha? [*With a return to his angry manner as he crosses down left.*] If your father and mother—

MARTHA. [*Interrupting with a touch of quiet dignity.*] Don't say anything against them, please.

FRANK. [*More gently.*] I'm not going to say anything against them. They're dead. You were hungry—he fed you. I've done as much for a hungry dog before now.

MARTHA. [*Softly.*] Frank, if they had sent me to that poor-house that time, I would have died there.

FRANK. [*Going to her and speaking with great tenderness.*] Don't you believe I would have done as much for you as—

MARTHA. [*Winds her arms around his neck, and says softly.*] You've got to do more for me now, Frank, you've got to give me back to him. [*They are down right centre.*]

FRANK. [*Looking at her earnestly.*] Do you believe you're going to be happy as his wife?

MARTHA. [*Simply.*] No—I don't. But I'm afraid I wouldn't be happy as your wife—now.

FRANK. [*Astonished.*] What?

MARTHA. I don't understand why, but I feel it's true. Nor would you. He'd go away—we'd never see him again—we'd always think of him as a lonely, disappointed man.

FRANK. [*Realizing that all argument is useless, and accepting the situation.*] Well, here's an end to all our boy and girl life. [*He laughs bitterly.*] We *played* man and wife. [*He takes a tiny jeweler's box out of his pocket and gives it to* MARTHA.] Here, give this to Ben. I've got no use for it now.

MARTHA. [*Opens the box which contains a wedding ring. She is deeply moved and cannot keep back her tears.*] Oh, Frank —when did you buy this?

FRANK. Yesterday. [*He is almost at the point of breaking down himself, and tries to hide his feelings with a bitter laugh.*] Wasn't it lucky I thought of 'it? You and Ben couldn't get married without a ring, you know.

MARTHA. [*With tender reproach.*] Ah, don't be bitter. Poor old Ben, he's more to be pitied than either you or I. [*She kisses the ring tenderly.*] I'll keep this, and some day—

FRANK. [*Turning to her quickly, and speaking with quiet forcefulness.*] No, Martha, no day—no one—never!

MARTHA. [*Goes to him, puts her hand on his shoulder, and turns his face to her. She speaks with great tenderness.*] Oh, yes. You're young—some girl will come into your life, and you will love her. Not just as you've loved me, perhaps—and I will love her, and you'll marry her with this ring.

[TURNER *enters from the house, upper left. He carries a bunch of keys, and speaks as he comes in.*]

TURNER. Now Ben— [*He stops surprised as he sees* FRANK *and* MARTHA.] Where's Ben? [*As soon as* MARTHA *and* FRANK *hear* TURNER'S *voice, they separate a little consciously.* MARTHA *goes to the bench, right.*]

FRANK. [*Curtly, pointing centre right.*] Out there.

TURNER. [*Crossing to* FRANK *centre, astonished at his manner.*] What's the matter with you?

FRANK. [*In the same curt manner.*] Do you see anything the matter with me? [*He turns away from his father, and goes down left.*]

TURNER. [*Rebuking him quietly.*] I see that you're disrespectful to your father. [*He crosses to* MARTHA *and says very kindly and gently.*] Are you crying, Martha?

MARTHA. [*Smiling and trying to hide her tears.*] Do I look as if I were, Uncle Billy?

TURNER. [*Peering at her doubtfully.*] Well, of course, my eyes ain't—I thought you looked— [*With a glance at* FRANK.] Then this surly—

FRANK. [*Regretting his show of rudeness and making an effort to speak gently.*] I didn't intend to be surly, Father.

TURNER. Ben never spoke a surly word to me in his life.

FRANK. [*Impatiently breaking out again as he turns up centre.*] Oh, Ben's got wings!

TURNER. [*Sharply.*] And you run to tongue, don't you?

[ELIZABETH *enters from the house, through the door, left.*]

ELIZABETH. William, Albert Truax is here again. He's been over to that dock three times this morning.

TURNER. [*Crossing to* ELIZABETH *and speaking querulously.*] Why don't he come when the steamer's in? I ain't goin' to live on the dock for Al Truax nor nobody else. [*He goes towards the door, left.*]

ELIZABETH. [*Following him.*] If his fruit spoils, he'll sue the company.

TURNER. Let him sue. We hire a lawyer by the year. [*He goes off, left, followed by* ELIZABETH.]

ELIZABETH. [*Speaking as she goes.*] Go 'long and get the man his stuff. 'Twon't kill yeh to walk over to that ol' shed, I guess. [*They are both off by this time, and she is heard outside saying:*] I'm ashamed to have folks running here after you every five minutes of the day.

MARTHA. [*Crossing to right centre.*] You shouldn't have been so impatient with your father, Frank. [*She sits on the topmast, right.*]

FRANK. [*Coming down left centre, and speaking with great bitterness.*] I spoke as I feel—I wish I were dead!

MARTHA. [*Awed.*] Oh, Frank—that's a sin! If it were not, I could wish that I, too—

FRANK. [*Turning on her with a return to his angry manner.*] It's a sin to love one man and marry another!

MARTHA. [*With quiet impressiveness.*] Frank, do you believe in dreams?

FRANK. [*Standing centre.*] I d'know. Sailors believe in most everything, I suppose.

MARTHA. Well, your mother came to me last night, and kissed me—and put my hand in Ben's.

FRANK. [*Wistfully.*] Mother never knew me—I was a baby when she died. If she'd known me, perhaps—

MARTHA. [*Trying to speak cheerily in an effort to get* FRANK *out of his sombre mood, rising and going centre.*] Let's get into a boat and row out on the bay!

FRANK. [*Gloomily, dropping down left.*] No, what's the use of prolonging a fellah's misery? He'll be here directly, and well—I'm not going to cry— [*Softening.*] If I could cry, I'd get over it. I haven't cried since the first time I left you to go to sea, until yesterday.

MARTHA. [*Curiously.*] Yesterday? What made you cry yesterday?

FRANK. I d'know—I cried as I stepped off the train.

MARTHA. [*Deeply moved, going to him and kissing him.*] You're crying now, Frank.

FRANK. [*Ashamed of his tears, pulls away from her quickly.*] No, I'm not! I'll never cry again. [*He goes to the bench, left.*]

[BEN *enters through the centre doors from the right.*]

MARTHA. [*Turns and sees him, and tries to speak cheerily and naturally.*] Why, here's Ben, now. [*She crosses to him and they meet centre.*] We were just talking of you.

BEN. [*At* MARTHA'S *right, taking her hand and speaking with great tenderness.*] Were you—what were you saying?

MARTHA. [*A little at a loss, hesitates.*] Well, we—ah—

BEN. [*Smiling at her, and mustering all his cheerfulness.*]

Did you tell Frank what I said to you yesterday afternoon?

MARTHA. [*Evasively.*] Well, not all. I told him part of it.

BEN. *The* part?

MARTHA. Yes.

BEN. [*As before.*] Well, what is he going to do—shoot me?

MARTHA. [*Surprised.*] Shoot you—what for?

BEN. [*Half laughing.*] For trying to steal his Sunday girl.

MARTHA. [*Pretending not to understand what he means.*] Who is his Sunday girl?

FRANK. [*Breaking in with a short sarcastic laugh.*] A sailor has a girl in every port, you know. He oughtn't to quarrel over any *one* girl. [*He crosses to the right, and sits on the topmast.*]

BEN. [*Going to* FRANK *and putting his hand on his shoulder.*] Frank, yesterday afternoon, I asked Martha to be my wife.

FRANK. [*Sullenly, without looking at him.*] I know you did.

[MARTHA *crosses to the upper end of the bench, left, and stands watching the two men a little uneasily.*]

BEN. I didn't know then that she was in love with you.

FRANK. [*With a significant glance at* MARTHA.] I don't know it now.

BEN. [*He is so intent on his own thoughts that the import of* FRANK'S *speech escapes him. He speaks with generous heartiness.*] Of course this ends your going to sea. You've got to give that up. [*With an affectionate glance toward* MARTHA.] You've been away from her so much that, well—I don't think it's safe to leave her alone any longer [*Laughs.*] —not even with me.

FRANK. Who do you mean by "her"?

BEN. Why, Martha.

FRANK. Oh!

MARTHA. [*Smiling.*] You've taken pretty good care of me so far, haven't you, Ben?

BEN. [*Looking over at her wistfully.*] Have I?

MARTHA. You know you have. You gave me a home—

BEN. I d'know as I deserve any credit for that. You've earned pretty much all you ever got, I guess. [*He turns to* FRANK *again.*] However, Frank can't support a wife on seaman's wages.

FRANK. [*Sarcastically.*] I may marry a girl that's got money.

BEN. [*Ignoring* FRANK'S *attitude.*] Frank, the best thing for you to do now is to settle right down, and go into business here with me. There's work enough for all of us. When you're married, I hope you'll live with us, same as ever. [*He looks over at* MARTHA *and speaks feelingly.*] I don't believe the house would be the same without her—but if you feel that you'd like your own little home, why—

MARTHA. [*Amazed, crossing to* BEN *centre.*] I thought you asked me to be *your* wife?

BEN. I did, but as I say—I— [*He hesitates as though at a loss, looking from one to the other.*]

MARTHA. [*Summoning up her courage.*] I haven't given you my answer yet, have I?

BEN. [*Puzzled.*] No, but I thought that he— [*Indicating* FRANK.]

FRANK. [*Breaking in, sullenly.*] Suppose you think for yourself and let me do the same!

MARTHA. [*Hastily to* BEN, *to cover* FRANK'S *anger.*] Do you want my answer now?

BEN. [*Looking at her, sadly.*] I have it. [*He takes the locket from his pocket, and holds it out to her.*]

MARTHA. [*Very much startled, taking it.*] Where did you get this?

BEN. You dropped it in the yard. [*He crosses* MARTHA, *and drops down a little below left centre.*]

MARTHA. [*Trying to make light of the situation, goes to* FRANK *and says with a little laugh:*] Well, Frank, I guess you didn't think your little present was going to make trouble between Ben and me, did you?

FRANK. [*Coldly, without looking at her.*] No—perhaps I wouldn't have sent it, if I had.

MARTHA. [*Turning to* BEN, *with a note of tender reproach in her voice.*] Why, Ben, you're not jealous of Frank's picture, are you?

BEN. [*Standing at workbench, left. His manner is very gentle, but frank and straightforward.*] No, I'm not jealous at all. It set me thinking, that's all. I was wondering why you never showed it to me.

[MARTHA *is on the verge of tears. She is confused and troubled, and hardly knows what she is saying. She makes a pathetic effort to get hold of herself, and tries to speak lightly. She is standing right centre.*]

MARTHA. Well, I don't know—I wanted—I intended to show it to you yesterday, and to read you his letter, but you— you—[*Laughs.*]—didn't give me a chance—[*Laughs.*]— y'know.

BEN. [*Slowly and thoughtfully.* MARTHA'S *attitude deceives him, but he still has some misgivings.*] How long have you had it?

MARTHA. [*With nervous lightness, quickly.*] I've had the picture a long time. He sent me the locket from Yokohama. Don't you see it's a Japanese curiosity—the setting is?

BEN. [*Who is seated on the bench, left.*] I didn't see the

setting. [*Wistfully.*] I saw nothing but his handsome, young face, and my plain, old one.

MARTHA. [*Who is standing centre, between the two men, is touched by* BEN'S *attitude, and says gently:*] Yours is not an old face, Ben, nor a plain one. You asked me not to say no, if I could help it. Well—I'm going to say—

BEN. [*Rising, and going to her, centre.*] Wait! [*With great earnestness.*] Are you doing this because you love me—or because I've been good to you?

MARTHA. Both. I couldn't love you if you were not good to me, and you—you couldn't be good to me and I not love you.

BEN. And you and Frank are not—

MARTHA. [*Evading a direct answer, but not so much as to be noticeable.*] Why—I'm going to marry *you*, am I not?

BEN. [*Going to* FRANK, *right, and laying his hand on his shoulder, speaking gravely.*] Is this a sacrifice you two are making for me?

[*In spite of himself,* FRANK *is touched by* BEN'S *manly, generous attitude, and now he speaks with a great effort, as though impelled to do so by something beyond himself. He rises as he speaks, and his hands are clenched at his sides.*]

FRANK. Sacrifice? Humph! Why should I make a sacrifice for you? Because you're my brother? If I wanted a girl, and that girl wanted me, all the brothers on earth couldn't take her away from me.

BEN. Frank, I love you—not because you are my brother, but because you are—yourself. I love her. I don't believe it's just because she's a young girl, although youth has a great charm for one who has got beyond it—but I've loved her ever since I first held her in my arms, a baby. She's a part of me now— [*He laughs and goes to her, puts his hands on her shoulders, and looks her full in the face.*] Martha, I want you—if you can come to me of your own free will and because you want to be my wife. But I *don't* want you if you

come through a sense of duty or obligation. You owe me
nothing. [*He turns up centre, towards the doorway.*]

[CAP'N DAN *and* FREEMAN *enter through the door on the
right, and stand watching the scene with intense interest.*]

FRANK. [*Crossing to* MARTHA, *says to her warningly in a
low voice,*] You'd best think twice. [*He drops down left,
below the summerhouse.*]

[MARTHA *stands for a moment in deep thought. Then, as
though she had made up her mind, she turns quickly and goes
to* BEN *with her hands outstretched. She speaks from the
depths of her heart.*]

MARTHA. Ben, I come to you of my own free will. I want
to be your wife.

[*As* FRANK *hears* MARTHA'S *decision, he drops his head on
his breast, utterly crushed.*]

BEN. [*Who is standing right centre, says to* MARTHA,] Remember, I'm no longer a boy.

MARTHA. No, you're a great, big, splendid man. [*With deep
feeling.*] Do you remember Whitcomb Riley's poem "Jim"?

> "When God made Jim, I'll bet you
> He didn't do anything else that day
> But just set around and feel good."

Well, that's you, Ben. You're Riley's "Jim."

[BEN *looks at* MARTHA *a second, then takes her greedily, as
if clasping a jewel he had believed lost, and holds her close.*]

CAP'N DAN. [*Who is still standing by the door up right with*
FREEMAN, *says to him quietly,*] Did yeh ever see him?

FREEMAN. [*Without taking his eyes off* BEN *and* MARTHA.]
Who?

CAP'N DAN. Riley's Jim?

FREEMAN. No, not to know him. Have you?

CAP'N DAN. No, not 'at I remember. Hush! [*He is anxious
not to lose a word of what is going on.*]

[MARTHA, *a little spent, moves down right, and leans against the bench.* BEN *crosses to* FRANK *and puts his hand on his shoulder. He is greatly reassured and, with a resumption of his cheery manner and laughing joyously, he says to* FRANK :]

BEN. Why, what a durned fool I've been for making such a fuss over your picture! It got me all mixed up. I don't blame you for being angry with me. You'll stay here and share the business with me, won't you?

[FRANK'S *bitterness against* MARTHA *and his jealousy of* BEN *surge over him in a fury, and his first impulse is to smash* BEN *in the face with his fist. He masters this, and says in a dull and colorless voice:*]

FRANK. I don't know's I'll do that—but I'll do something, Ben. [*He turns away from* BEN *and drops down left, near the bench.*]

[GEORGE SALTER *enters through the centre doors from the right, accompanied by the two carpenters, and at the same time* WILLIAM TURNER *comes from the house with a bale of new rope.*]

TURNER. Ben, why didn't yeh come over an' get your freight? There's some of it. [*He drops the rope on the floor, and mops his forehead.*]

GEORGE. [*Speaking almost at the same time* TURNER *does.*] Ben! Cap'n Peterson's here with his boat. Shall we—

BEN. [*Interrupting* GEORGE, *in an excited and important manner.*] Hold on, boys, there isn't going to be another stroke of work done here today— [*To* GEORGE.] George, run over to the Nassau House and get me a bottle of champagne. [*He goes down to* MARTHA, *who is still standing at the bench, right.*]

[*Everyone catches* BEN'S *mood of excitement.* CAP'N DAN, *who has been observing* FRANK *closely, is not quite satisfied in his mind that all is going as it should. Now, he calls after* GEORGE *thoughtfully,*]

CAP'N DAN. Say—git two of 'em—one for me—cha'ge it.

GEORGE. [*Laughing.*] Champagne's always charged! Quarts or pints?

BEN. Quarts!

GEORGE. Kee-rect! [*He starts to go off through the centre doorway, just as* ELIZABETH ANNE *enters centre from the left. They run into each other.*]

ELIZABETH. Why, George Salter, where are you going in such a hurry?

GEORGE. 'Scuse me, Miss Turner, can't stop. I've got to get two quarts of champagne. [*He runs off centre to the right.*]

ELIZABETH. [*Coming down stage, and looking wonderingly from one to the other.*] What in time are you going to do with that stuff?

BEN. [*Triumphantly.*] We're going to drink the health of the happiest man alive—that's me—and of the only girl in the world, and that's Martha. [*He holds out his hand, and* MARTHA *goes to him.*] She and I are going to get married!

EVERYBODY. [*Except* FRANK,] Good!

[CAP'N DAN *puts his arm around* ELIZABETH *and brings her down left centre.*]

FRANK. [*Coming a little centre and facing them all. He speaks in a tone of forced gayety, and has hard work to keep the tears out of his voice.*] And while you're about it, you might as well drink the health of the jolliest Jackie in the United States Navy—that's me—and *I'm* going to get married!

ALL THE MEN. [*Laughing.*] To who?

FRANK. [*Recklessly.*] I don't know. [*They all think he is joking and laugh loudly.*] To the first girl that'll have me. [FRANK *drops down left again.*]

[GEORGE *enters right, carrying a number of goblets on his*

arm, piled up as waiters pile them.[1] *He is followed by* HOSEA
STEVENS, *a red-headed, freckle-faced barkeeper. He wears
a barkeeper's white coat and apron, very much soiled; his
trousers are turned up at the bottom, and his shoes are spattered as if with the drinks that had slopped off the counter.
A soiled towel is on his arm, a stump of a cigar is in his
mouth. He carries two dirty, dented, tin wine coolers, con-
taining ice, and two bottles of champagne. His manner is
very important and assured.*]

GEORGE. [*Speaking as he enters.*] Here's y'r champagne!

HOSEA. How d'do, ladies and gents. [*They all bow to him indifferently.*] My boy's off watch—come myself.

[HOSEA *comes down centre, and they all crowd around him.*
WILLIAM TURNER *is at* HOSEA'S *right, with* GEORGE *standing
next to him and the two ship carpenters at the right of*
GEORGE. BEN *stands a little below the carpenters, between
them and* MARTHA, *who is still leaning against the bench,
right. To the left, above* HOSEA, *stands* FREEMAN, *with* CAP'N
DAN *and* ELIZABETH *a little below him.* FRANK *stands apart
from the rest, lost in his own gloomy thoughts. With the exception of* MARTHA, BEN *and* FRANK, *they are all very much
excited. This is a most unusual event in their lives.*]

FREEMAN. [*To* CAP'N DAN.] I thought champagne allus came
in bottles?

CAP'N DAN. [*Ingenuously.*] Don't it?

FREEMAN. He's brought his'n in two tin buckets.

TURNER. [*Anxiously.*] Come now, let's get 'r drinked up,
'fore the boat gits in. Have yeh got a corkscrew?

HOSEA. [*In a grandly patronising manner.*] Do'want no corkscrew for champagne.

TURNER. How d'yeh git the cork out?

HOSEA. I'll show yeh.

    [1] *NOTE:* George should not bring on champagne goblets, but very
coarse, cheap, drinking goblets.

[*They all crowd around* HOSEA *and watch him as he tries his best to open one bottle of champagne. Meantime,* ELIZABETH *takes* CAP'N DAN *a little away from the others.*]

ELIZABETH. [*In a low voice.*] Dan'l Marble, you ain't going to drink any of that champagne?

CAP'N DAN. Well, I thought I would.

ELIZABETH. Isn't it intoxicating?

CAP'N DAN. [*Very innocently.*] I never heard it was. It's champagne.

HOSEA. [*As the cork breaks in the bottle.*] Well, I'm blamed! That's the fust bad cork I see in a case o' that wine. [*He takes a corkscrew out of his pocket, and starts to open the bottle with it.*]

CAP'N DAN. You're such an easy liar, Hosea, there's no believin' you.

HOSEA. Git y'r glasses ready! It may fly some. [*They all hold out their glasses.*]

[CAP'N DAN *hands a glass to* ELIZABETH. GEORGE *passes the second bottle of champagne to* CAP'N DAN.]

ELIZABETH. [*Doubtfully.*] I'm afraid to drink it.

CAP'N DAN. [*Forcing the glass on her.*] 'Twon't hurt yeh, it's champagne.

HOSEA. [*Pulling the cork.*] Look out, ladies and gents, here she comes! [*There is a loud pop as he draws the cork out. All laugh, and hold their glasses to be filled. He pauses and says very impressively*] Wait now, there's a way to serve out champagne. This ain't beer nor cocktails, it's champagne!

FREEMAN. [*Warningly.*] She's a-drippin'.

HOSEA. Let her drip. Ben, hold y'r glass. [BEN *comes forward and* HOSEA *pours a little of the champagne into his glass.*]

BEN. [*In humorous protest.*] Oh, Gosh, fill'r up!

HOSEA. After the ladies. That's so's if they's any cork or anythin' in the bottle, the gent'll git it, see? [*As he passes the bottle to* BEN.] Now serve the ladies.

[BEN *pours champagne into* MARTHA'S *glass, and then serves* GEORGE, *his father, and the two carpenters. Meantime,* CAP'N DAN *is trying to open the second bottle.*]

HOSEA. [*Looking about.*] Where's the other bottle?

CAP'N DAN. [*Trying to hold the cork down.*] I got it. Look out, I can't hold it in—it's comin'—you'll get splattered! [*He pulls the cork, the champagne pops and sizzles, and he holds his hand over the bottle as he says, chuckling:*] I got mine out 'thout no corkscrew!

[*They all laugh.*]

HOSEA. Take y'r hand off'n it.

CAP'N DAN. It'll splatter!

HOSEA. It's all right.

[CAP'N DAN *fills* ELIZABETH'S *glass, and then* FREEMAN'S. *He goes to* FRANK, *who is paying little attention to the scene, and fills his glass.*]

HOSEA. Well, I got to run. Take good care of them cham-pagne glasses. I'll charge it, Ben. One to you and one to the Cap'n. Dollar apiece. [*He hurries off by the door, right.*]

[*By this time, everyone's glass is full.* CAP'N DAN'S *bottle is still partly filled.* FREEMAN, ELIZABETH *and* CAP'N DAN *stand apart from the others by the summerhouse, down left.*]

BEN. [*Holding up his glass.*] Here's to the new firm—Ben Turner and Brother!

GEORGE. Rah! Rah! Rah!

ALL THE MEN. [*Except* FRANK.] Rah! Rah! Rah! They're all right—Rah! Rah! Rah! [*They all drink. They sip their wine as if they had never tasted champagne before, and were curious.*]

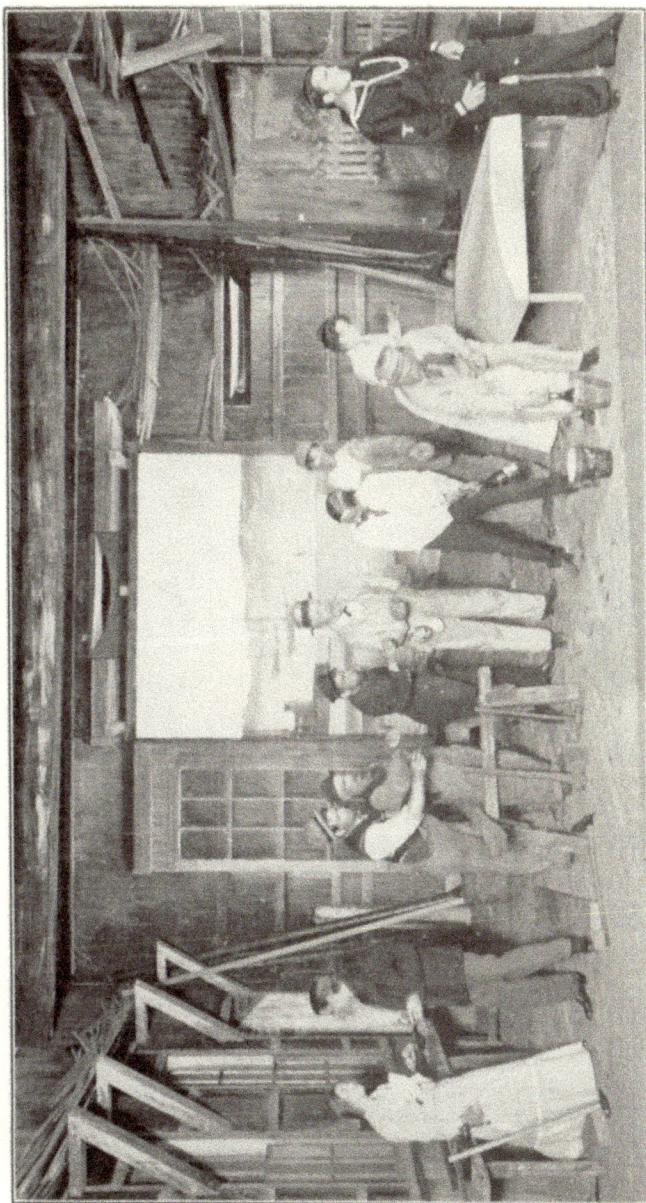

SAG HARBOR. ACT 2

FREEMAN. [*To* CAP'N DAN.] No great shucks, is it? [*Sipping it again.*] I'd as lief have cider.

CAP'N DAN. [*Tasting his.*] It goes up my nose like soda. If I'd 'a' knowed it cost a dollar a bottle, I'd have ordered cider.

GEORGE. [*Holding up his glass, and chanting in a singsong voice.*] Here's to the vine that grew the grapes that made this bottle of champagne.

ALL. [*As before, except* FRANK, *sipping the champagne.*] Rah! Rah! Rah!

FREEMAN. [*Holding up his glass.*] Here's to— [*He sees it is empty and turns to* CAP'N DAN.] Give me some. I want to make a speech. [CAP'N DAN *pours a little champagne into* FREEMAN'S *glass.*] Here's to Martha Reese—what's the matter with her?

ALL THE MEN. [*Except* FRANK.] She's all right! Rah! Rah! Rah! [*They all drink.*]

TURNER. [*Holding up his glass.*] Here's to the fast-sailin' steamer "Antelope." [*They all start to drink as a steamboat's whistle is heard in the distance.* TURNER *starts, listens, pulls out his watch, looks at it, and says disgustedly:*] Half an hour ahead of time! [*They all laugh uproariously. He starts to go, stops, empties his glass hurriedly, and rushes over to* BEN *who still stands with a half-empty champagne bottle in his hand.*] Here, give me that bottle! [*He grabs the bottle and runs off, centre to the left.*]

BEN *and* GEORGE. Oh! Here—hold on—

[BEN, GEORGE *and the two carpenters rush out after* TURNER. FREEMAN, CAP'N DAN *and* ELIZABETH, *who have been hobnobbing over their drinks, pay no attention.* FRANK *slowly comes centre. The men can be heard outside, shouting:*]

THE MEN. What's the matter with the "Antelope"—she's all right. Rah! Rah! Rah! [*Their laughter and voices die away in the distance.*]

[MARTHA *puts her glass of champagne, which she has not touched, down on the bench, right, and goes to* FRANK. *They meet centre.*]

MARTHA. [*With deep feeling.*] Frank, you're the bravest and handsomest boy in the world. [*She puts her arms about him.*] And I love you ten times more than ever. [*They are oblivious of the little group down left, who are equally oblivious of them.*]

FRANK. [*With a sudden outburst of rage, raising his glass, which he has not touched, says between his teeth,*] I've a good mind to smash this on his—

MARTHA. [*Frightened.*] Oh, Frank— [*She takes his glass, and puts it on the bench, right.*]

BEN. [*Calling off left.*] Martha, come here a minute, I want you.

MARTHA. [*Calling.*] All right, Ben. [*Coaxingly to* FRANK.] You come, too, Frank!

FRANK. Let me alone! You've made your choice, stand by it. [*He turns away from her, goes up stage, leans his arm on the doorpost, right centre, drops his head on his arm and sobs.* MARTHA *follows him and stands beside him on his right, trying to soothe him.*]

[JANE CAULDWELL *enters from the house, left. She is radiant with smiles as she enters, but her face changes as she sees* FRANK *and* MARTHA.]

JANE. [*Going up centre.*] Why—what's the matter here?

MARTHA. [*Going to her and clinging to her, tearfully.*] Jane dear, I'm the most unhappy girl in the world.

JANE. [*Putting her arms around* MARTHA, *and looking significantly at* FRANK.] Why? You ought to be the happiest.

MARTHA. [*Solemnly.*] I'm going to be married—[JANE *looks at* FRANK, *certain he is to be the bridegroom.*]—to Frank's brother. [JANE *gives a low exclamation of horror.* MARTHA *quickly puts her hand over* JANE'S *mouth.*] Hush! [MARTHA *goes off left centre.*]

[JANE *stands for a moment, looking pityingly at* FRANK. *Then she goes to him, and puts her arms around his neck.*]

JANE. Poor Frank.

FRANK. [*Who did not know she was there, turns and looks at her vacantly.*] Oh! I—?

JANE. [*In a voice that is vibrant with tenderness.*] I'm so sorry.

FRANK. [*Ashamed of having shown his feelings, says a little irritably,*] Don't pity me please. I hate to be pitied.

JANE. [*Awed.*] This won't drive you away to sea again, will it?

FRANK. [*Indifferently.*] I don't know, and I don't care. [*He goes off through the door on the right.*]

JANE. [*Heartbroken for* FRANK, *looks about her crying and laughing at once, and says half to herself,*] What a mixed up mess! How ever is it all going to end, I wonder? [*She goes off left centre.*]

[FREEMAN, CAP'N DAN *and* ELIZABETH *come centre.* FREEMAN *gets down to the topmast, right centre.*]

CAP'N DAN. Say 'Lizbeth, they was one spell there, I didn't know just how it was goin' to end between Ben and Martha and Frank, did you?

ELIZABETH. [*Who is centre, with* CAP'N DAN *on her left, speaks casually.*] Never can tell when it's between a woman and two men.

CAP'N DAN. I hope she knows her own mind.

ELIZABETH. She's old enough.

FREEMAN. [*Sitting on the topmast. He is slightly affected by the champagne.*] Say, the blame stuff's strong, d'yeh know it?

CAP'N DAN. [*Sipping the champagne. He is also a little affected.*] It is sort of insiduous.

FREEMAN. It's gone to my head.

ELIZABETH. [*Who has not emptied her glass, gingerly sipping her champagne. She is in a complacent mood.*] No wonder, you've drank a quart of it.

FREEMAN. [*Scornfully.*] Them bottles don't hold a quart.

[CAP'N DAN *attempts to pour some more champagne into* ELIZABETH'S *glass. She stops him by putting her hand over it.*]

ELIZABETH. Don't give me any more, please.

CAP'N DAN. [*Looks at the bottle and sees it is empty, chuckles.*] By Gosh! They ain't no more into it. [*He reads the label.*] "Sarah-cuse Wine Co., Limited—Extry Dry"—[*To* FREEMAN.] What's that mean?

FREEMAN. [*Dryly.*] Means the bottle's empty—you've played the limit. [CAP'N DAN *throws the bottle on the floor.* FREEMAN *rises and yawns.*] Well, this ain't paintin'. [*He goes to the bench right, as though to put down his glass. He speaks casually.*] Say, you two goin' to the fun'ral tomorrow?

CAP'N DAN. Whose?

FREEMAN. Whose? You ain't livin' in New York where you can have your choice of three or four fun'rals a day. [*As he puts his empty glass down, he sees the full glass which* MARTHA *has placed on the bench, right.*] Hello! Somebody's left a hull tumbler full o' champagne. [*To* ELIZABETH, *as he crosses centre.*] Want it?

ELIZABETH. [*Who is now in a very dignified mood.*] No, indeed, thank you.

FREEMAN. [*To* CAP'N DAN.] You have some of it, Cap'n?

ELIZABETH. [*With great dignity, putting her hand over* CAP'N

DAN'S *glass.*] No, he's had all that's good for him. [*She takes another sip of her champagne.*]

CAP'N DAN. [*Chuckling.*] I guess I have about all I can manage.

FREEMAN. [*Laughs.*] I'll drink it myself, says the little red hen. [*He drinks, and begins to sing as he crosses to the summerhouse.*] "Maid of Athens, ere we part"—I s'pose you two'll stand up with 'em? [*He picks up a paint pot lying near the summerhouse, as he sings:*]

"Give, oh give me back my heart."

[*He looks around.*] Ain't no more limited layin' 'round loose, is they? [*He goes up centre singing:*]

"Or since that has left my breast,
Pity me and take the rest."

[*He goes off through the door on the left.*]

ELIZABETH. [*Crossing down left and wiping her forehead with her handkerchief.*] My, just look at the perspiration on my forehead!

CAP'N DAN. [*Yawning.*] It's the weather. Dog day sort o' day.

[CAP'N DAN *sits on the freshly painted summerhouse, and* ELIZABETH *sits on an empty box at his left. She sips her champagne very gingerly. The taste is pleasant, and she does not realize the effect.*]

CAP'N DAN. [*Taking a bag of salted peanuts out of his pocket and handing it to her.*] Here!

ELIZABETH. [*Eagerly.*] What be they—caramels?

CAP'N DAN. No—salted peanuts.

ELIZABETH. [*Taking the bag.*] D'know's I ever et any.

CAP'N DAN. It's a new industry—they say they're healthy.

[*They lapse into silence and eat the nuts, occasionally sipping the champagne.*]

ELIZABETH. [*Who is now in a sentimental mood.*] Dan'l, you've always been awful good to me.

CAP'N DAN. [*Frankly.*] Allus mean to be.

ELIZABETH. I haven't always deserved it.

CAP'N DAN. [*With a laugh.*] Yeh have, too.

ELIZABETH. No, I haven't. I've been real mean to you sometimes.

CAP'N DAN. [*Heartily.*] I disremember when.

ELIZABETH. [*In a matter-of-fact manner.*] Want to eat a fillipeen? [*She offers him a nut.*]

CAP'N DAN. Yes yes. [*He takes the nut.*] What is it—give or take?

ELIZABETH. Yes or no. [*They eat the nuts.*]

CAP'N DAN. All right.

ELIZABETH. What's it for?

CAP'N DAN. Pair of gallusses.

ELIZABETH. [*Primly.*] A pair of gloves.

CAP'N DAN. Um'm! [*There is a pause. They eat more nuts.*] Will yeh stand up with 'em if they ask yeh?

ELIZABETH. Yes, won't you?

CAP'N DAN. 'Course, if you do. [*There is a pause.*] You know that lot in Hog's Neck you like so much?

ELIZABETH. [*Correcting him.*] North Haven, if you please!

CAP'N DAN. [*With a sly smile.*] It's Hog's Neck on the chart. Well, I've bought it.

ELIZABETH. [*Delighted.*] You haven't?

CAP'N DAN. Yes, I have! An' I'm goin' to build onto it.

ELIZABETH. Oh my, when?

CAP'N DAN. Soon's the season's over.

[*He rises and goes to the bench, left. He has a little difficulty in walking steadily. He takes a drawing from the
bench, returns with it to the summerhouse, and sits down
again.*] Here's a picture of the house. [*Proudly.*] There, what
do you think of that for a cottage by the sea?

ELIZABETH. [*Looking at the drawing, delighted.*] Oh! A
Queen Annie—who made this?

CAP'N DAN. Len Howells drawed that. They ain't no better
site on the Neck—an' they won't be no pootier place. Lots of
'em'll cost more.

ELIZABETH. I've always been wild to live on that Neck.

CAP'N DAN. [*Pointing to the drawing.*] There's your room.

ELIZABETH. [*Pleased.*] Beautiful! Looks right out on the
bay.

CAP'N DAN. [*Smiling slyly and pointing.*] That's you in the
window a-watchin' for me. There's the "Kacy" just roundin'
the P'int. That's me standin' in the riggin'.

ELIZABETH. [*Blinking her eyes, but with perfect uncon-
sciousness.*] There's two of you!

CAP'N DAN. [*Innocently.*] No, there's only one o' me. Al
Holmes is a-steerin'.

ELIZABETH. [*Innocently, rubbing her eyes.*] I swan! I
thought I saw two of you. I wonder if anything's the matter
with my eyes?

CAP'N DAN. [*Cheerfully.*] I dunno, why don't you see an
optomist?

ELIZABETH. [*Looking at the drawing again.*] What's that on
the beach?

CAP'N DAN. That's y'r bathhouse. [*Again indicating the drawing.*] That's the "Kacy's" moorin'.

ELIZABETH. [*Pleased and complacent.*] Why, you'll have everything—won't you?

CAP'N DAN. [*With an insinuating smile.*] Yes yes—when I get you.

ELIZABETH. [*Consulting the drawing, unconsciously.*] Which's your room?

CAP'N DAN. [*Nonplussed.*] Eh?

ELIZABETH. Which is your room?

CAP'N DAN. [*Dryly.*] I thought I'd sleep aboard the boat for a spell—jes' come in to my victuals.

ELIZABETH. [*Ingenuously.*] Oh, no, I wouldn't do that. Why don't you take this one? [*Points to the drawing.*]

CAP'N DAN. [*Disgustedly.*] That's way 'round on the other side o' the house—northern exposure.

ELIZABETH. Well, what o' that?

CAP'N DAN. [*Pointing.*] This is a nice room—next to yours.

ELIZABETH. [*With calm unconcern.*] Yes, that'll make a nice guest-chamber.

CAP'N DAN. [*His spirits greatly dashed.*] Yeh goin' to have guests?

ELIZABETH. [*With quiet positiveness.*] Always'll have *some* company.

CAP'N DAN. [*With determination.*] Then I'm comin' visitin'.

ELIZABETH. [*Sweetly, but ingenuously.*] You'll be the host.

CAP'N DAN. [*Pleadingly.*] I'd rather be a guest. Why don't yeh plan to take boarders?

ELIZABETH. Oh, no, we don't want to do that just yet—not so long's you're doing as well as you are now.

cap'n dan. [*Putting his arm around her.*] I am doin' pooty well now—ain't I?

elizabeth. [*Looking down at his arm, quizzically.*] Better than you expected to when you got up this morning, I guess. [*She laughs.*]

cap'n dan. [*In a humorous manner, that has a little touch of pathos.*] Say, 'Lizbeth, I don't care a durn where my room is—yeh can put me in the cellar, or in the garret, so long's I know I've got you in my house somewheres. That's all I want. I'm lonesome, 'Lizbeth. 'Tain't so bad summers—they's more or less company on the boat—but winters—scallopin's cold, lonesome work. I've got to that time o' life when it ain't good for a man to live alone no longer.

elizabeth. [*She is now in a motherly, tender mood.*] Well, Dan'l, when you get that house finished, p'r'aps you shan't live alone any longer.

cap'n dan. [*Joyously.*] By Gosh! I'll start the *arch*-i-tects tomorrow mornin'!

elizabeth. [*Complacently.*] That don't scare me.

cap'n dan. Yeh dasn't set a day.

elizabeth. [*Spunkily.*] I dare, too.

cap'n dan. I double stump yeh!

elizabeth. [*The champagne has made her daring.*] I won't take a stump from anybody. First Monday in September.

cap'n dan. That's Labor Day.

elizabeth. I don't care if it is.

cap'n dan. Will yeh have a justice of the peace or a minister of the gospel?

elizabeth. Why, I'll have our minister, of course. [*Proudly, with a foolish laugh.*] When I get married, I'll get married in church. [*Pompously.*] I'll be all in white—[*Giggling.*] —and you'll have to wear a swallow-tail suit.

CAP'N DAN. [*Joyously.*] Oh Gosh! I'll wear anythin'! Yeh dasn't seal the bargain?

ELIZABETH. [*Once more relapsing into her dignified mood.*] I have no sealing wax. [*She gives a silly laugh, and puts* CAP'N DAN'S *hat on.*]

CAP'N DAN. I have! [*He sees the hat on her head and shouts warningly,*] Say, look out—that's a forfeit!

ELIZABETH. [*Innocently.*] 'Tisn't, is it?

CAP'N DAN. They say it is. [FREEMAN *enters left, and* CAP'N DAN *calls to him, as he points to the hat.*] Freeman, ain't that a forfeit?

FREEMAN. [*Coming centre, and speaking with profound seriousness.*] Well—some says it is, an' some says it isn't. It all depends. If 'twas *my* hat, I'd claim fo'feit.

CAP'N DAN. [*Turning to* ELIZABETH.] So'll I.

ELIZABETH. Well, you shan't, unless you're stronger than I am—and I'm afraid you are. [*She throws the hat down, puts down her glass, and rises with great dignity. Then she crosses to* FREEMAN *and says in withering tones:*] Freeman Whitmarsh, I knew a man once who got rich minding his own business.

[*As* ELIZABETH *crosses,* CAP'N DAN *rises, and picks up the empty peanut bag, and blows into it, until it is puffed up with air.*]

FREEMAN. [*Cheerfully.*] 'Twan't me, by Gosh!

ELIZABETH. No, it certainly was not you.

[ELIZABETH *goes up stage towards the door, left. She is followed by* CAP'N DAN, *who is still holding the bag. As he turns up stage, the audience sees that his clothes are covered with paint where he has been sitting on the freshly painted summerhouse. At the door* ELIZABETH *turns and says,*]

ELIZABETH. Dan'l—[*Laughs mysteriously.*]—turn one of

your stockings wrong side out, tonight, and put it under your pillow. Tell me your dream in the morning, and I'll tell you mine. [*She goes out, left.* CAP'N DAN, *all smiles, stands looking after her, filled with complacent satisfaction.*]

FREEMAN. D'you wear stockin's?

CAP'N DAN. I don't wear nothin' but wings—I'm in Heaven, I be! [*He begins to sing.*]

> "Oh there was a little man,
> And he had a little gun,
> And its bullets was filled with lead, lead, lead."

[*As he reaches the final line, "And he shot him right through the head, head, head," he claps his hands together, and the paper bag bursts with a loud noise.*[1]]

QUICK CURTAIN

[1] *NOTE:* Cap'n Dan and Elizabeth must handle this scene very delicately. The slightest exaggeration will make it offensive. The actors must remember that these simple people have never before tasted champagne or liquor of any kind.

ACT THIRD

The living room of the Turner home.

SCENE: *The room is parlor, library and dining room combined, and its whole atmosphere is one of comfort. The walls are papered simply, but tastefully, and the carpet is of a quiet tone in harmony; the furniture is good, but not expensive, and, with the exception of two large, old-fashioned easy chairs, which are upholstered, is quite modern. There are several small chairs in Colonial style, a cane-seated rocker, one or two artistic wooden chairs of cherry or mahogany, and one or two bits of Chippendale furniture, showing* MARTHA'S *modest good taste. There are several good engravings on the walls, and a few fine ornaments on the mantelpiece.*

The room itself is an old-fashioned one, Colonial in type. A wooden wainscot, painted white, runs halfway up the walls. The old-fashioned fireplace is down right, with an armchair in front of it. There is a cheery log fire on the hearth. Above the mantelpiece is a door leading to a hallway. In the upper right-hand corner of the room is a stairway. It is painted white, and has a handrail of mahogany. It runs up a few steps to a landing, then makes a sharp turn, and runs straight up the right-hand wall. In the corner made by the landing is a door leading to MARTHA'S *bedroom. A little to the left of the stairway, at the side of the room facing the audience, is a bay window, with a cushioned window seat. At the left-hand corner of this wall is a door leading outside. Between this door and the bay window is a small writing desk. Against the left wall, at right angles to the centre door, is an upright piano with a bench in front of it, and beside it, a stand for music. Below the piano is an armchair. The*

194

*lower end of the left wall juts into the room, making a cor-
ner, and down left against that part of the wall facing the
audience, at right angles to the piano, is a Chippendale sideboard. Below this, at the extreme lower left, and at right
angles to the sideboard, is a door which leads to the kitchen.
In the centre of the room is a mahogany dining table, with
drop leaves.*

*At the opening of the act it is late in the afternoon, and
through the bay window a light snowstorm can be seen falling outside. Evening comes on during the act, and the lamp
is lighted and the buff window-shades, which have been up,
are drawn down.*

At the rise of the curtain, MARTHA *is discovered standing
centre behind the dining table, cutting out baby clothes.
(There is no cover on the table.)* ELIZABETH *is seated at the
left of the table, sewing.* MRS. RUSSELL, *who is spending
the afternoon, is seated in the cane-seated rocker, right of the
table, knitting. There is a workbasket on the table contain-
ing sewing materials of every kind. On the floor beside*
ELIZABETH *is a small valise.* WILLIAM TURNER'S *slippers stand
on the rug by the fireplace on the right.*

MRS. RUSSELL. [*Watching* MARTHA *as she works, admiringly.*] Isn't Martha handy with her scissors? I d'know's I
ever saw a girl so—

ELIZABETH. [*Placidly.*] Comes natural to her.

MRS. RUSSELL. 'Tisn't every girl's got the knack.

[MARTHA *smiles; she knows she is clever.*]

ELIZABETH. She can cut and fit me better than any dress-
maker. She made my wedding dress.

MARTHA. [*Smiling at her tenderly.*] And now I'm making
your baby clothes.

[*All laugh.*]

ELIZABETH. [*Half laughing, half blushing.*] Seems ridiculous,
don't it?

MRS. RUSSELL. It's the natural sequence, as Cap'n John used to say when he was playin' whist.

MARTHA. [*Holding up a baby's garment, one that her own baby used to wear.*] Now, you're sure you want it exactly like this, are you, Aunt 'Lizbeth? You see, there are strings on this, no pins, and all the fullness goes right in here, under the arms.

ELIZABETH. [*Delighted.*] Yes, just like that. I think that's just too cunning for anything. [*To* MRS. RUSSELL.] Don't you?

MRS. RUSSELL. Funny—[*Smiling reflectively.*]—babies are most generally always born about the same size.

MARTHA. [*Busily cutting.*] There's nothing in the world like babies, bless 'em.

MRS. RUSSELL. Seems as if there were more babies born this year than any year I know.

ELIZABETH. [*Holding up the baby's shirt she is working on.*] What mites they be! Who'd ever imagine that'd go on any human being!

[*All smile.*]

MARTHA. I guess we've all been there, Aunt 'Lizbeth.

[*All laugh.*]

MRS. RUSSELL. I've got some of Cap'n John's baby things. His mother gave 'em to me. They ain't no bigger than those. [*Smiles.*] La! He was six foot four.

MARTHA. I saw some of Washington's baby clothes in the Old South Church at Boston.

MRS. RUSSELL. [*To* ELIZABETH.] What does Cap'n Dan'l say —isn't he just about crazy?

ELIZABETH. [*Laughing shyly.*] He don't know a thing about it.

MARTHA. [*Laughing.*] Oh, I think that's awful mean, Aunt 'Lizbeth.

ELIZABETH. [*Laughs, but with a note of affection in her voice.*] Old fuss-budget! He does half the housework now. [MARTHA *and* MRS. RUSSELL *laugh understandingly.*] Wants to carry me up and down stairs if I have a headache. Why, he wouldn't let me lift my little finger. I'd never get him out of the house at all if I told him.

MARTHA. He'll pay you up when he does find out.

[WILLIAM TURNER *is heard stamping his feet outside the door upper left, to knock the snow off. Then he enters cheerily. He is dressed in a short overcoat, and his undercoat shows below it. He wears a cap and boots. He is not dressed for winter, but for a cold night in spring. He carries a folded newspaper.*]

TURNER. [*Unwrapping himself as he speaks.*] Snow in Aprile. What do yeh think o' that? [*He sees* MRS. RUSSELL.] Good evenin', Mrs. Russell. [*He goes briskly into the hallway, right.*]

MRS. RUSSELL. [*Who is extremely polite and always rises when some one enters or leaves the room.*] Good evenin', William. [*She sits.*] Is it cold out?

TURNER. [*Speaking outside.*] No-o-o! Us young fellahs never mind the weather. [*Laughs.*] Only it seems s'funny to have snow in Aprile.

ELIZABETH. What's the news up street, William?

TURNER. [*Who has left his outer things in the hall, now enters carrying the newspaper and blowing his nose on a red handkerchief.*] Oh, Klondike—Klondike! Gosh! Everybody's gone crazy. [*He crosses to the fireplace, right, and seats himself in the armchair, and begins to read his paper.*]

ELIZABETH. They say it's terrible cold up there.

MRS. RUSSELL. And butter's two dollars a pound!

ELIZABETH. Mercy, I should think they'd starve. Is that the paper you've got there, William?

TURNER. Yes. [*Reads.*] "*Sag Harbor Express,* Saturday eve-nin', Aprile 18th, 1897." Listen to this! [*He reads, and the three women listen with great interest as they continue their work.*]

"We were informed last week, on creditable authority, of the death of William Wright, and so gave the public the benefit of the news through our enterprisin' colyumns. Yesterday, Mr. Wright walked in and informed us that he is still alive. We apologize to the relatives and friends."

MARTHA. [*Smiles.*] How funny!

ELIZABETH. [*Dryly.*] I should think they'd apologize to the corpse.

TURNER. [*Reading.*]

"Potatoes are sellin' at eighty cents, wholesale."

[*There is a slight pause as he scans the paper, then he continues.*]

"Last Monday afternoon, Mrs. John H. Pierce hung out her wash and left it over night. Some scamp threw sand upon the clothes as they hung there, so that in the mornin', when she went to take them in, they were so badly soiled that she was obliged to do her washin' all over again. Mrs. Pierce thinks she knows the person who did it."

ELIZABETH. [*Indignantly.*] I don't think there's any punish-ment too good for that miscreant.

TURNER. If it was my boy, I'll bet you he'd eat his victuals standin' up for the next month. [*Reading.*]

"Pete Jagger has the contract for buildin' Judge Nelson's new house."

MRS. RUSSELL. Beats all how they are a-buildin'.

TURNER. [*Glancing down the columns of the paper.*]

"The pulpit of Unity Church will be occupied by Rev. Henry
Nevin of Water Mill."

[*Pause.*]

"Salvation Army meetin'."

ELIZABETH. Well, if I've got to play a tambourine to get to
Heaven—

TURNER. [*Reading.*]

"Mr. William Owen has presented us with a large sea shell
on which he has painted a Hudson River scene. Thanks, William,
awfully."

MRS. RUSSELL. I'd like to see that.

TURNER. [*Reading.*]

"Henry Seymour's havin' a tasteful coat of paint applied to
his barn."

MRS. RUSSELL. That's an *ex*-cellent paper—I like it better
than I do the New York papers. It has more home news.

TURNER. It has an im-mense circulation. Hunt's fearless—
says what he thinks. He's for the people!

MARTHA. [*Beginning to fold up her work.*] Well, Aunt 'Lizbeth, I guess we'll have to quit for tonight. It's getting on
to suppertime. [*She gives the sewing to* ELIZABETH. *Then
she carries her workbasket to the sideboard, left, and puts
it in the cupboard. She takes a tablecloth from the sideboard
drawer, and carries it to the table.*[1]]

[ELIZABETH *picks up her work and puts it, together with the
sewing* MARTHA *gave her, into the valise by her side.*]

ELIZABETH. [*Laughing.*] Have to put the work out of sight,
so's Dan'l won't go poking round and find it.

[1] *NOTE:* The tablecloth and napkins are of a good material,
snow-white, and must be laundered for every performance.

[*All the women laugh.* ELIZABETH *takes the valise and goes off through the door, lower left. She returns immediately without the valise, but carrying a lighted lamp, which she places on top of the piano, left. Then she goes to the sideboard for the silverware and napkins, and sets the table during the next scene.*[1]]

[MRS. RUSSELL *moves her chair right, close to* WILLIAM TURNER'S, *and they chat together.*]

[BEN *is heard stamping his feet outside the door, upper left. He enters, dressed in a comfortable working suit of dark grey. He wears a cap and muffler, but no overcoat.* MARTHA *goes to him and they kiss each other complacently.* BEN *gives* MARTHA *his cap and starts to take off his muffler. They are both standing left centre.*]

BEN. Gosh! Plenty of snow, if we don't get anything else. [*To* MARTHA.] Frank got in?

MARTHA. No, not yet.

BEN. [*Curiously.*] What's the matter with him, Martha?

MARTHA. [*Disturbed, but concealing it.*] I don't know—I haven't noticed—

BEN. [*Giving* MARTHA *his muffler.*] He acts so funny. Sometimes he hardly speaks to me, and then at others, he almost eats me up. [*Laughs.*]

MARTHA. [*Who understands it all;* FRANK *and she have had several stormy scenes since he has been at home.*] Why, that's singular! [*She takes* BEN'S *muffler and cap into the hall, right, returns immediately, and busies herself helping* ELIZABETH *with the table.*]

[BEN *goes down to the fireplace, right, and greets his father and* MRS. RUSSELL. *As soon as* BEN *joins them,* TURNER *rises and gives the armchair to him, and sits in the smaller*

---

[1] *NOTE:* The crockery used in this scene is of neat pattern, the table-ware is plated, and the glassware is imitation cut glass.

chair at the lower end of the fireplace with his back to the audience.]

[FRANK *enters by the door, upper left. He is comfortably dressed in a ready-made suit of dark blue serge; he has made no effort to look smart, but his clothes fit him well. He puts his hat on the piano, then goes down to* MRS. RUSSELL *and shakes hands cordially.*]

BEN. [*Heartily.*] Hello, Frank!

FRANK. [*Indifferently.*] Hello. [*Turning to* MARTHA.] Martha, is the attraction of this family at home this evening?

MARTHA. [*Coming down left.*] Yes, I'll get her. [*She starts towards the kitchen.*]

FRANK. [*Crossing below the table and stopping her.*] Let me get her. [*He tries to take her hand; she avoids him.*]

MARTHA. [*Coldly.*] Certainly, if you want to.

[FRANK *goes off lower left.* MARTHA *goes back to her work at the table, and she and* ELIZABETH *discuss its arrangement in low tones.*]

BEN. Well, Father, "Antelope" get in today?

TURNER. Four hours and a half late. Danged old tub! Snow, they say. Thick weather on the Sound.

[FRANK *enters lower left.*]

FRANK. Baby's sound asleep.

ELIZABETH. Are you fond of babies, Frank?

FRANK. [*Dryly.*] D'know—I guess I'm fond of this one.

[*He sits on the bench at the piano and plays a few chords in a desultory way.*]

CAP'N DAN. [*Calling from the kitchen, lower left.*] Is my wife here?

ELIZABETH. Oh! There's Dan'l now. [*She hurries off into the kitchen. There is the sound of a loud kiss, and then the crash of a saucepan.*]

ELIZABETH. [*Outside.*] Oh! you great rough bear. Behave yourself, Dan'l Marble!

[*The following five speeches are spoken at once in a loud hearty manner, with a general laugh.*]

MRS. RUSSELL. Save the pieces!

TURNER. Take in y'r jib!

MARTHA. Mercy on me!

FRANK. Luff'r, Cap'n, luff'r!

BEN. [*Singing.*] "I'll have peanuts when your peanuts are gone!"

[*In the midst of the laughter and noise,* CAP'N DAN *appears at the door, lower left. He wears a short rubber coat, a sou'-wester, dark blue trousers and waistcoat, a blue flannel shirt, a black tie, and rubber boots.*]

CAP'N DAN. [*With a broad grin on his face.*] May I come in?

MARTHA. [*Who is standing back of the table.*] Come in? [*They all laugh.*] I should say you *are* in!

[SUSAN, *the hired girl, enters from the kitchen, lower left, with a tray on which are cups, saucers and plates. She places them on the table, and then returns to the kitchen.*]

CAP'N DAN. [*Coming left of the table.*] Martha, I brought yeh the finest mess o' scallops yeh've had this season. Ain't late, be I?

MARTHA. [*Cheerily.*] No!

MRS. RUSSELL. Pretty cold on the bay today, wa'n't it?

CAP'N DAN. [*Smiling quizzically.*] Well, we didn't need no fans.

MARTHA. [*Roguishly.*] Where'd you leave Aunt 'Lizbeth?

CAP'N DAN. [*Pointing off left.*] Out there. She's mad. [*They all laugh. He goes down left and calls off.*] Come in, 'Lizbeth, they all seen you do it! [*They all laugh.* CAP'N DAN *pulls off his coat and hat.*] Well, Frank, hain't got the gold fever yet, have ye? [*He takes his hat and coat off into the hall, returning immediately and going down to* BEN *at the fireplace.*]

FRANK. No, have you? [*He rises and walks up to the window, and stands looking out.*]

CAP'N DAN. Not yet, scallopin's good enough for me. Where's the baby?

BEN. Asleep. What do you think of her?

CAP'N DAN. Think of her— Gosh!

BEN. What's the matter? Don't you like her?

CAP'N DAN. Like her— Gosh! I wish she was mine. Martha, are her ears punched yet?

MARTHA. [*Smiling at his joke.*] No, not yet.

CAP'N DAN. Well, let's have 'em punched. I've got a pair of Cornelian earrings 'at belonged to my gran'mother. She may have 'em.

MARTHA. [*Laughing.*] All right.

CAP'N DAN. [*At the fireplace, warming himself, to* BEN.] Ben, that's the only thing in this world that I envy you. [*He nods in the direction of the kitchen.*] 'Lizbeth, she's one o' the best women God ever put the breath of life into, an' if I only had a baby—

BEN. What would you like, boy or girl?

CAP'N DAN. Wouldn't care. Anythin', s'long's it was a baby.

MRS. RUSSELL. [*Glancing at him with a knowing, tender little smile.*] Rome wasn't made in a day, Cap'n Dan'l.

BEN. Why don't you adopt one?

CAP'N DAN. [*Smiling and shaking his head.*] 'Twouldn't be the same. Um'm!

[*There is a loud knock on the door, upper left.* MARTHA *goes to the door to open it. At the same time* ELIZABETH *enters with the bread, butter and milk, which she places on the table.*]

BEN. [*As* MARTHA *goes to the door.*] There's Freeman, I'll bet a cookie.

TURNER. I'll bet it's that Smith boy, come to borry our axe agin.

[MARTHA *opens the door;* JANE CAULDWELL *and* FREEMAN WHITMARSH *are standing outside.* FREEMAN *wears a heavy overcoat;* JANE *wears a cape and has a scarf wrapped around her head, and she carries a leather music roll. They are both lightly covered with snow.* MARTHA *is delighted to see them, and greets them warmly.*]

MARTHA. [*To* FREEMAN, *shaking hands.*] Oh! I was just wondering if you had deserted. [*Laughs.*] Why, Jane Cauldwell! [JANE *enters, followed by* FREEMAN.] Oh, how delightful!

[MARTHA *gives both hands to* JANE *and kisses her warmly, overjoyed to see her. There is a general murmur of greeting from the others.*]

JANE. To-morrow's Easter, you know, and I'm going to sing in church. We have a rehearsal tonight, and—

FREEMAN. I took the liberty of fetchin' Miss Cauldwell in to clam pie. [*He drops down left and begins to take off his gloves.*]

CAP'N DAN. You're always takin' some liberties.

BEN. That's right.

MARTHA. [*To* JANE, *as they stand up left centre.*] Take off your things.

[MARTHA *helps* JANE *off with her wraps.* JANE *is wearing a very pretty dress.* ELIZABETH *and* FRANK *come up and greet* JANE. *The talk now becomes general, not boisterous, but cheery.* MARTHA *takes* JANE'S *cape, scarf and music roll into the hall, right.*]

ELIZABETH. [*To* JANE.] Go down to the fire. You must be frozen. [*She leads* JANE *down to the fire.*]

JANE. [*As they go down.*] Thank you, I'm not a bit cold.

[JANE *shakes hands with* MRS. RUSSELL, BEN *and* WILLIAM TURNER. ELIZABETH *gets a knife, fork and napkin from the sideboard and sets a place at the table for* JANE. *Then she places chairs about the table.* MARTHA *returns from the hall, and helps* ELIZABETH.]

JANE. Somebody take Mr. Whitmarsh's things.

FRANK. [*Going to* FREEMAN *down left.*] Give 'em to me, Freeman.

[FREEMAN *hands him his overcoat and hat. He has taken off his gloves, and put them in his overcoat pocket. He is wearing what are obviously his best clothes. They are ready-made, and fit him very badly. His light trousers are much too short, and his dark cutaway coat is too tight. His collar, a very high one, is also too tight, and his black string tie has a habit of getting around under one ear. Whenever* FREEMAN *turns around, the loop attached to his coat collar at the back can be seen standing straight up. However, he is perfectly unconscious of this, and firmly believes that he is most correctly attired. His manner exudes self-satisfaction. He takes out a freshly-ironed handkerchief, shakes it, and wipes his nose and mouth.*]

FRANK. [*Sniffing.*] Phew! What kind of perfume's that?

FREEMAN. [*Nonchalantly.*] Pichulee.

[FREEMAN *crosses below the table, and joins the group at the fireplace.* FRANK *takes* FREEMAN'S *coat and hat into the hall, right, and returns almost immediately. He goes to the piano and seats himself.*]

JANE. [*To* BEN.] How's baby tonight?

BEN. Oh! Fine—

JANE. [*Cheerily.*] I love babies.

MARTHA. [*Smiling at* JANE.] Then you'll make a good mother. [*She and* ELIZABETH *are placing chairs around the table.*]

JANE. [*Laughing.*] Think so? [MARTHA *nods.*] That's what I want to be. [*NOTE:* JANE *must play this entire act with spontaneity, cheer and vivacity, and with merry, rippling laughter.*]

FREEMAN. [*Pompously.*] I should want the mother o' my children to be—

JANE. [*Laughing.*] Your children!

CAP'N DAN. I tell my wife—

JANE. [*Laughing.*] Captain, you imagine you've got the only wife in the world. [*She leaves the group at the fireplace, crosses left below the table, and joins* FRANK *at the piano.*]

CAP'N DAN. [*Good-naturedly.*] No, I don't—but I've got the best one!

[*During the scene between* JANE *and* FRANK, MARTHA *and* ELIZABETH *busy themselves at the table, and* BEN, CAP'N DAN, FREEMAN, WILLIAM TURNER *and* MRS. RUSSELL *converse in low tones among themselves.*]

JANE. [*Smiling at* FRANK *fondly.*] Well, Frank!

FRANK. [*Still seated on the bench at the piano; with little interest but not impolitely.*] Well, Miss Cauldwell!

JANE. [*Pouting.*] *Miss* Cauldwell— [*Laughs.*] I think you might have come over to see me.

FRANK. [*Laughing.*] What? 'Way over to Bridgehampton?

JANE. [*Laughs.*] 'Way over—four miles—I've been over here—[*Counts on her fingers.*]—six times.

FRANK. [*Smiling.*] It's easier coming than going.

JANE. [*Simply.*] Yes. I like to come, I hate to go.

FRANK. [*Casually.*] P'r'aps I'll walk home with you after church tomorrow.

JANE. [*Eagerly.*] Will you! [*Disappointed.*] Oh, my! And I've gone and got company!

FRANK. [*Laughing.*] There you see—

JANE. [*Pouting.*] I didn't know that you— I'll get rid of him.

FRANK. [*Laughs.*] No, no, no! Not on my account.

JANE. [*Laughs.*] Yes, yes, yes! I will, too.

FRANK. [*With a humorous glance at* FREEMAN.] Besides, Freeman might put something in my tea.

JANE. He— [*Laughs.*] The old flirt. He has a new string to his bow every day or two.

FRANK. That so? I thought he and you—

JANE. [*Quickly.*] You didn't think anything of the kind. [*Coyly.*] You used to be fond of me when we were children.

FRANK. [*Innocently.*] How old are you?

JANE. [*Laughs.*] What a question! [*With a meaning glance at him.*] I'm old enough to know better. [*Laughs.*] You know how old I am—Martha and I are the same age.

FRANK. I'm coming to church to-morrow to hear you sing.

JANE. [*Pleased.*] You've heard me sing lots of times.

FRANK. That's the reason I'm coming to-morrow.

JANE. [*Laughing delightedly.*] That's a real compliment, isn't it?

FRANK. I wish I could sing. I love singing.

JANE. I'll give you lessons. Free gratis, for nothing. [*Laughs. From now on, the talk between* JANE *and* FRANK *is not heard by the audience.*]

[SUSAN *enters from the kitchen, lower left, and brings on the teapot, which she places on the table, and then goes off into the kitchen again.*]

CAP'N DAN. [*Drawing* FREEMAN *down right, away from the others.*] Keepin' company with Miss Cauldwell now?

FREEMAN. [*With an air of ownership.*] Well, yes—I guess so.

CAP'N DAN. Stiddy?

FREEMAN. Yes. There's money into her. She's got a voice like a nightingale.

CAP'N DAN. You're a mighty lucky man, if you get her, Freeman.

FREEMAN. *If*—there's no if about it. When I want a girl, all I've got to say is—"Come here."

JANE. [*Coming down to them right centre below the table, and speaking playfully.*] What are you two talking about?

CAP'N DAN. [*To* JANE.] What do you think of Frank?

JANE. [*With girlish enthusiasm.*] I think he's handsomer than ever. Don't you, Freeman?

FREEMAN. [*With a touch of jealousy.*] I never could see he was so awfully handsome.

JANE. [*Amused.*] Oh, my! [*Teasingly.*] I do hope he'll sit next to me at supper, don't you?

FREEMAN. [*Crossly.*] No, I don't. Miss Cauldwell, I 'scorted you here.

JANE. [*Looking very innocent.*] Well, what of that?

FREEMAN. [*Loftily.*] It's considered ettikwet to ask the gentleman who—

JANE. [*Laughing.*] Oh, bother ettikwet! I'm going to have a good time. [*She leaves* FREEMAN, *and crosses to left centre below the table.*]

MARTHA. [*Coming down stage and standing by the right-hand chair at the foot of the table.*] Come to supper, please!

[*They all rise and move towards the table.* BEN *stands be-*

side his place at the head of the table, with WILLIAM TURNER *at his right and* ELIZABETH *at his left.*]

MARTHA. Frank, will you seat Miss Cauldwell? [*She indicates the seat at the end of the table, on the left-hand side.*]

JANE. [*Delighted with this arrangement.*] Martha, you're a mind reader!

[FRANK *pulls out a chair for* JANE. FREEMAN, *who is standing down right, looks exceedingly crestfallen.*]

MARTHA. [*Smiling.*] Am I? [*She turns to* FREEMAN *and, with a twinkle in her eye, says mischievously:*] Mr. Whitmarsh, will you do the honors for Mrs. Russell? [*She indicates the two seats next to* TURNER, *on the right-hand side of the table.*]

[MRS. RUSSELL *promptly advances to* FREEMAN, *and takes his arm with a little air of proprietorship.*]

FREEMAN. [*Sulkily.*] I don't guess I'll eat anything. [*All laugh, and exclaim "Sit down! Sit down!"*]

FREEMAN. I don't feel a bit clammy.

CAP'N DAN. Take your med'cine like a little man, Freeman! [*They all laugh.*]

[FREEMAN, *with very bad grace, escorts* MRS. RUSSELL *to the table. She sits next to* TURNER, *and* FREEMAN *sits below her and next to* MARTHA. *With the exception of* ELIZABETH *and* CAP'N DAN, *they all seat themselves, and the talk becomes general.* FREEMAN *slumps in his chair, oblivious to what is going on.*]

ELIZABETH. [*Drawing* CAP'N DAN *down left, says in a low voice.*] Dan'l, you'll sit next to Martha. [*She indicates the chair on* MARTHA'S *right, at the foot of the table.*]

CAP'N DAN. [*In a tone of disappointment.*] Ain't I goin' to sit next to you?

ELIZABETH. No.

cap'n dan. Well, how are we goin' to hold hands under the table?

elizabeth. We're not going to, to-night.

cap'n dan. [*Disgustedly.*] Oh Jinks! That spiles the hull thing.

[*He takes his seat at* martha's *right, at the foot of the table.* elizabeth *takes her place at* ben's *left.* frank *is seated between* elizabeth *and* jane.]

martha. [*Calling to Susan, off stage.*] Now, Susan, the clam pie!

[*There are exclamations of delight from everyone except* freeman. susan *enters with a smoking hot clam pie in a deep dish. She is greeted with a round of applause in which everybody at the table joins with the exception of* freeman. susan *sets the pie in front of* ben, *who helps to it.*]
[*During the next scene,* susan *busies herself waiting at the table, passing tea, bread and butter, and coming and going with food.* martha *pours the tea, and* elizabeth *helps to applesauce from a dish which is placed in front of her. They all eat heartily, and there is a general atmosphere of good cheer.* jane *is of course delighted to sit next to* frank, *and they converse together in low tones.* freeman *alone does not eat, and remains sunk in gloom. When occasion demands, he is frigidly polite to* mrs. russell, *who good-naturedly ignores his resentment.*]

cap'n dan. [*Eating.*] It's worth walkin' a mile to eat one o' Martha's clam pies.

ben. [*Who is serving the clam pie and talking at the same time.*] What'll you have, Miss Cauldwell, a wing or a piece of the breast? [*Laughs.*] Now, folks, if you don't see what you want, ask for it!

cap'n dan. I never stand on no ceremony in this house. Ben, did you know George Holman's goin' to the Klondike?

ben. [*Laughing.*] Why, he's eighty years old.

cap'n dan. That don't bother him. He's goin' all the same.

turner. [*Eating busily.*] Everybody's goin'. The Higgins boys is goin', Rufe Haynes is goin', Bill Matteson's goin', an' I don't know who all ain't a-goin'. There's a reg'lar epidemic. There won't be a decent man left in Sag Harbor by the first o' June, if it keeps on. George Salter says he'd go if he had the money. Jackass, he never did have no sense.

ben. I'd go, if it weren't for my wife and baby.

martha. [*Laughing.*] We'll go with you, Ben.

cap'n dan. Oh, that ain't no place for a woman. You don't catch me takin' 'Lizbeth there—not for all the gold in the diggin's. I'm afraid they'd keep her. [*Laughs.*]

mrs. russell. [*Passing the celery to* freeman.] Have some celery, Mr. Whitmarsh, it's good for the nerves.

[freeman *does not reply and she jogs his elbow. He comes to with a start, and takes a piece of celery, which he does not eat.*]

jane. [*Laughing, to* frank.] I was planning how to get a seat next to you.

frank. Were you—well, you got there. [*Laughs.*]

jane. I'm going to ask Martha to invite me every Saturday night while you're at home.

frank. I'll invite you.

jane. [*Pleased.*] Thank you.

martha. [*Who observes for the first time that* freeman *is not eating.*] Aren't you well, Mr. Whitmarsh?

[freeman *does not hear her, and* mrs. russell *nudges him.*]

mrs. russell. Martha's talkin' to yeh.

freeman. [*Starts and sits bolt upright.*] Eh? Oh! I beg pardon.

martha. Aren't you well?

FREEMAN. First rate. That is, no—I et some canned lobster, and—

[*There is a general murmur of sympathy from everyone.*]

MRS. RUSSELL. Take a dose of Bromo Seltzer.

FRANK. [*To* JANE, *laughing.*] I guess, *you're* the canned lobster.

JANE. [*Laughs.*] Not I—but you.

[*Their voices sink again.*]

BEN. How are the clams tonight, Cap'n?

CAP'N DAN. There ain't no bad clams—all good. Some better than others—but all good!

[SUSAN *enters with a plate of ginger bread, cut into large slices.*]

BEN. Cap'n, help to the ginger bread, will you?

CAP'N DAN. Certanimo, as the Portageese say. [*He passes the ginger bread as he sings.*]

> Of all the birds that fly the air,
> The green, the blue, the red,
> Of all the cakes my mammy makes,
> Give me the ginger bread!

[*They all help themselves to ginger bread,* CAP'N DAN *rises, leans across* MARTHA *and passes the plate to* FREEMAN.]

CAP'N DAN. Freeman! Freeman! [FREEMAN *pays no attention.* CAP'N DAN *turns to the others, and says with a chuckle:*] He thinks he's in church and I'm passin' the plate.

[*They all laugh.*]

TURNER. Say, Ben. Culver lost one of his hosses to-day.

BEN. What's the trouble?

TURNER. Colic.

MRS. RUSSELL. [*Innocently, to* FREEMAN.] When anyone has colic where I be, I just take hot camphire an' rub 'em well.

FREEMAN. [*Sullenly.*] Well, you needn't rub me—I've got no colic!

FRANK. [*To* JANE.] I should think you'd hate to have to go to church.

JANE. [*Laughs.*] Oh, it gets to be a business like everything else.

MARTHA. Who's going to church to-morrow?

[*The six following speeches are spoken together.*]

MRS. RUSSELL. I am.

FREEMAN. If I didn't have to, I wouldn't.

BEN. We're all going.

FRANK. Well—

ELIZABETH. Dan'l and I are going.

TURNER. I'm goin' fishin'.

JANE. Well, I *will* have an audience.

[*There is a knock at the door, upper left.*]

BEN. Come in!

[HOSEA STEVENS *enters through the door, upper left, in an overcoat and a dress suit. He carries a lantern, and has the stump of a cigar in his mouth, as usual.*]

HOSEA. Uncle Billy, is there a case of bottle goods in the freight house for us?

TURNER. Yes, come in this afternoon.

HOSEA. Why didn't you send it over?

TURNER. [*Testily.*] Why didn't you come after it?

HOSEA. Didn't know it was there.

TURNER. That's your business.

HOSEA. Can we get it to-night?

TURNER. No. [*Crossly.*] What do you fellahs think I'm made of?

HOSEA. Can we get it in the mornin'?

TURNER. I'm goin' fishin' in the mornin'. I'm not goin' to break the Sabbath for you nor nobody else.

HOSEA. We're all out of case goods.

TURNER. You've no right to sell rum on Sunday anyway.

HOSEA. Well, good night.

BEN. Won't you have a cup of tea, Hosea?

TURNER. Do you want to poison him?

HOSEA. No, thank you. I've got to take my girl to the show. Good night. [*He goes out through the door upper left.*]

TURNER. [*After* HOSEA'S *exit.*] He don't get none the better o' me—Jackass!

FRANK. My gracious, I forgot there was a show to-night. Will you go, Miss Cauldwell?

JANE. Yes, if Freeman will let me off that old choir rehearsal. Will you, Freeman?

CAP'N DAN. Say, Freeman, let her off that choir rehearsal so she can go to the show with Frank!

FREEMAN. [*Unable to control his rage any longer, rising and almost upsetting the table.*] That settles it. I've got to go home. [*He crosses down right.*]

ALL. [*Protesting.*] Oh!

MARTHA. We're not through supper yet.

JANE. Oh! Freeman, we've just come!

FREEMAN. [*With great dignity.*] Miss Cauldwell, I've no jurisprudence over you.

JANE. [*Laughing.*] You 'scorted me here. It's ettikwet—

FREEMAN. [*Witheringly.*] Sarcasm doesn't become you, Miss Cauldwell. If you're going with me, you've got to go now.

[FREEMAN *goes off, right, for his hat and coat.*]

ALL. [*In protest.*] Oh, no, no, no! [*The supper is abruptly ended.*]

JANE. [*Rising hastily and laughing.*] Oh, he's a perfect tyrant! Where are my things?

MARTHA. [*Rising.*] In here. [*She starts off with* JANE *towards the hallway, right, speaking as she goes.*] Must you go?

JANE. Oh, my, yes! Didn't you hear him say so? [MARTHA *and* JANE *go off, right, into the hall.*]

[BEN *rises and goes up to the window,* ELIZABETH *and* SUSAN *begin to clear the table.* FRANK *rises and goes to the piano, and plays softly.*]

MRS. RUSSELL. [*Rising.*] I must be goin' too. The Doctor'll think I'm lost. [*She joins* BEN *at the window.*]

BEN. Cap'n Dan and I'll walk a piece of the way with you, Mrs. Russell. [*He goes off into the hall, right, and returns immediately with his cap and muffler.*]

CAP'N DAN. 'Course we will!

TURNER. [*Rising and yawning.*] I'm goin' to bed. Got to get off at three o'clock to get the tide. Good night everybody. Thank yeh for a pleasant evenin'.

ALL. Good night.

[TURNER *goes up the stairway and off.*]

[FREEMAN *enters, right, with his hat and coat on. He comes down right.* CAP'N DAN *crosses to him, below the table.*]

CAP'N DAN. [*To* FREEMAN.] Next Saturday night, you'd better stay to hum, you long-legged, red-headed gawk. You've sp'iled everythin'. [*He goes into the hall, gets his hat and coat, then returns and joins* BEN *and* MRS. RUSSELL *at the window.*]

[JANE *and* MARTHA *re-enter from the right.* JANE *has on her cape and scarf.* MARTHA *is carrying* JANE'S *music roll, which is open as if they had been looking over some of the songs. She also carries* MRS. RUSSELL'S *bonnet and cloak.*]

MARTHA. [*Crossing above the table to* FRANK, *and giving him the music roll.*] Frank, roll this up, please! [*She goes to* MRS. RUSSELL *at the window and helps her on with her bonnet and cloak.*]

[*During the next scene,* ELIZABETH *and* SUSAN *continue to clear the table.* MARTHA, BEN, MRS. RUSSELL, JANE *and* CAP'N DAN *chat together at the window.*]
[FRANK *takes the music roll, drops down left a little and proceeds to roll up the music.* FREEMAN, *who has been standing down right, sees what he is doing and crosses to him quickly, going below the table.*]

FREEMAN. [*To* FRANK, *sulkily.*] I'll take charge o' that.

FRANK. [*Good-naturedly.*] Is it yours?

FREEMAN. Well, I 'scorted it here, all the way from Bridgehampton.

FRANK. My! [*The wind can be heard whistling outside.*] You've got a long, cold walk, haven't you? [*He smiles. He has strapped the music roll by this time, and now he hands it to* FREEMAN, *who unrolls it and then does it up again.*]

FREEMAN. [*Coldly.*] There *is* hosses and wagons in Sag Harbor.

[FRANK *laughs, then turns away and joins the group at the window.* CAP'N DAN *comes down to* FREEMAN, *left.*]

CAP'N DAN. [*Smiling and nodding towards* JANE.] Have you asked her to have you yet?

FREEMAN. No, not yet.

CAP'N DAN. Well, if I was you, I d'know's I would.

FREEMAN. D'know's I will.

[*There is a general movement of departure.*]

JANE. [*To* FRANK, *extending her hand, warmly.*] Good night, Frank. You don't know how I've enjoyed myself.

FRANK. [*Shaking hands.*] I'm glad—I'll see you to-morrow.

JANE. I'll expect you. Good night, everybody. [*She kisses* MARTHA *and* ELIZABETH.] I've had a splendid time.

ALL. Good night.

MARTHA. I'm glad—it's been a treat to us, I'm sure.

[*These lines are spoken together.*]

JANE. [*Carelessly.*] Come, Freeman dear!

[JANE, MRS. RUSSELL, CAP'N DAN *and* BEN *start to go by the door, upper left.*]

CAP'N DAN. Freeman dear don't seem to be in the best o' spirits. [*Laughs.*]

[CAP'N DAN *and* BEN *follow* JANE *and* MRS. RUSSELL *off.*]

FREEMAN. If you'd et canned lobster—

[*He follows the others off, and they are heard laughing and talking until their voices die away in the distance.* MARTHA *closes the door after them, then she and* ELIZABETH *go to the window, let the curtains up and, shading their eyes from the light inside, they enjoy the scene out of doors, laughing with the others.* FRANK *drops on the bench beside the piano.*]

[*During this,* SUSAN *is clearing the table, and carrying off the dishes.*]

CAP'N DAN. [*Outside. The wind is heard blowing loudly.*] Phew! Blizzardy!

JANE. [*Outside.*] Oh, the snow, the beautiful snow!

CAP'N DAN. [*Outside, singing.*] "Spring, spring, gentle spring!" [*All laugh.*]

BEN. [*Outside.*] My, look at that drift, will yeh?

MRS. RUSSELL. [*Outside.*] Some o' you men'll have to lend me your rubber boots or carry me.

[*All laugh.*]

CAP'N DAN. [*Outside.*] I'll carry yeh, Mrs. Russell.

[*All laugh.*]

[*Their voices die away.* MARTHA *and* ELIZABETH *draw the curtains.*]

MARTHA. [*Who has enjoyed the evening, and is filled with bright, good thoughts for everybody.*] They're a jolly party, aren't they?

ELIZABETH. Yes, everybody's happy to-night, anyway, if they never are again. I guess.I'll help Susan with that pile of dishes. [*She goes off into the kitchen, lower left.*]

[*By this time the table has been completely cleared except for the cloth.* MARTHA *folds this as she talks, and puts it in the sideboard drawer.*]

MARTHA. [*To* FRANK, *very cheerily.*] Haven't we had a grand evening?

FRANK. [*Still seated at the piano, half-heartedly.*] You have, I guess.

[*Now that* JANE *has gone, he relapses into his old mood of sullen resentment.*]

MARTHA. [*Trying to draw him out of himself.*] Haven't you?

FRANK. [*As before.*] No, can't say that I have.

MARTHA. [*Smiling significantly.*] You seemed to enjoy yourself.

FRANK. I had to be polite—to your guests.

MARTHA. [*Lightly.*] Oh, Frank, honest now—don't you think Jane is a magnificent girl? [*She busies herself setting the chairs back in their right places.*]

FRANK. [*Grudgingly.*] She's handsome, if that's what you mean.

MARTHA. And as bright as a new dollar. [*A trifle significantly.*] She's going to make some young fellow very happy one of these days.

FRANK. [*Who is not interested in* JANE, *nor in* MARTHA'S *eulogy of her.*] Yes, she made Freeman happy to-night.

MARTHA. [*Laughing, as she puts down the drop leaves of the table.*] Oh, she doesn't care anything about him. He finds he can't twist her round his little finger—it nettles him, that's all. He'll have another girl before to-morrow night. [*She comes down right of the table.*] Help me set this table back.

[FRANK *comes down left of the table, and they each take an end and set the table back in its place up centre near the window.* MARTHA *looks earnestly at* FRANK *and says gently*]

MARTHA. When are you going to be your cheery old self again?

FRANK. [*In cold measured tones, looking at her hard.*] When your husband is dead and buried, I guess.

MARTHA. [*Horrified, drops the table with a loud crash.*] Why, *Frank!* You ought to be ashamed of yourself.

[*They pause for a moment, gazing at each other like two antagonists.*]

FRANK. [*Defiantly.*] I dare say I had, but I'm not!

[MARTHA *goes down to the sideboard, left, gets a scarf from the drawer, returns to the table and arranges the scarf on it. She is almost crying, and her action is mechanical. She hardly knows what she is doing.*]

MARTHA. I don't see how you can hold my baby in your arms, and harbor such thoughts against her father. [*She must find work to do in this scene, so she will at no time be idle.*]

FRANK. [*Gloomily.*] The baby put 'em there, I guess. [*He goes slowly down to the fireplace, right.*]

MARTHA. [*Rebuking him gently.*] Oh, Frank!

FRANK. [*Turning and facing her again.*] I'm human, Martha! I can't sit here and see you and him—

MARTHA. [*Who is still at the table, stopping him with a note of warning in her voice.*] Are you going to begin all over again? This is the third time since you've been home that we've gone over all this. Ben'll overhear you sometime, and then— [*Appealingly.*] Why don't you be brave and live the thing down?

FRANK. [*Impetuously.*] I've tried to—I can't!

MARTHA. [*Impatiently.*] Oh pshaw! I've done it.

FRANK. [*Walking restlessly up and down.*] Well, I can't. I'm all right when I'm away.

MARTHA. [*Slightly exasperated.*] Then why didn't you stay away?

FRANK. [*Raising his voice, astonished.*] Because you wrote and asked me to come.

MARTHA. [*Alarmed, with a quick look toward the kitchen.*] Hush! Don't raise your voice so. [*She speaks in a lower tone.*] I did it for your sake. [*She has in mind* JANE CAULD-WELL, *to whom she hopes to marry him.*]

FRANK. [*Contemptuously.*] Humph!

MARTHA. [*Gently.*] And for Ben's.

FRANK. [*Mockingly.*] Ben's!

MARTHA. He worries about you, Frank.

FRANK. [*Bitterly.*] He needn't worry about me, he's got you.

[*He is still pacing up and down.*]

MARTHA. [*Who is thoroughly unnerved by this encounter, and almost at her wits' end in dealing with* FRANK, *now assumes a tone of forced lightness.*] Shall I tell you why I wrote for you to come home?

FRANK. [*Pausing in his walk and facing her.*] If you like.

MARTHA. [*Smiling.*] You won't be angry?

FRANK. That all depends.

MARTHA. [*Laughing.*] Well, I'm a regular old matchmaker. I'm going to marry you off to some—

FRANK. [*With a harsh laugh.*] Oh! Dispose of me for a second time, eh? [*He goes down to the fireplace, and seats himself on the arm of the chair.*]

MARTHA. [*Laughing.*] Sarcasm doesn't become you, Mr. Turner! Seriously, you're morbid, Frank, and I've made up my mind to try and get you interested in some one besides yourself and me.

FRANK. [*Sullenly, looking away from her into the fire.*] You may spare yourself the trouble. If I were to marry now, I'd always hate the girl.

MARTHA. [*Cheerily.*] Oh, no, you wouldn't.

FRANK. [*Bitterly.*] Yes, I would. I'd hate her as much as I hate myself.

MARTHA. [*With increasing nervousness, and a rising note of hysteria in her voice.*] You're morbid, I tell you, and you're making life very hard for yourself—and for me. And you're worrying Ben. Sometimes you won't speak to him. Then again—

FRANK. I know it. [*He is still looking away from her.*] I can't speak to him sometimes. I was walking behind him in the yard today, and I thought how easy it would be to pick up an adze and— [*He rises.*]

MARTHA. [*Terrified.*] *Kill* him? [*She walks down to him, takes both his wrists, holds his arms at his sides, and turns him, forcing him to face her. She speaks accusingly, and her voice trembles with horror.*] Frank Turner, there's murder in your heart! [*She has allowed her voice to get louder than she intended it to.* ELIZABETH *looks in from the kitchen, left, sees they are both excited, and closes the door very softly again.*] [*For a moment,* FRANK *and* MARTHA *face each other. He sees that he has shocked her, and is a little ashamed; he says with a half-laugh:*]

FRANK. Don't be silly! [*Softly.*] I could no more kill him than I could you. [*He leaves her and moves a few steps towards centre.*]

MARTHA. [*She is greatly shaken, her eyes are wide with fear, and she realizes that she has let matters drift too long. She says, more to herself than to* FRANK:] I'll tell Ben everything to-night. There's got to be an end to this.

FRANK. [*Angrily.*] You know what that'll mean?

MARTHA. [*Desperately.*] I don't care. [*She bursts into tears.*] When I married Ben, I did what I believed right and best, for both you and me—you consented.

FRANK. [*Stubbornly.*] I did not consent.

MARTHA. Well—you—you didn't prevent it.

FRANK. I couldn't prevent it.

[BEN *and* CAP'N DAN *enter through the door upper left. They both have smiles on their faces which give way to expressions of horror as they realize the meaning of the scene before them.* CAP'N DAN *wishes to interrupt* MARTHA *and* FRANK, *but* BEN *will not permit it. They stand at the door, watching the others, who are so absorbed that they are not aware of the presence of* BEN *and* CAP'N DAN.]

MARTHA. [*Quickly.*] You could—and now you torture the very heart and soul out of me. It's cruel.

FRANK. [*Crossing to her, right centre, and speaking in a low tense voice.*] Martha, do you love me?

MARTHA. [*Indignantly.*] I won't answer you.

FRANK. [*Brutally, taking hold of her wrists.*] You will!

MARTHA. [*Quietly.*] Let go of me, you hurt me! [*She masters him and he drops her hands, ashamed. She adds with finality.*] I've no right to love you.

FRANK. [*Flinging angrily away from her, left centre.*] You've no right to love him!

MARTHA. [*Trembling with fear and anger, her voice shaking with sobs, follows him centre.*] Frank Turner, you've got to go away from here, and stay away from here! That's your salvation and mine.

FRANK. [*Turning to her, with determination.*] Then you'll go too. I won't leave you here with him.

MARTHA. [*With a skeptical laugh.*] What—desert my baby?

FRANK. [*Recklessly, hardly knowing what he is saying.*] We'll take the baby with us.

MARTHA. [*Gasping at the folly of his suggestion.*] And run away from my husband?

FRANK. [*Furiously.*] He stole you from me!

MARTHA. [*Laughing hysterically.*] Now I know you're crazy!

[BEN, *who can contain himself no longer, starts down to* FRANK. CAP'N DAN *tries to stop him, but* BEN *flings him off.* CAP'N DAN *remains up stage, a silent spectator, his face drawn with anguish.* BEN'S *anger and indignation are at white heat, but he forces himself to speak quietly.*]

BEN. [*To* FRANK.] Do you know what I ought to do to you?

[MARTHA, *with a hysterical cry, runs to* BEN, *and throws her arms around his neck, as if he were the only one who could save her from herself.*]

MARTHA. Oh, Ben, I'm so glad!

BEN. [*Harshly, disengaging her arms from his neck and pushing her aside, but not too roughly.*] Let me alone, Martha,—[*With chagrin and bitterness*]—you've fooled me for two whole years.

MARTHA. [*She is utterly crushed.* BEN *has failed her for the first time in her life.*] Oh, Ben! [*Completely spent, she drops into the armchair by the fireplace.*]

BEN. [*Who has scarcely noticed* MARTHA, *all his fury concentrated on* FRANK.] I ought to kill you.

[ELIZABETH, *dressed for the street, enters from the kitchen. She stops, aghast, down left when she sees what is going on.*]

FRANK. [*Standing up to* BEN *without flinching, and giving him blow for blow.*] I ought to have killed you two years ago!

[CAP'N DAN *comes down between the two men, lays a hand upon the shoulder of each, and says very gently and quietly,*]

CAP'N DAN. Boys, I guess I'm the one that ought to have been killed two years ago. But, just now, you're killin' her— [*He points to* MARTHA]—the woman who loves both of you.

[BEN *and* FRANK *glance at* CAP'N DAN, *then at* MARTHA, *and realize he is speaking the truth.* FRANK *drops his head, ashamed;* BEN *gets himself under control, goes to* MARTHA *and speaks quietly.*]

BEN. Martha, do you love my brother, Frank?

MARTHA. [*Without looking at him, says in a flat, dead voice,*] I can't tell you to-night—Ben—I want you to leave me alone —to-night—please!

[CAP'N DAN *goes to* BEN, *takes his arm, and leads him away, saying in a voice of soft pleading,*]

CAP'N DAN. Ben, leave her alone to-night—she can't talk to-night. She's got to think. You two come home with me. [*With his other arm he takes hold of* FRANK, *and leads the two men to the door upper left.* BEN *acquiesces reluctantly;* FRANK *doesn't care. As they go up,* CAP'N DAN *continues,*] We're aground, boys, we're aground, and we've got to wait for the tide to float us—come— [*They reach the door, upper left.* FRANK *picks up his hat from the piano.*]

ELIZABETH. [*Gently, full of love for her great, big husband.*] Do you need me, Dan'l?

[CAP'N DAN *leaves* BEN *and* FRANK *standing at the door, and comes down left to her.*]

CAP'N DAN. [*Hesitatingly.*] No—I guess not. You stay here with her.

ELIZABETH. [*Very softly.*] Ain't you going to kiss me good night?

CAP'N DAN. [*With a glance toward the two men.*] I'm afeared it'd look kind o' selfish in us. [*He crosses to* MARTHA, *puts his hand on her hair, and says very tenderly.*] Good night,

Martha. Easter Sunday in the mornin' y'know. Those same angels'll be flyin' over Calvary—just as they did nineteen hundred years ago—angels never get old. I d'know's I ever see an old angel. [*He turns to* BEN *and* FRANK.] Ready, boys?

[*They go out. The wind howls and blows the door to with a loud bang. The curtain starts to fall slowly.*]

ELIZABETH. [*With a start.*] Oh! [*She looks quickly around, realizes it was the door that slammed, and says to herself,*] How careless to let that door slam!

[MARTHA *is immovable. The wind increases.*]

CURTAIN

[*On the second curtain,* ELIZABETH *goes to* MARTHA *and comforts her.*]

ACT FOURTH

THE *next day. "Easter Sunday."*

The scene is the same as in Act Third.

SCENE: *The storm of the night has passed, the snow has all gone, and the sun is shining brightly through the bay window. The room has been set in order, and a fire burns cheerfully on the hearth. The piano is closed. The dining table has been moved into the corner made by the turn in the stairs, right. There is a small chair beside the table, and another small chair stands down left centre.*

At the rise of the curtain, ELIZABETH *is standing at the window, with* MARTHA'S *baby in her arms. The baby is freshly dressed.* ELIZABETH *is holding the baby up, and is talking to her.*

ELIZABETH. "There!" she says—"Now I's a nice clean baby, and I's ready to be kissed, or to go to church, or any old sing."

[CAP'N DAN *enters through the outside door, upper left. He wears his Sunday suit of blue, a white shirt, and a bright red necktie. His shoes have been freshly polished, and a clean handkerchief is tucked in the pocket of his coat. He is as cheerful as ever, though not quite as merry.*]

CAP'N DAN. Good mornin', 'Lizbeth. [*He looks around surprised.*] Why, where is everybody?

ELIZABETH. [*Holding up the baby.*] "Good morning, Uncle Dan'l—I's everybody." [*She kisses him.*]

CAP'N DAN. [*Pinches the baby's cheek, then takes her in his arms and kisses her.*] You'd be everybody if you were in our home. I know somebody's nose that'd be out of j'int.

226

ELIZABETH. [*Rearranging his necktie and fixing him up here and there.*] Where did you get that tie, Dan'l?

CAP'N DAN. [*Very much pleased with himself.*] Top bureau drawer.

ELIZABETH. [*Dryly.*] I thought so. It's mine.

CAP'N DAN. Well, I like it, 'cause there's so much red into it.

ELIZABETH. Phew! You've got cologne enough on you, anyway.

CAP'N DAN. [*Defensively.*] It's Easter Sunday an' I like it. Here, take your ol' baby. [*He hands the baby back to ELIZABETH, then says wistfully,*] Gosh, I wish that was our baby, don't you, 'Lizbeth?

ELIZABETH. [*Smiling at her own thoughts.*] No—I dunno as I do.

CAP'N DAN. Well, by Gosh, I do. Where's Martha?

ELIZABETH. [*Pointing to the door on the stair landing, right.*] Upstairs. [*She comes down to the fireplace with the baby, and seats herself in the armchair.*]

CAP'N DAN. [*Following ELIZABETH down to right centre.*] Has she been to bed?

ELIZABETH. No.

CAP'N DAN. Neither have they. Has she said anything?

ELIZABETH. No.

CAP'N DAN. Neither have they.

ELIZABETH. [*Disappointed.*] Oh, my—

CAP'N DAN. Ben jes' sot there—*rum*-inatin' to himself, an' Frank sot there waitin' for him to speak—

ELIZABETH. And you?

CAP'N DAN. I sot there keepin' 'em company.

ELIZABETH. Where are they now?

CAP'N DAN. Comin' along.

[MARTHA *enters through the door on the stair landing, right. Her dress is in order, but it is the same one she wore in Act Third, indicating that she has not been to bed. Her manner is composed, but very serious. If anything, her personality should be more attractive than ever.*]

[CAP'N DAN *goes towards* MARTHA *and smiles affectionately.*]

CAP'N DAN. Good mornin', Martha.

MARTHA. [*Simply.*] Good morning, Captain. [*She comes down the stairs.*]

CAP'N DAN. Fine mornin'—[*He hesitates a second*]—after the storm.

MARTHA. [*Looks at him significantly, and smiles a little sadly.*] Yes. [*She goes to the window and stands looking out.*]

[*Distant church bells are now heard. (This is kept up for at least five minutes.)* BEN *enters through the outside door, upper left, followed by* FRANK. *There is an uncomfortable pause.* MARTHA *continues to stand with her back to the room, and seems unaware of her husband's presence.* FRANK *goes down to the piano, and seats himself on the bench, looking at no one. He is ready to fight at a word.* BEN *remains standing at the door.* BEN, CAP'N DAN *and* ELIZABETH *look silently from one to the other, as if asking: "Who is going to begin it?"*]

CAP'N DAN. [*Breaking the silence, pleasantly.*] Won't you draw your chairs up to the fire, gentlemen, and make yourselves at home? [*He goes to* BEN, *puts an arm over his shoulder, and draws him towards his old seat by the fire.*] It's jes' as cheap settin' down as standin' up, y'know.

[*As* BEN *comes towards the fireplace,* ELIZABETH *rises and takes the baby into the kitchen down left. At the same time* MARTHA *comes down left centre, and sits in the chair which is standing there.* BEN *seats himself in his armchair by the fire.* CAP'N DAN *goes up to the window and stands looking out.*]

ELIZABETH *re-enters, and stands in the doorway for a moment, giving a quick, solicitous glance at* MARTHA *and the two men. Then she goes quietly to the window and sits down. The church bells continue to ring in the distance.*]

CAP'N DAN. This is one o' God's days, sure enough, ain't it? [*He smiles. There is a pause. He looks hopefully from one to the other, expecting some one to speak.*]

[*After a little, people are seen passing the window on their way to church. The people must be simple, typical, native people, none of them the characters of the play, dressed for Sunday, and must be carefully rehearsed to be in conversation, serious and light, all varying in walk, talk and expression. After the bells have rung for sufficient time to impress the situation upon the audience,* CAP'N DAN *continues his talk.*]

CAP'N DAN. George! If there *is* a soothin' sound in this world, it's church bells on a Sunday mornin', at a distance, y'know. [CAP'N DAN *must be sure to say "At a distance, y'know" simply, and not with a double meaning.*] You don't want to be too near 'em. Wonder what luck Uncle Billy and them'll have? [*Pause.*] Did anybody see 'em go? [*Pause.*] They've got a fine day. Couldn't have picked a finer. [*Pause.*] Ben, what'd you ever do with that spear o' yours? I'd kinder like a mess of eels—[*A very slight pause.*]—some day. [ELIZABETH *shakes her head at him; he nods at her reassuringly, as if to say he knows what he is doing.*] I see by to-night's paper—I mean last night's paper, that Osborne and Thompson'll get into new and commodious quarters about the first of May.

[*The bells have stopped ringing; a few late churchgoers pass hurriedly. There is another pause.*]

BEN. [*Rising and crossing to* MARTHA. *His manner is very grave.*] Martha, last night—you asked me to leave you alone—

[*As soon as* BEN *speaks,* CAP'N DAN *relapses into a tense silence, and throughout the next scene, he is keenly observ-*

*ant of all that passes, never relaxing his attitude. His love
for the three people involved gives him a poignant interest
in their problem, and their varying moods are reflected in
his face. Occasionally, he and* ELIZABETH *exchange glances.
As the scene increases in tension, he looks more and more
worried and anxious.*]

MARTHA. [*Quietly, without bitterness.*] Yes, I couldn't talk
to you last night.

BEN. Can you talk this morning?

MARTHA. Yes.

BEN. We didn't kiss each other last night, did we?

MARTHA. [*Sadly.*] No, we didn't.

BEN. Didn't even say good night?

MARTHA. No.

BEN. First time in twenty years. Did I push you away from
me last night?

MARTHA. Don't you know you did?

BEN. [*Very candidly and openly.*] No. The Captain said I
did.

MARTHA. [*In a heartbroken voice.*] You did. I needed you
last night, Ben, more than the poorhouse baby needed you
years ago. I went to you with my heart open. I wanted to tell
you everything—I put my arms around your neck—and—
you—

BEN. Pushed you away.

MARTHA. Yes.

BEN. [*Deeply moved.*] I didn't know it. I'm sorry. [*He goes
to the fireplace, right.*]

MARTHA. So am I.

BEN. [*With a look towards her.*] You don't doubt that I
love you, do you?

MARTHA. [*With great sincerity.*] If I did, I couldn't live with you, Ben.

BEN. [*Thoughtfully.*] Is that so?

MARTHA. That is so. Doubt would kill me.

[BEN *sits in the armchair and looks into the fire. After a moment's thought, he says:*]

BEN. I want you two to go over to the lawyer's with me to-morrow.

MARTHA. [*Startled.*] What for?

BEN. I want to make over the business here and what little I have to you—and Frank.

FRANK. [*Sullenly.*] You needn't make anything over to me —I don't want it.

MARTHA. Why are you going to do that?

BEN. I'm going to make what compensation I can for coming between you, as I have.

FRANK. [*Contemptuously.*] Compensation— Humph! A little old country shipyard!

BEN. [*Without noticing the interruption.*] And then I'm going away.

[*Everybody is startled.*]

MARTHA. [*Aghast, rising.*] Ben!

BEN. That's what you said you would do, if—

MARTHA. [*Appalled.*] Do you doubt me, Ben?

BEN. [*For the first time showing his bitterness and suffering.*] I know you love him.

MARTHA. [*Firmly.*] How do you know I do?

FRANK. [*Coming down to the left of* MARTHA.] *I* know you do.

MARTHA. [*Turning on him indignantly.*] You do not.

FRANK. [*Trying to justify himself.*] You—did.

MARTHA. Well, I don't now. If I did, what harm? You can't expect the bird not to love the spring. You were the first boy I ever knew.

BEN. [*A little bitterly, reflecting on the difference between his age and* FRANK's.] And I the first man.

MARTHA. The first man, and the only one. [*Glancing at* FRANK.] This "little old country shipyard" has been my world, and I wouldn't exchange it and my memories of it for the finest mansion over there on the Neck. If I could paint, I'd paint it and my life in it. But I couldn't paint it with one of you in it and not the other. Do you wonder then that I love you both? [*She cries.*]

BEN. [*Deeply affected, rises and walks up and down, right.*] Oh, Martha, if you had only told me then. I'd have given you to Frank, and—I'd have lived here with you just the same.

MARTHA. [*Through her tears.*] Ah, no, you wouldn't! You know you wouldn't. You'd have left us then, just as you're going to do now. [*She sits in the chair, down left.*]

BEN. No, I wouldn't.

MARTHA. Yes, you would. I was only a girl, but I saw that. He saw it too. [*With a look towards* FRANK.]

FRANK. [*Stubbornly, like a perverse child.*] I would have been glad of it.

MARTHA. [*Smiles protestingly.*] Ah, Frank! No! [*In a tone of finality.*] At all events, it's too late now. I did what I believed best for all of us. [*To* BEN.] I married you.

BEN. [*In a hard voice.*] That's the mistake you made.

MARTHA. [*Hurt.*] Perhaps so, but you've no right to censure me for it.

BEN. After I'm gone a spell—

MARTHA. Where are you going?

BEN. To the Klondike— [MARTHA *stares at him incredulously.*] You can get a divorce and—

MARTHA. [*With womanly indignation.*] Divorce? Ben, you talk like a child. Do you suppose I'm going to allow you to disgrace yourself and me?

BEN. Why, what'll you do?

MARTHA. [*Smiling as if it were a matter of course.*] Go with you.

BEN. I won't take you.

MARTHA. [*Very gently, but firmly.*] Then you shan't go.

BEN. [*Angrily.*] Who'll stop me?

MARTHA. [*Rising.*] I will.

BEN. How?

MARTHA. [*Desperately.*] I don't know, but I'll do it.

BEN. [*Going to her, slowly.*] Martha, if you attempt this—

FRANK. [*Going to* MARTHA, *impatiently.*] Why don't you let him go?

MARTHA. [*Turning sharply on him.*] Frank! Please! [FRANK *drops down left, again;* MARTHA *turns to* BEN.] Do you mean what you said just now?

BEN. Yes.

MARTHA. You're determined to leave me?

BEN. [*Evasively, crossing down right.*] I'm going away.

MARTHA. [*She is now stern and cold.*] Very well. I'll go with you to the lawyer to-morrow, and you make the business over to me.

BEN. Better let me make it over to Frank and you.

MARTHA. [*With quiet dignity.*] No. You'll make it over to me. Frank has nothing to do with this. He'll have to leave here when you go.

BEN. I don't see why.

FRANK. [*Angrily.*] I see why.

MARTHA. I'm not going to give people a chance to talk.

BEN. Who'll carry on the business?

MARTHA. I will—best I can.

[BEN *and* FRANK *stare at* MARTHA, *amazed at the fearless spirit she is showing for the first time in her life.* CAP'N DAN *and* ELIZABETH, *who are sitting in the window, glance at each other approvingly.* CAP'N DAN *nods and smiles at* ELIZABETH *as if to say "By George, that is a level-headed scheme."* MARTHA, *unaware of the effect she is producing, continues to speak, walking up and down excitedly. She is deeply wounded by* BEN'S *attitude, and her womanhood is on the defensive.*]

MARTHA. I'm not going to sit down here and eat my heart out, because my husband doesn't choose to live with me. I've got a child to bring up and educate, and I'm going to do it, if God spares me.

[CAP'N DAN *nods to* ELIZABETH, *as if to say "That's grit, pure grit."*]

BEN. [*Bitterly, in self-justification.*] I can't stay here after what's happened. I've been lied to, and fooled, and—I dare say laughed at.

MARTHA. [*Turning and facing him.*] Now—stop! You've said enough. You've settled it. You're going away, Frank's going—and I'm going to stay here and keep my home.

FRANK. [*Hotly.*] What's the use of arguing with him? Let him go! [*He turns impatiently up to the piano.*]

[CAP'N DAN *rises, and comes slowly down to* BEN. *In contrast to the angry mood of the others, his manner is easy-going and genial, and his voice has a leisurely reminiscent drawl.*]

cap'n dan. Say, Ben, d'you ever know a family—Gosh! couldn't think of the name for a minute—ol' Cap'n Smith, Patchogue, y'know— [*They are all a little taken aback at the interruption.* frank, *with a bored look, sits on the bench at the piano.* ben *turns away impatiently.* martha *stares wonderingly at* cap'n dan. *He reassures her with an affectionate smile and says gently:*] Sit down, Martha. [*She takes the chair down left. As he talks,* cap'n dan *takes out his pipe and a small pouch of tobacco, and begins to fill his pipe. His action is mechanical, and he is hardly aware that he is doing this.*] He had one boy, Ed—the best boy that ever stepped into shoe leather. Boy? Well, he was a man, time I speak of— Never went to church nor nothin'—but was just born good—naturally. Well, by'n by ol' man Smith died. Ed, he took the boat and the business and took care of his mother an' all that. There was a shiftless sort of a family there named—named—Jones! Gosh! it's hard to remember names. A man and his wife and a little girl. They was as poor as Job's off ox, and Ed used to help 'em one way and another, an' take the little girl out, an' git her ice cream soda an' things, till he got awful fond of her and she of him. After a while, the Joneses died, and left Liza—that was her name,—a girl of—ah—I d'know, fifteen or sixteen I guess, without no means nor friends, and Ed took her home to his old mother and sorter 'dopted her. Sent her to school and she growed up to be a woman. [*Smiles; pauses.*]

martha. [*Interested.*] Is that all?

[ben *sits in the armchair, right.*]

cap'n dan. [*Rousing himself.*] No. Next door to the Joneses, there was a family named Brown—I always can get their name—and they had a boy named Charlie, han'some as a picture, about the same age as Liza. The children sorter grew up together, and finally they just naturally fell in love, and they was engaged, but didn't let anybody know it. Ed didn't know it, nobody knew it. Ed, he was in love with her himself, but he always thought he was too old for her. He *was* some older; and so he never said nothin' to her about it, although it was just about eatin' him up y'know. About this time Charlie shipped in a—a—whaler I guess—shipped for five years. Now, there was an old busybody there—everybody knew him, I forget his name, but he knew everybody's business. He got the idea into his head that Ed ought to marry Liza, so he ups and tells Ed that she's dead in love with him, and proved it to him. And once Ed got it into his head, he couldn't get it out. So, finally, one day he ups and asks her to marry him. Well, you can imagine. She worshipped him, he'd been everythin' to her; but there she was —she loved Charlie. Well, sir, first she thought she wouldn't say a word, but just marry him—sort of lie, y'know—but she couldn't, so she told him. He laughed, and pretended he knew it all the time, and that ended it. He was just as good to her as ever, but he got so's he couldn't eat nor sleep, and his poor old mother begun to worry, and finally died, and left him and Liza alone together. About this time, there come reports that Charlie was lost at sea. The whole village was up, 'cause, as I said, he was han'some and everybody liked him; and when Liza heard the news she turned pale and she looked at Ed, and you couldn't tell just what was in her mind—whether she considered it Providence or not. And she asked Ed to find out, and he went up to York to the company's office, but he couldn't get no positive news—only that Charlie's ship had been lost. That was certain. And, sir, he came home and he told her it was true, Charlie was *drowneded*.

FRANK. [*Contemptuously.*] The old liar!

CAP'N DAN. I guess he thought she—

BEN. I'd have thought so too—the way she looked at him.

MARTHA. I don't believe she knew.

CAP'N DAN. Well, anyway, after a while, Ed and she was married. And a baby come. [*Looks at them curiously.*] She was happy; so was he, apparently, but he got awful nervous. One day she was down in the village on some business, some woman's business I guess, and she come where they was diggin' a hole in the street for a sewer or somethin'. There was a crowd lookin' on, and she stopped to look too, when some one touched her on the shoulder and she looked around, and there was Charlie. She never stopped—she run home as hard as she could run, and she called out, "Ed, Ed, Ed!" He was upstairs 'r somewheres I guess. Anyhow, he heard her, and, sir, he knew in a minute she'd seen Charlie and he dasn't face her—'shamed y'know—so he hid in the wood-house or some place till it was dark, and then he stole out and he enlisted in the Secesh War. There wa'n't no Klondike then, or I s'pose he'd gone there. And he was killed in one o' them battles. Well, sir, he'd no sooner got out of sight of the house, than he was sorry he went; sorry he hadn't stayed and faced the thing out like a man. Y'see he couldn't get that baby out of his head. [*Reflectively.*] Babies is wonderful things. Sing'lar that they be, too, there's so many of 'em. Well, sir, as soon as he was gone, and she realized she'd lost him for good—she begun to mourn for him—got sorter hungry after him, y'know—the place wa'n't the same, and Charlie wa'n't the same—and by'n by, she begun to under-stand that she'd loved him all the time and didn't know it—and then she wished she'd married him first off—had lied to him—so's he wouldn't have had t'lie to her about Charlie, y'know, 'cause she knew Charlie'd get over it some time. Then she set to work to bring the boy up to be like him. He was the dead image of his father anyhow. [*To* BEN.] Jes' as your baby is o' you. And last I heard, she was keepin' a millinery shop or somethin', and the boy was goin' to school. But, say, the cur'ous part of it is, that that ol' busy-body down there must have seen that in her, somehow—he couldn't tell you how—but he seen it, yes sir, jest as sure as you're born.

[*When* CAP'N DAN *finishes his story, there is a pause.*

They are all profoundly moved, and sit lost in thought. CAP'N DAN *stands, pipe in hand, looking into the distance.* ELIZABETH *tiptoes up to him, and says softly,*]

ELIZABETH. Dan'l, may I kiss you now?

CAP'N DAN. [*Humorously, after a glance at the others.*] Yes yes.

[ELIZABETH *kisses him; then she takes his arm and leads him towards the kitchen door, down left.*]

ELIZABETH. [*Gently, speaking as they go.*] I'm going to tell you something this evening.

CAP'N DAN. Tell me now.

ELIZABETH. No, this evening—at our home.

CAP'N DAN. [*Pausing, and looking at her anxiously.*] Say, how did that sound to you?

ELIZABETH. [*Ingenuously.*] Why, it made me cry.

CAP'N DAN. That so? [*Smiles.*] D'know how I ever made it up. Couldn't do it again to save my life. [*They go off into the kitchen.*]

[*There is a long pause. Then* FRANK *takes a deep breath, squares his shoulders, and comes down left towards the others. There is a new manly note in his voice, as he says quietly*]

FRANK. Ben, your going away isn't going to get us out of this muddle. It will simply break up the home. She couldn't marry me now, if you were dead.

BEN. [*Slowly and thoughtfully.*] I'm not Ed Smith, of course.

FRANK. Well, you are and you're not. But she's Liza and I'm Charlie—[*Sadly.*]—and that ends it.

BEN. I'm sort of ashamed to stay now.

FRANK. Better be ashamed than sorry.

MARTHA. [*Who is still seated, looks up at* BEN *and says*

gently.] Ben, if this had to be done over again, and you knew
—would you—

BEN. I don't know—would you?

MARTHA. [*Looking at him frankly and earnestly.*] Yes.

FRANK. [*Who has been watching them both, with a tragic
little smile.*] He's the one you've loved all the time, isn't he?

MARTHA. [*Simply and pathetically.*] I guess he is. Don't
blame me—I didn't know it. I couldn't help it.

FRANK. [*Abstractedly.*] I don't blame you. [*He goes up
towards the window.*]

CAP'N DAN. [*Putting his head in at the kitchen door, and
calling cheerfully.*] Say, do you folks know that you ain't
had a mouthful to eat today?

MARTHA. [*Jumping up.*] Why, that's so. [*She laughs in an
effort to be her happy, natural self.*] Well—and I'm starved!

CAP'N DAN. 'Lizbeth and me's got some hot coffee out here.
[*He disappears.*]

MARTHA. [*Trying to throw off her depression, crosses to
BEN and takes his hand.*] Ben, let's go and get a cup of hot
coffee. [*She pulls him out of his chair.*] Come, Frank!

FRANK. [*At the window.*] You go. I'll be there by the time
you've got it poured out.

BEN. [*Turning towards FRANK, and speaking gravely and
kindly.*] Frank, I want to have a good, long talk with you,
by and by.

FRANK. All right.

[MARTHA *and* BEN *walk together towards the left. As they
get to the door,* BEN *pauses, looks* MARTHA *full in the face
and says*]

BEN. Martha, I'm going to try and be the big Ben you married.

MARTHA. [*Looking up at him with all the tenderness and affection of which she is capable.*] Oh, he's been away. I expect him home by this evening. I'll introduce you to him. You'll like him. I'll let you hold his baby. [*They go off together lower left.*]

[FRANK *drops down to the fireplace, and stands looking into the fire.*]

[JANE CAULDWELL *passes outside the window towards the door, upper left. She knocks on the door; there is a pause, then the knock is repeated.*]

FRANK. [*At the fire, indifferently, without looking up.*] Come in.

[JANE *enters in her new Easter gown and hat, and carrying a small, folded umbrella. She radiates health and cheer.*]

JANE. [*Speaking as she enters.*] I thought you were all coming to church this morning to hear me sing? [*She looks about and sees that* FRANK *is alone.*] Why, where are all the folks?

FRANK. [*Turning towards her.*] Martha and Ben are at breakfast.

JANE. [*Laughs.*] Breakfast?

FRANK. [*Ironically.*] Yes, we have breakfast late some Sunday mornings.

JANE. Why, what time did you get up, for pity's sake?

FRANK. We didn't get up. We haven't been to bed.

JANE. What!

FRANK. [*In an effort to change the subject.*] Many in church?

JANE. Everybody, except you.

FRANK. I'll tell them you're here. [*He starts to cross left, towards the kitchen.*]

JANE. [*Stopping him.*] No, no, no,— I'm in no hurry. I'll wait. [*Then she says half pouting, half coquettishly*] But you might offer me a chair.

FRANK. [*With grave courtesy.*] Oh, excuse me. [*He brings forward the chair that* MARTHA *has been sitting on.*]

JANE. [*Sits.*] Thank you. [*There is a slight pause.* JANE *senses something in the air, and says seriously*] Something dreadful has happened here, Frank. What is it?

FRANK. [*Takes* JANE'S *umbrella and gloves, placing them in the armchair left. He makes an attempt to speak casually.*] Oh, nothing much. After you left here last night, Martha and I got talking. Ben came in and overheard us. [*He crosses to the fireplace, right.*]

JANE. [*Simply, with an understanding smile.*] It's a tragedy, isn't it?

FRANK. [*Reflectively, sitting in the armchair, right.*] Sort of. She never really loved me.

JANE. [*Very tenderly.*] Poor Frank! My heart just aches for you.

FRANK. Humph! I don't know that I've any right to be considered.

JANE. [*Rising and going to him, speaking comfortingly.*] Why, you're the one to be considered! You've been the only real sufferer. They've had each other, and that baby. You've been alone. [*She hesitates, then asks half shyly,*] Do you love her still?

FRANK. [*Doubtfully.*] N-n-no! [*With a return to his old bitter manner.*] What's the use? But I suppose I resent it; any fellow would, you know.

JANE. I suppose you'd laugh if I were to tell you it's all for the best. [*He turns and looks at her incredulously, and she nods her head at him emphatically.*] It is. You were never meant to be man and wife.

FRANK. [*With an unhappy laugh.*] A blind man can see that—now.

JANE. [*Earnestly.*] I saw it years ago.

FRANK. Why didn't you say so?

JANE. You wouldn't have believed me. [*Smiles.*] Neither would she. [*She turns and crosses to the chair, left.*] I knew that Ben was the man for her. Besides, I didn't want you to think I—[*She gives a little embarrassed laugh*]—was trying to grind my own axe.

FRANK. [*Thoughtfully.*] I wish I'd known it.

JANE. Do you?

FRANK. Yes.

JANE. [*Anxiously.*] What are your plans now?

FRANK. [*Rising and crossing to the window.*] I'm going to the Klondike.

JANE. [*Pained and startled.*] Oh!

FRANK. [*Walking restlessly up and down.*] That's all there is left. I'm sick of going to sea, and I can't stay here.

JANE. [*Leaning on the back of the chair, left centre.*] Why can't you stay here?

FRANK. [*Still walking up and down.*] Why? Because I— [*Laughs bitterly.*] What difference does it make? Who cares where I go?

JANE. [*Quietly.*] I do.

FRANK. [*Stops, and stands looking at her amazed.*] You do?

JANE. I do. [*She gives a little embarrassed laugh, then summons all her courage, and says earnestly,*] I don't ask anything of you, only that you'll let me come into your life—let *me* play a part in this domestic drama—[*With a little laugh.*] —"Two Loves and a Life."

FRANK. [*Catching the infection of her mood, smiles as he says:*] Half an hour ago, I didn't believe I should ever laugh again.

JANE. [*Rising and going towards* FRANK, *who is standing*

at the fireplace, right.] Favorable symptom. The fever's broken. Let me feel your pulse. [*She takes his hand and pretends to count his pulse.*] Humph! Normal. [*She begins to laugh;* FRANK *hesitates, then laughs with her.* JANE *turns away and walks up left towards the piano, as she says:*] Don't blame Martha, she's as true as steel. Ben is a splendid man, and you— [*Laughing, with shy enthusiasm.*] Well, I just think you're—

FRANK. [*Now thoroughly roused from his sombre mood, sits in the armchair and says with a confidential air*] What would you do if you were me?

JANE. [*At the piano, smiles significantly at him.*] If I were you—well, I'd— [*She laughs.*] Do you really want me to tell you?

FRANK. I wouldn't ask you if I didn't.

JANE. And you won't think I'm selfish?

FRANK. [*With a protesting laugh.*] You selfish!

JANE. Well, I'd stay right here and go into business with my brother—and—that's practical advice, isn't it? [*She smiles and sits on the arm of the chair, left.*] Sag Harbor isn't much of a place in the eyes of the world, but God is here just the same as He is everywhere, y'know.

FRANK. [*Reflectively.*] And you're here.

JANE. [*Laughing joyously.*] Oh, yes, I'm very much here! That is, I'm in a suburb—Bridgehampton.

FRANK. [*Looking thoughtfully into the fire.*] I wonder if anybody could ever love me?

JANE. [*Simply.*] I've always loved you. Didn't you know it?

FRANK. [*Surprised.*] No—I—

JANE. [*Rising and going a few steps towards him.*] I always thought you did, and that you didn't want me to.

FRANK. [*Ingenuously.*] No, it never entered my head.

JANE. [*Simply.*] I'm sorry. [*She turns up to the piano.*]

FRANK. [*Smiling at her.*] So am I.

JANE. [*At the piano.*] You've heard the story of the man who wandered all over in search of the Kingdom of Heaven, and found out at last that it was in his own heart all the time? [*She laughs significantly.*] Well—

FRANK. [*Rising and taking a few steps towards her.*] Honestly, now, don't you think the best thing I can do is to go away?

JANE. [*Very earnestly.*] No, I do not. I suppose I'm selfish, but I do not.

FRANK. [*Half doggedly.*] Well, I won't go into business with Ben—not right off, anyway. [*He returns to the fireplace, and sits in the armchair.*]

JANE. [*Approvingly.*] If you feel that way, perhaps it's just as well not.

FRANK. [*Thoughtfully.*] If I were to begin keeping company now, folks'd say—

JANE. [*Laughing.*] I never care what folks say—so far as I'm concerned.

FRANK. [*Hopefully.*] The Montauk Steamboat Company has made me a good offer.

JANE. [*Coquettishly.*] That will take you to the City three days in every week, won't it?

FRANK. [*Looks at her, smiles, and says meaningly and slowly,*] Yes, but I'll be here the other four.

JANE. [*After reflection.*] I think I'd take it. [*She goes towards him.*]

FRANK. [*Rising and going towards* JANE.] I will. [*They meet centre and he says cheerily,*] I'm glad I had you to tell all this to. [*They clasp hands.*]

JANE. [*Laughing.*] You had to tell it to some one, didn't you?

FRANK. [*Tenderly.*] Yes, and you're so wise, Janey.

JANE. [*With a teasing laugh.*] Oh, I'm Janey again, am I?

FRANK. [*With a quizzical look at her.*] Some years since I called you Janey, isn't it?

JANE. [*Lightly.*] Oh, years don't count. [*They are quite unconscious that they are still standing close together, holding hands.*]

FRANK. Will you kiss me for auld lang syne?

JANE. [*Looking at him coyly.*] I'll kiss you for new lang syne.

FRANK. [*Hesitates and shakes his head doubtfully.*] No-o-o —not yet—for auld lang syne.

JANE. [*Laughing.*] Oh, well, any old lang syne! [*They kiss. She is suddenly overcome with shyness, breaks away from him, and goes left. She says with an effort to overcome her embarrassment.*] Don't put that in *The Express.*

FRANK. [*Who is also embarrassed, laughs back.*] Don't you. [*He turns and goes down right.*]

[MARTHA *enters from the kitchen, lower left. She is quite her cheerful self again.*]

MARTHA. Frank, your coffee is getting cold. [*She sees* JANE.] Why, Jane! [*Goes to her left centre, with outstretched hands, and kisses her.*] How long have you been here?

JANE. [*Laughing a trifle hysterically.*] I don't know. Seems as if I hadn't been away!

MARTHA. We must apologize for not coming to church, but Ben had a business matter to settle, and—

[BEN *enters from the kitchen, lower left.*]

JANE. Good morning, Ben.

BEN. Good morning, Jane. Fine morning.

[BEN *crosses up right towards the stairs, and goes off through the door on the landing.* JANE *follows* BEN *up a little, and remains standing centre.* MARTHA *goes to* FRANK, *right, takes his arm, and leads him in the direction of the kitchen.*]

MARTHA. Now, Frank, run along and get a cup of coffee. I'm sure it will be cold if you wait any longer. [*She pushes him off affectionately, lower left.*]

[*As soon as* FRANK *has left the stage,* JANE *rushes down to* MARTHA *and the two girls meet left centre.*]

JANE. [*Bubbling over with joyous excitement.*] Martha, I'll tell you something—I'm the happiest girl in Sag Harbor.

MARTHA. [*Comprehending at once.*] Has he—? [*She nods in the direction of the kitchen.*]

JANE. [*Hardly able to control herself.*] N-n-no—not yet— [*Laughs.*]—but I think he—will— [*Slightly hysterical and embarrassed, and at a loss what to say, she finishes lamely as she turns up stage.*] He's handsomer than Ben, isn't he?

MARTHA. [*Watching her and laughing sympathetically.*] Well, I think he's more to your taste.

JANE. [*As she comes down right to the fireplace.*] Oh, I know he's that. [*She laughs; then she looks about as though surprised to find* FRANK *gone.*] Where is he?

MARTHA. In the kitchen.

JANE. I'm going in there. [*Laughs.*] May I?

MARTHA. Why, certainly.

[JANE *dashes clear across the stage and off lower left.* MARTHA *turns and watches her, smiling with pleasure.*]
[BEN *enters through the door on the stair landing, right, carrying a freshly folded handkerchief, which he shakes out as though he had gone into his bedroom to get it.*]
[*At the same time, there is a knock on the outside door,*

upper left. MARTHA *goes up and opens the door, admitting*
MRS. RUSSELL, *dressed in her holiday best.*]

MARTHA. [*Greeting her delightedly.*] Good morning, Mrs.
Russell, I'm so glad to see you.

MRS. RUSSELL. [*Beaming upon* MARTHA *and* BEN.] I missed
you in church, and thought I'd tell you what a wonderful
sermon we had.

[BEN *comes up stage and greets* MRS. RUSSELL. *At the same
time,* FRANK, JANE, CAP'N DAN *and* ELIZABETH *enter from the
kitchen, lower left.* ELIZABETH *wears her outdoor wraps,
and* CAP'N DAN *is carrying her small valise. They all go to
the window and greet* MRS. RUSSELL *heartily, and the conversation becomes general.*]
[*There is another knock on the outside door, upper left.*
BEN *opens it, and* FREEMAN *enters, accompanied by* MISS
BAILEY. MISS BAILEY *is a very tall woman of the masculine
type. She wears glasses and chews gum. Both she and* FREE-
MAN *are dressed for bicycling in fashionably cut tweeds.*
MISS BAILEY *wears an ankle length skirt, and* FREEMAN *has on
knickerbockers and golf stockings. There is a general murmur of welcome from everyone, and* MARTHA *drops down
stage a few steps to greet the newcomers.*]

FREEMAN. [*To* MARTHA, *in a very pompous and important
manner, as if he were making a public announcement.*] Mrs.
Turner, this is Miss Bailey of Gloversville. [*With a flourish
of his hand towards her.*] You must have seen her pictures
around the store windows. She's going to lecture in Masonic
Hall.

MARTHA. [*Taking* MISS BAILEY *in from head to foot.*] Oh,
yes!
[MARTHA *shakes hands with* MISS BAILEY, *then draws her
towards the window, and introduces her to* BEN *and the
others. During the next scene,* MISS BAILEY *examines their
hands, and explains her method of manicuring them. They
listen incredulously;* MARTHA *and* JANE *exchange sly smiles.*]

[CAP'N DAN *takes* FREEMAN *down left, and as he does so, the valise he is carrying bursts open without his being aware of it.*]

CAP'N DAN. [*In a confidential undertone.*] Say, Freeman, who did you say she was?

FREEMAN. [*Bursting with self-importance.*] Miss Bailey of Gloversville. She's taken parlors at the Nassau.

CAP'N DAN. [*Very seriously; he is deeply impressed.*] Goin' with her now?

FREEMAN. [*Tentatively.*] Well, yes.

CAP'N DAN. Stiddy?

FREEMAN. She's only been in town three days. There's money into her—she's a manicure.

CAP'N DAN. What's that?

FREEMAN. [*Solemnly.*] Cleans folks 's nails. [*He notices the open valise.*] Y'r grip 's open.

CAP'N DAN. [*Closing the valise.*] Gosh! Have folks got so lazy they can't clean their own nails?

FREEMAN. She does it scientifically, see! [*He shows* CAP'N DAN *his hands which have been perfectly manicured.*] She's going to lecture on "Degeneration." Free to women Tuesday night, and men Thursday night.

CAP'N DAN. I'll come on Tuesday night.

FREEMAN. [*Shaking his head, very gravely.*] I can't let you in.

CAP'N DAN. [*After a glance at* MISS BAILEY.] Good-lookin', don't you think?

FREEMAN. [*Doubtfully.*] Well, she's what I call intellectual. [CAP'N DAN's *valise bursts open again.* FREEMAN *notices it.*] Y'r grip's open. What's in it, anyway?

CAP'N DAN. I d'know. She's got it packed so dang full— [*He pulls some of the things out, and tries to stuff them into smaller space. A baby's shirt falls out. He sets the bag down*

on the chair, *left centre, and picks up the shirt. He gazes at
it wonderingly, then holds it out to* FREEMAN.] What in the
name of time is that?

FREEMAN. [*Inspecting it soberly.*] I should say it was a
baby's unmentionable.

MISS BAILEY. [*Coming down centre towards them, and speaking in a loud and domineering voice.*] Mr. Whitmarsh, if
we're going to make this century run—

FREEMAN. [*To* CAP'N DAN, *in a shocked, hurried whisper.*]
Don't let Miss Bailey see that! [*He hastens towards her,
takes her up stage, and says with an air of proprietorship*]
Yes, dear.

CAP'N DAN. [*Very much puzzled, still holding the shirt, turns
towards* FREEMAN.] Well, how'd it get in this bag? [FREE-
MAN *is occupied with* MISS BAILEY *and does not answer.*
CAP'N DAN *calls to* ELIZABETH.] 'Lizbeth, how'd this thing
get into— [ELIZABETH *comes down quickly and takes the
shirt from* CAP'N DAN. MRS. RUSSELL *turns and comes down a
little right centre, and watches* CAP'N DAN *and* ELIZABETH
with wistful interest. BEN, MARTHA *and the others are still
too busy talking to* FREEMAN *and* MISS BAILEY *to notice what
is taking place.*]

ELIZABETH. [*With a little, embarrassed laugh.*] Dan'l Marble,
I wish you'd let things alone! [*She gives him a significant
look.*] That's my sewing! [*She turns away from him, and
puts the shirt back into the valise and closes it.*]

[*For a moment,* CAP'N DAN *stares at* ELIZABETH, *wondering
and silent; then he falls into a muse and, as he grasps the
full meaning of her words, a smile of happiness breaks over
his face. He stands there, positively beatified, like one in a
dream. After a time he says, half to himself,*]

CAP'N DAN. Well, by Gosh! If this don't beat the Dutch!

[MRS. RUSSELL *goes over to* CAP'N DAN *and stands at his
right. She is deeply moved, and speaks very gently.*]

MRS. RUSSELL. She's told yeh, hain't she? You look just like Cap'n John did. Our baby was a year old when he saw her.

[CAP'N DAN *makes no reply, but stands like a man in a daze.*]

ELIZABETH. [*Coming to* CAP'N DAN, *left, and taking his arm.*] Dan'l, don't stand there as if you were petrified. Everybody'll be staring at you in a minute.

CAP'N DAN. [*In a voice filled with tears.*] I be, 'Lizbeth, I be petrified.

ELIZABETH. Hush! Don't say nothing.

CAP'N DAN. [*Taking her in his arms and kissing her tenderly.*] I can't, 'Lizbeth, I just can't.

[CAP'N DAN *and* ELIZABETH *start to go towards the door upper left.* MRS. RUSSELL *stops them.*]

MRS. RUSSELL. [*To* ELIZABETH *in an undertone, with a glance at the others.*] Why don't you take him out the kitchen way? They'll see his eyes if you go out the front way.

ELIZABETH. [*Very gently, as though talking to a child.*] Come, Dan'l!

[ELIZABETH *and* CAP'N DAN, *arm in arm, walk slowly towards the door, lower left.*]

[*At the same time,* MARTHA *leaves the group up stage, and seats herself at the piano.* BEN *follows her over, and stands above her, looking down at her affectionately.*]

CAP'N DAN. [*To* ELIZABETH, *as they go out.*] George! You could just knock me down with a feather! [*They go off lower left.*]

MRS. RUSSELL. [*Looking after them, and smiling wistfully at their happiness.*] I never see a man take it so to heart. [*She turns and drops into the chair by the fireplace, and sits nodding her head and smiling, lost in memories.*]
[MARTHA, *at the piano, begins to sing "All through the night," playing her own accompaniment.* FREEMAN, MISS

BAILEY, FRANK *and* JANE *are chatting together in the window. As* MARTHA *starts to sing,* WILLIAM TURNER *appears outside the window with a long string of fish. He raises the window and looks in.*]

TURNER. [*Holding up the fish.*] Say—if you folks want to see some fish, look here! [*He stops on hearing the singing.* FREEMAN, MISS BAILEY, FRANK *and* JANE *crowd around him and congratulate him in low voices.* TURNER *is introduced to* MISS BAILEY, *and begins to tell them all about his fishing trip.*]

[MARTHA *continues her song.*]

MARTHA. [*Singing.*]

> "Sleep, my love and peace attend thee
>   All through the night.
>   Guardian angels God will lend thee
>   All through the night.
> Soft the drowsy hours are creeping
> Hill and vale in slumber steeping;
> Love alone his watch is keeping
>   All through the night."

[*The curtain falls slowly on the last line.*]

THE END OF THE PLAY

HEARTS OF OAK

A Drama in Six Acts

By

JAMES A. HERNE

CHARACTERS

TERRY DENNISON, *"The sailor miller."*
NED FAIRWEATHER, *"The boy he brung up."*
OWEN GARROWAY, *"Who never speaks without his I. O. U."*
UNCLE DAVY, *Terry's father, "who does all the work."*
MR. ELLINGHAM, *An attorney.*
FOREMAN OF THE MILL.
CLERK OF THE MILL.
CHRYSTAL, *"The sweetheart."*
AUNT BETSEY, *"An old maid."*
TAWDREY, *"The model help."*
LITTLE CRYSTAL, *"A sunbeam."*

THE BABY.

Sailors, Fishermen, Mill Hands.

ACT I.   The seacoast near Marblehead, Massachusetts.
         A summer evening, just before sunset.
            "The Wreck."

ACT II. The interior of Terry Dennison's mill.
         The next morning.
            "The Mill."

ACT III. The living room of Terry's home.
         An evening in early spring, two years later.
            "The Baby."

ACT IV. A lane near Whalers' Wharf.
         Several weeks later.
            "The Lane."

ACT V.   A country churchyard.
         Six years later. A morning in early summer.
            "The Wedding."

ACT VI. Owen Garroway's hut.
         Late afternoon, the same day.
            "The End."

TIME—1859.

PLACE—Marblehead, Massachusetts.

HEARTS OF OAK

ACT FIRST

"The Wreck"

The *seacoast near Marblehead, Massachusetts.*

A summer evening, just before sunset.

SCENE: *A wild and picturesque seacoast. On the left is an incline with steps cut in the rock, leading to a promontory above. On this promontory is a small cannon, equipped with life-saving apparatus. On the right and at back is a view of the open sea with a lighthouse [practical], in the distance, left centre. The beach forms the foreground of the scene. It is strewn with bits of wreckage, old hawsers, anchors, ships' blocks, and fishing nets. To the right and left are small rocks [practical] on which the characters sit during the action.*

Before the rise of the curtain, and at intervals during the act, the noise of the surf breaking upon the beach can be heard, and the sea is continually in motion.

[NOTE: All the effects used in the act, the movement of the sea, the noise of the surf, the rain and storm effects are practical. The storm, from the moment it begins, increases gradually, until the end of the act, when it becomes furious.]

The overture concludes with a symphony of the chorus of the "Mill Song" to which the curtain rises.

OWEN GARROWAY *is discovered sitting on a rock, right, mending a net. As the curtain goes up the chorus is heard in the distance, singing the "Mill Song."*

*[*OWEN *is a gnarled, heavy-set fisherman in his late fifties, who seems older because of his weather-beaten appearance.*

257

He is bluff, hearty, full of broad, rough-and-ready humor, and devoted to TERRY DENNISON.]

CHORUS. [*Sung off stage.*]

> Click, clack, click the mill goes,
> On and on the stream flows,
> To the river that runs to the sea.
> Still while the stream flows.
> Round and round the wheel goes,
> And merry, happy boys,
> Happy, merry boys,
> Merry, merry boys are we!

OWEN. [*Laying down his net and coming centre, and speaking through the chorus.*] There, that's done. [*He turns right, to put the net on a rock.*]

[TERRY DENNISON *enters left, during the singing, pauses and looks out to sea.* OWEN *is busy with his nets; his back is towards* TERRY, *and he does not see him.*]

[TERRY *is a stalwart man in his early forties, simple and kindly in manner, frank, honest and generous. There is a flavor of the sea about him. He wears a blue flannel shirt and trousers, high rubber boots, and a sou'wester. He carries a rubber coat which he throws on the ground as he comes down.*]

[*As the song finishes,* TERRY *crosses to* OWEN *and slaps him on the shoulder.*]

TERRY. [*Laughing.*] Hello, Owen!

OWEN. [*Turns and grasps his hand, laughing heartily.*] Terry! I was just this minit a-thinkin' o' you.

TERRY. [*Good-naturedly.*] Was you? Well, you know the old sayin'—"Talk o' the devil"—

OWEN. An' ye're sartin to find him at your elbow! [*They both laugh.*] Yes—well, I was just a-sayin' to Will Barton —he was tellin' me about your givin' him that new boat o' yourn—

TERRY. [*Trying to change the subject.*] Did yer ever hear such a chatterbox in all your born days?

OWEN. There ye go again, Terry—another heart made light and happy!

TERRY. And why not? Aren't he a little waif thrown in our midst without kith or kin? Besides, although I'm not rich by no manner o' means, I've enough and to spare. I've the best set of mill hands as ever done a day's work for a master.

OWEN. Aye—that ye have, Terry.

TERRY. The oldest dad in the neighborhood—

OWEN. An' the best un.

TERRY. An aunt as never was married- –

OWEN. No; nor never likely to nuther! [*Both laugh.*]

TERRY. I don't know about that—they say she's got an eye on you, Owen. [*Laughs.*]

OWEN. [*Laughing.*] Avast! Avast! No! No! No!

TERRY. A lad that's the best seaman and truest friend as ever trod a deck and a—a—a— [*Stops, scratches his head, then looks* OWEN *in the face.*] A—a—

OWEN. A lass that ye love better'n a nigger loves a holiday—

TERRY. [*Blushing.*] Hold hard, Owen—hold hard! That's a queer word—a very queer word—I don't know which is the queerest, the word or the feelin'. [*Laughs.*] But I guess you're right—*she's pretty precious to me.* [*Shakes his head.*] But I'm afeared—I'm afeared—

OWEN. Afeared?

TERRY. You've said it.

OWEN. Of what?

TERRY. [*Slowly.*] Of that little word.

OWEN. [*Chuckling.*] What little word?

TERRY. [*Sheepishly.*] L-o-v-e. [*Laughs.*]

OWEN. Well—ye—needn't be—all's I got to say is, Heaven bless the gal as you'd take hum for a wife. [*Confidentially.*] And it's my opinion that the happiest moment of Chrystal's life'd be when the parson j'ined your hands together.

TERRY. [*Starts, breathes quickly.*] One moment, Owen—say it gently—if you don't want to choke me. Why man, the bare thought on't—the bare thought on't is—as refreshin' as a breeze after a calm—a doctor's cheerin' word to a dyin' patient—a dose of physic to a bilious man. That's exactly how I feel, only I'm wuss nor all three on 'em put together, an' I'm afeared my cure ain't to be found on this side of Eternity.

OWEN. [*Laughing and slapping him on back.*] Your physic's nigher'n you think for. Owen Garroway says that and he never says a thing 'less he's sure of it—

TERRY. [*Looking as if in doubt.*] Say, Owen, be you in arnest—or be you only jokin'?

OWEN. [*Very serious.*] Jokin'? Terry Dennison, if ye ax me that question—'cause I happened to laugh and speak the words lightly—I forgive ye. But—if ye ax 'cause ye thought I were a triflin' with ye—why, there'll be trouble atween us.

TERRY. [*After a slight pause.*] Then Owen, do yer wust, I can't believe ye.

OWEN. [*With surprise and a pretended angry movement towards him.*] Hey! What d'ye mean to call me?

TERRY. [*Grasping his hand.*] My friend—Owen—my friend every day o' the week. Only what ye've said can't be true. Why—I'm too old—too rough—too ignorant—too—too—I can't think of anything half bad enough—ever to mate with my little Chrystal. And yet, you'll never guess half the love I feel for her. The Lord forgive me, I'm afeared she's in my thoughts more'n he is—and you ought to know what that means in a rough nature like mine. [*In a whisper.*] But I can never hope to win her—never hope to be more than a friend to her and when the day comes I'll give her to the man of her choice—whoever he may be—

OWEN. [*Boisterously.*] Steady—steady—hold hard—and stand by—till I prove to ye—ye piratical son of a sea cook, and show you how Owen Garroway knows what he talks on and never opens his mouth without he's got his I. O. U.

TERRY. Prove? Prove what?

OWEN. That Chrystal loves ye, ye swab! Loves ye with her whole heart and soul. [*He gives* TERRY *a dig in the ribs.*]

TERRY. Loves me— [*Wipes his forehead.*] Phew! Say, Owen, why don't ye take away a fellow's breath at once and done with it?

OWEN. You only hear me out—and you'll be breathless for the balance of yer nat'ral life—ye lubber—

TERRY. [*Excited.*] Go on—go on I say—I'm afire.

OWEN. [*Very boisterously and with great wisdom. Positive of being right and knowing it all. Waving his hands.*] Then clear the decks—clear the decks and give me sea room!— Hem! Ahem! Ahem!!! This arternoon, as I were passin' the old mill—who should I meet standin' in the rud that faces the sea, shadin' her eyes with her hand, and lookin' in the direction you went this mornin'—[*Again digging* TERRY *in the ribs*]—ye rascal—who but Chrystal? [*Impressively.*] There she stood as still and motionless as a cat watchin' a mouse, an' never took her eyes from the sea—nor her lips from suthin' she held in her right hand. [*Chuckling.*] So, what does I do but steals right up behind her to take her onawares like—and what does she have in her hand but—

TERRY. [*Impatiently.*] What?

OWEN. A pictur'—

TERRY. A picture?

OWEN. Yes— [*Poking him in the ribs.*] Your'n.

TERRY. [*Astonished.*] Mine?

OWEN. H'm, H'm! [*Smilingly noticing Terry's perplexity.*] That's not all—

TERRY. No?

OWEN. No—another look—what did my skylights detect this time—atween the glass and the pictur'—*two locks of hair.*

TERRY. Two locks o' hair?

OWEN. H'm, H'm! Tied in a true lover's knot— [*Chuckles, and nudges* TERRY.] Just at that moment a puff of wind took her hat clean into the middle of the rud—when I brung it back to her the pictur'—*yourn*—was gone—there. [*Pointing to his bosom.*] That's whar the women folks puts everythin'—you know.

TERRY. [*Pleased.*] It can't be— It can't be—why how could she come by a lock o' my hair? Besides, I never give her no picture—

OWEN. No, nor she never axed yer leave to git it either. Can't ye see or won't ye see? [*Wisely.*] She's had the pictur' taken' from the one as hangs over the chimney place—and as for the hair, she's cut that off when ye've been asleep sometime. There—I've ciphered it all out—I've unfathomed it all—she loves ye I tell ye—[*With another nudge.*] and I feel jest as happy an' sheepish as if she loved me.

TERRY. [*Who has been walking up and down.*] Owen—pinch me—darn it, man, knock me down—

OWEN. [*Gives him a terrific thump in the breast.* TERRY *staggers back.*] D'ye feel better?

[CHRYSTAL'S *music.*]

TERRY. Much.

OWEN. I'm glad on't [*Looking off left*] for here comes Chrystal.

TERRY. [*Frightened.*] Chrystal! [*He starts to rush off, right, in a panic of shyness.* OWEN *stops him.*] What's to be done?

MRS. JAMES A. HERNE, AS CHRYSTAL,
IN HEARTS OF OAK, ACT I

OWEN. Why, pop.

TERRY. Pop—when?

OWEN. Now.

TERRY. How?

OWEN. Ax her to be your wife o' course.

TERRY. I can't—I haven't the courage.

OWEN. [*Disgusted.*] Then I will. [*Going left.*]

TERRY. [*Stopping him.*] I'll be durned if ye do.

OWEN. I'll be durned if I don't, 'less you do; will ye, yes or no?

TERRY. I'll try.

OWEN. Good, and mind, Terry [*Confidentially*] don't let on as if I'd told ye anythin'.

TERRY. All right—I'll be as ignorant as a clam. [*Sits on a rock, centre.*]

OWEN. Hush! Mum's the word— [*He sings, and resumes the business of mending the net as if he had been at work all the time. The music grows louder.*]

[*Enter* CHRYSTAL, *at the top of the cliff, left. She is a lovely young girl, simply but daintily dressed. She starts to run down the steps. Midway she stops.* OWEN *looks up and sees her. She shakes her finger at him, motioning him to take no notice of her.*]

TERRY. [*Pretending not to know that* CHRYSTAL *is there.*] Yes, we may expect her now at any moment. The "Charlestown" got in about a month ago, and the "Nantucket" is the next ship. Well, the sooner the better. [*During this,* CHRYSTAL *has stolen down on his left, and now she shouts in his ear, "Booh!" He starts as if greatly frightened.* OWEN *and* CHRYSTAL *laugh heartily.*]

CHRYSTAL. [*After the laugh.*] I thought I'd frighten you!

TERRY. I should say you did frighten me!

OWEN. [*Laughing.*] He jumped like a skun frog.

TERRY. Yes, and you'd have jumped too if you hadn't knowed she was comin'. [OWEN *laughs.*] Chrystal! You here?

CHRYSTAL. [*Playfully.*] Yes, and I might have stood here till doomsday it seems, for all the notice you'd take of me. [*Gaily.*] Where have you been, sir, all this blessed day? Shortly after breakfast we saw you pulling away for dear life towards the lighthouse. Does Ida, the lightkeeper's pretty daughter, cause you to have so much business in that direction of late? [*Laughs.*] Come now, Terry, own up! You're caught.

OWEN. [*Coming forward and laughing boisterously.*] Ah, yes—own up, you're cotched. [*Aside.*] What did I tell ye? She watches ye— [*Digs him in the ribs.*] She's *jealous* on ye.

TERRY. [*Aside.*] Be quiet, Owen, she'll hear you.

OWEN. [*Aside.*] How can she hear me, when I'm a-talkin' in a whisper?

TERRY. There! There! [*Aloud.*] Chrystal, I'll tell you—you remember a month ago when the "Charlestown" got in?

CHRYSTAL. [*Knowingly.*] Yes.

TERRY. Well, Jack Dalton brought me a letter from Ned, tellin' me we might expect him any time within a fortnight. I said nothin' to you about it, but thought I'd keep a sharp lookout and add to your happiness by havin' him pop in on you unawares and of a sudden like. [CHRYSTAL *smiles, takes a letter from her bosom, shakes it, unseen by* TERRY, *kisses it and replaces it in her bosom.*] And that's what's caused me to have such pressin' business in the neighborhood of the lighthouse.

CHRYSTAL. Forgive me, Terry, I was only joking. Dear old Ned! It's three years since he left us, isn't it?

TERRY. Three years, day after to-morrow—eh, Owen?

OWEN. *More*—it's nigh on to twenty month. [TERRY *and* CHRYSTAL *laugh.*]

TERRY. Twenty months—there's nice arithmetic for you! Why, it's three years, you durned old multiplication table—

CHRYSTAL. How old was he then?

TERRY. Twenty—the very day he set sail.

OWEN. And just as purty—yes—purtier nor any pictur' book, as I ever looked at, wa'n't he? Eh!

CHRYSTAL. [*Seems pleased and blushes.*] And how old was I?

OWEN. You! Oh! la! you wan't no old; you was in short frocks and pantalettes. Why we couldn't keep no shoes nor stockin's on your feet half the time—ye would run barefooted in spite of us. [*He chuckles.*]

CHRYSTAL. I'm a good deal *changed,* ain't I, Terry?

OWEN. Oh, yes, you wear shoes an' stockin's *all* the time now.

TERRY. No, she don't, she only wears 'em daytimes. [*Laughs.*] Why, yes, you're a young woman now.

CHRYSTAL. [*Shyly.*] D'ye think he'll know me?

TERRY. [*To* OWEN, *laughing heartily.*] Oh! Sal—i—ma—gun —di—!

OWEN. [*Laughing.*] Oh! Al—a—ma—goo—zle—um—! By chowder, that's a good un! Ned not know Chrystal! [*Sits on a rock right centre.*]

CHRYSTAL. I wonder if he's much changed?

OWEN. Well, I hope so, or he'll be a-wantin' to romp all over the country with you on his back, just as he used to do. It were all right in them days—but it wouldn't look just the ticket now. I say, Chrystal, I ain't a-goin' to forget the Sunday afternoon as he were a-carryin' you pickaback across the mill stream. You was all in your Sunday go to meetin's, your best bib and tucker, and laughin' fit to kill yourself, when all of a suddint—kerplunk, kersplash, in ye both went and if I hadn't been there to fish ye out—I don't know what might 'a' happened! I got ye out somehow and I spread ye out on the bank in the sun to dry—and when you was dry on one side I rolled ye over so's to get ye dry on t'other. I gin ye each a handful o' cherries and in a few minutes I heerd ye a-chatterin' and crowin' away as if ye hadn't just gotten yer second baptism. [*Sighs, rises.*] Ah, well, them's childhood's pranks an' it won't do for a horny-fisted salt water cuss like me to recall 'em too much or folks'll say I'm a-gettin' old. [*Laughs.*] I must be off now—I've my nets to set yet and evenin's a-comin' on.

> "Work is work and play is play,
> We're here to-morry and gone today."

[*Picks up his basket and net and prepares to go.*]

TERRY. [*Who has been nervously scanning the sea and sky, pretending to be amused, but in reality anxious to get rid of him.*] D'ye see that sky to the westward there, Owen? I don't like the looks o' that 'ere.

OWEN. [*Looking.*] It does look a leetle thick.

TERRY. On your way up I wish ye'd stop at the station and tell Joe to have the men ready—it won't do to be caught with our eyes shut on this coast—ye know—

OWEN. Them's my sentiments to a T. In time o' war—prepare for peace. All right, I'm off— [*Aside to* TERRY.] Now's yer time. Buckle on yer armor—gird up yer l'ins, ax her to be yer wife, an' she's yourn. [*Pokes* TERRY *in the ribs, chuckles.*] Good night, Chrystal— [*As he crosses her to go up the incline left he salutes her respectfully.*] When Ned comes hum—I ain't a-goin' to say nothin' to him about the mill stream, it might recall unpleasant reminiscences. [*He laughs and goes off up the rocks, singing and winking at* TERRY.]

"Oh, of all the fish that's in the sea,
The red, the green, the blue,
Of all the birds that's in the air,
There's no bird love like you!"

[*After* OWEN'S *exit, and during the scene between* TERRY *and* CHRYSTAL, *the storm begins to come up, and the stage gradually darkens.*]

TERRY. Phew! Well, I did think he never would go—

CHRYSTAL. Were you impatient? Why, I could listen to him by the hour.

TERRY. So could I sometimes—but just now I wanted to be alone with you, I wanted to talk with you about—about—

CHRYSTAL. [*Innocently.*] About—what?

TERRY. About— [*Goes towards her, hesitates, chews a straw, finally blurts out.*] Ned!

CHRYSTAL. [*Overjoyed, but without showing it.*] Ned?

TERRY. Yes— [*Hesitates.*]

CHRYSTAL. [*Aside.*] Dear Ned! [*Feels in her bosom as if to assure herself the letter and picture were still there.*]

TERRY. [*Aside.*] I must tell her. [*Aloud.*] Yes, Ned; the day after to-morrow'll be his birthday, and I've been pre-parin' a bit of a surprise for him. I just thought I'd make this his last voyage to sea. I've had a new sign painted for the old mill—it reads "Dennison and Fairweather," and the first sight that catches his eye on reachin' home, 'll be his name and mine, as business partners. What d'ye think of it?

CHRYSTAL. [*Who has been eagerly drinking in every word, which she must be careful not to let him see, turns to him with tears in her eyes.*] Oh! Terry, how good—how gener-ous—how like—*you*—*only* you—

TERRY. But that's not all.

CHRYSTAL. No?

TERRY. No—suppose we were to just stagger him with another surprise—

CHRYSTAL. What other surprise? [*She is almost frantic now with eagerness to know, half imagining her hopes and his thoughts are one.*]

TERRY. Why—a sort of matrimonial birthday—a weddin' atween—

CHRYSTAL. Yes— [*Eagerly.*] Yes—between—whom?

TERRY. Can't you tell?

CHRYSTAL. [*Pretending to be puzzled.*] No—no—

TERRY. Why, Chrystal—don't you know—haven't ye seen—that I—

CHRYSTAL. [*Chilled—immovable.*] Well!

TERRY. I—I—love you. [*Music.*]

CHRYSTAL. [*With a smothered cry.*] Love me? [*Slight pause, then as if comprehending,*] Love me—why of course you do. [*Laughs half hysterically.*]

TERRY. Understand me—not as a friend—not as a brother—as a husband—

CHRYSTAL. [*With a cry.*] Husband! [*Turns her face slowly from him without moving her body, speaks dreamily.*]

TERRY. [*Approaches her, takes her hand, turns her towards him.*] Answer me—you will be my wife—won't you? Think how happy the news'll make Ned when he returns.

CHRYSTAL. [*Aside. Stifling her sobs.*] Happy—Ned happy —ah!

TERRY. Still silent! [*He releases her hand and turns up stage; at the same moment* CHRYSTAL *with a suppressed cry, turns as if to call him back; simultaneously he turns and comes to her. As he speaks, he nervously crushes his hat between his hands.*] Forgive me, Chrystal—I'm only a rough, grizzly beary sort of a fellow at best—I don't know how to talk to a girl like you, don't know how to tell her what I think or feel, yet I must say suthin'—I can't help myself. I swear, I can't help myself. Look here—if you touch me, big and strong as I am, I tremble all over just like a bush on a windy day—if you speak to me, I tingle with pleasure. I'm only happy when I'm near you—I love you, Chrystal, oh, how I love you—I have loved you ever since you were a little child —no bigger than that—when I used to carry you in my arms along the beach, your little sunburned face pressed close to mine, and your arms clasped fast about my neck. But for the last five years you've been pretty much all my life. Oh, Chrystal, if I could only make you understand— [*She starts and gives a low cry.*] There now I've frightened you—I was wrong to ask you to speak—don't speak, don't answer, only hold out your hand, as a token. [CHRYSTAL *is half turned from him, kissing Ned's picture and sobbing over it; she slowly extends her hand to* TERRY *without looking at him; he seizes it and covers it with kisses.*]

TERRY. God bless you—my own little wife.

CHRYSTAL. [*With a passionate burst of tears, throws herself on the rock left, and unconsciously drops the picture.*] Forgive me, Ned—forgive me—

TERRY. [*Turns away to the right.*] Owen was right—she does love me. [*He turns to embrace her. At that instant a distant gun sounds off right.* TERRY *starts.*] A signal of distress!

[*He dashes up the cliff, left, and gazes out to sea. The storm increases, and the scene grows darker and darker.*]

CHRYSTAL. [*Following him.*] What is it?

TERRY. A vessel drifting headlong on the rocks! Quick— [*Thunder and lightning; the storm grows heavier.*]

CHRYSTAL. The station, the rocket, the life-line—quick! [*There is a rush of wind, the rain begins to fall. The gun goes off again, there is the flash of a blue signal light.*]

TERRY. Yes, quick! [CHRYSTAL *runs off, left. The storm increases, the signal lights flash more frequently.*] Yes, Owen was right. [*There is a tremendous crash.*] She's struck upon the reef! [*He rushes down to pick up his coat, and sees the picture* CHRYSTAL *dropped. He picks it up and examines it curiously.*] What's this? A picture? Chrystal must have dropped it. Can it be mine? O' course it is, the one Owen spoke of— [*There is a vivid flash of lightning.*] My God, it's Ned! Can it be that she loves him? [*There is another lightning flash.*] Yes—here are the two locks of hair— [*Lightning flash.*] One his, the other hers. [*He staggers.*] Oh! I see it all! Duty has impelled her to sacrifice herself to me—while all the time her heart was Ned's. [*Enter down left, a group of wreckers, and men and women mill-workers, wearing rubber coats and sou'westers, and carrying torches. They stand looking anxiously out to sea.*]

[*At the same time* OWEN *and* CHRYSTAL *appear at the top of the incline on the left.* OWEN *adjusts the life-saving apparatus.*]

OWEN. [*Peering through a spyglass.*] She's a bark, but I can't exactly make her out—

CHRYSTAL. Can you see her name, Owen?

OWEN. Bide a bit— [*There is a tremendous flash.*] My God —the "Nantucket"—

CHRYSTAL. [*With a shriek.*] The "Nantucket"—Ned's ship! Lost—lost! [*Half faints.*]

OWEN. [*Up at the cannon.*] Now, Terry, all's ready.

TERRY. [*He is dazed and hesitates.*] If I should miss—

OWEN. Why man—Terry, there's no time to lose! Come— quick!—come—

CHRYSTAL. Terry—quick for my sake— [*At the sound of her voice, he starts, rushes up the cliff, aims and fires the rocket. There is a tense pause, then a faint cheer is heard from the wrecked ship, off right. The rain descends in torrents. All the men and women standing on the beach raise their hands as if in prayer.*]

[TERRY *clutches at his throat as if choking.*]

TERRY. Thank God—thank God—

QUICK CURTAIN

SECOND PICTURE: *The bark can be seen floating in the distance a complete wreck. The men on the shore are hauling in the life-line.* TERRY *stands down left; he seems hardly aware of what is passing.* NED, *a handsome young sailor, stands centre, holding* CHRYSTAL *in his arms.* OWEN *stands right of* NED *with his hand on* NED's *shoulder. Everybody is shouting.*]

CURTAIN

ACT SECOND

"The Mill"

The *interior of* TERRY DENNISON'S *mill.*

The next morning.

SCENE: *An old-fashioned grist mill in full operation. There is a large open window centre, through which is seen the mill wheel, forced into rapid motion by a stream of real water. Beyond is a view of picturesque country. Beneath the window is a bench. A door on the right leads to the dwelling house, and another on the left leads out of doors. There is a rough chair left centre. Against the wall down right is an old-fashioned high desk; on it are writing materials and several ledgers. There is a high stool in front of the desk. A large heap of bags, filled with grain and flour and neatly piled, lies in the centre of the stage. Several smaller heaps are scattered about the scene. The floor is covered with white flour.*

At the rise of the curtain the scene is filled with movement and activity, and there is an atmosphere of noise and bustle. Several mill hands, dressed in white suits and paper hats are hurrying about, sorting and piling the bags of flour under the direction of the FOREMAN. *Others are carrying bags outside through the door on the left, to be carted away. A* CLERK *is at work on a ledger at the desk on the right.*

The noise of the mill wheel as it turns, and the rushing of the water, mingle with the voices of the men, who are singing the same song as in the opening of Act First. During the action the noise becomes subdued, and the song gradually dies away.

UNCLE DAVY *is busily engaged in superintending everything about the mill. He is a spry, wiry old man of seventy, fussy and mildly irascible in manner. He wears a white suit, and spectacles, and his face, hands and clothes are covered with flour. He runs from one man to another, examining their work and ordering them around. The mill hands take his interference good-naturedly. Finally he sinks on a pile of grain bags, left, completely exhausted.*

UNCLE DAVY. [*Wiping the perspiration from his forehead.*] Phew! [*Then, as though he were very tired and had done a great deal of work.*] We're up to our eyes in business. Phew! It's always the way; whenever we get taken like this, I has always to give the lads a hand, 'cause why? 'Cause, [*With pride.*] if I wasn't here, nothin' *would* be done. They're good lads, but they're lazy, lazy. Look at 'em now. [*Rises and looks towards the men.*] Ain't that laziness? They're doin' too much work, I won't stand it. [*Sits down again.*] I won't stand it! They ought to stop when I do and— [*Rises*] then commence again when I do, 'cause why? 'Cause they can't do anythin' unless I'm over them, and then I has to do it all myself.

FOREMAN. [*Coming down to him.*] What's the matter, Uncle Davy?

UNCLE DAVY. I suppose they'll tell Terry they've done all the work and I've done nothin'.

FOREMAN. [*Soothingly.*] What? I'd like to hear 'em. Why Uncle Davy, we couldn't get on without you—

UNCLE DAVY. I do all the work, don't I?

FOREMAN. [*Humoring him.*] Of course you do!

UNCLE DAVY. [*Shaking hands with the* FOREMAN, *chuckling and half dancing about, very much delighted.*] I knowed it, I knowed it! And if I had to work my fingers to the bone, I'd get the order filled. [*All the men laugh.*] What ye laughin' about? Go about your work. [*To the* FOREMAN,] What did I tell you? Lazy, lazy, every one of 'em! [*Bells in the distance ring for the hour of noon. The* FOREMAN *and all the mill hands stop their work and leave the scene.* TERRY *enters*

*left; he, like the others, wears a white miller's suit. He is very
pale and careworn. He goes down right and leans on the desk.*

UNCLE DAVY *watches him anxiously.*] I wonder what's the
matter with Terry? [TERRY *after an effort to shake off his
depression, covers his face with his hands.* UNCLE DAVY *after
looking at* TERRY *uneasily, goes to him and lays his hand on
his shoulder.*] Why, Terry, my dear boy—

TERRY. [*Abruptly turning away to conceal his emotion.*]
Don't speak to me!

UNCLE DAVY. [*Hurt.*] Eh!

TERRY. [*Turning to him kindly.*] Forgive me, Dad, if I'm a
trifle out of—of [*Laughing*] temper, but—

UNCLE DAVY. [*Shaking his head.*] You're not yourself.
[*Trembling.*] If anything was to happen to—to my Terry—

TERRY. [*Quickly putting his arm around* UNCLE DAVY'S *neck,
gives him a rough hug, and, throwing off his despondency,
laughs heartily as he brings him centre.*] That's just the way
with you, Dad, if I'm a bit pale or a trifle annoyed, you think
directly, Heaven bless you! that I'm going to die! [*He gives
another hearty laugh, in which* UNCLE DAVY *joins.*]

UNCLE DAVY. I know, but I can't help it. [*Laughing.*] Seventy
years of age and just as strong and as hearty as I were fifty
summers back, and why? Why? [*Patting* TERRY.] 'Cause my
boy—God bless him—God bless .him! [*Wiping his eyes*]
treats his old dad like a king. [*Trembling.*] 'And, if anything
were to happen to you, Terry—you know what would be the
result. For without your smiles and cheerin' words—your
poor old dad [*With pride*] with all his strength and all his
fortitude—would be as helpless as an infant. [*Laughing.*]
But I know what's the matter.

TERRY. [*Starting.*] You know?

UNCLE DAVY. [*Laughing.*] Yes, you hain't had your pipe!
You're never right till you've had your pipe. [*Chuckles.*]

TERRY. [*Relieved, humoring him.*] No more I am, Dad.

UNCLE DAVY. [*Laughing.*] O' course yer not—I'll just go and get it for you.

TERRY. No, ye shan't nuther.

UNCLE DAVY. Yes, I will tuther.

[UNCLE DAVY *crosses up, left centre, and gets his hat which he has left on the bench beneath the window. He puts it on, turns, looks at* TERRY *who has crossed to upper left, laughs and cries, goes to the door, right, turns again, laughs heartily and goes out.* TERRY *watches him off, sighs, sinks his head on his breast, puts his hands in his pockets, and goes off slowly through the door on the left. As* TERRY *goes off* CHRYSTAL *and* NED *are heard laughing, off right. Then* CHRYSTAL *comes quickly on from the right, as if she were running away, and* NED *were trying to catch her. She is followed by* NED; *both are laughing. When they are well down stage, they pause.* NED *makes a movement towards* CHRYSTAL. *He is about to take her in his arms when* UNCLE DAVY *enters through the door, right, puffing on* TERRY'S *pipe.* CHRYSTAL, *confused, moves towards the left.* NED, *with a cough, looks up at the ceiling.*]

UNCLE DAVY. [*Looking at them, aside.*] They've been at it. [*He laughs knowingly, looks around, misses* TERRY.] Well, I declare if Terry hasn't gone and forgot his pipe. [*He sits on the bags, centre, puffing on his pipe.*]

CHRYSTAL. [*Anxiously.*] Going, Uncle?

UNCLE DAVY. Yes! [*He does not move;* NED *and* CHRYSTAL *look at each other in dismay.*]

NED. [*Laughing aside.*] Oh, yes, he's going!

CHRYSTAL. Make haste, Uncle, make haste.

UNCLE DAVY. Well, I'm goin' as fast as I can. My hat, [*Rising and looking around*] wherever is my hat? [*He begins leisurely hunting for his hat.* NED *and* CHRYSTAL, *concealing their impatience, help him. After a moment,* NED *looks up and sees the hat on* UNCLE DAVY'S *head.*]

NED. [*Laughing.*] Why, it's on your head, Uncle Davy!

UNCLE DAVY. On my head? [*Feels.*] So it is. [*He joins in their laugh. They push him gently towards the door, right.*]

CHRYSTAL *and* NED. Now make haste, Uncle.

UNCLE DAVY. [*Aside.*] I wonder why they're in such a hurry to get ride of me?

[*As* CHRYSTAL *and* NED *are pushing* UNCLE DAVY *off,* AUNT BETSEY *suddenly appears at the door right and seizes him. She is a buxom woman of middle age, prim and old-maidish. She wears spectacles and old-fashioned side curls.*]

AUNT BETSEY. [*Severely.*] Davy, why don't you come to dinner? [*Turning to the others.*] Come, Ned, Chrystal, call Terry. Hurry up, or else it'll sp'il. [*She drags off* UNCLE DAVY.]

NED. All right, Auntie, we'll be right down. [*When they are off, he runs to* CHRYSTAL *and embraces and kisses her.*]

CHRYSTAL. [*Very happy.*] Dear, dear Ned!

NED. But where's Terry, eh, Chrystal? [CHRYSTAL *starts from his embrace.*] Lord bless his honest old heart, where is he?

CHRYSTAL. [*Aside.*] How shall I tell him?

NED. [*Taking her face between his hands.*] So I hold the soft, sweet face of my own little girl atween my hands at last! Yet it don't seem a whit sharper to my sight than when I've seen it leagues and leagues away, and almost fancied myself standing beside you in the church, your hand in mine, the parson— [*Suddenly sees* CHRYSTAL *standing stonily calm. He stops and looks at her.*] Why, how solemn you look, all of a sudden! Why Chrystal, wife!

CHRYSTAL. Wife! Ah! [*Placing her hand to her heart as if in pain.*]

NED. [*Not noticing her action.*] Well, I dare say that word does seem strange to you—it comes as natural to me as a shark after a dying man. My wife you'll be as soon as I can get hold of the license, and as for the ring, I bought it afore my last voyage, and I've worn it here ever since. [*He puts his arm about her waist, brings her forward and shows her the ring which he wears suspended by a ribbon around his neck. Music.*]

CHRYSTAL. [*Shuddering.*] Don't speak of that, Ned, don't speak of that!

NED. [*Laughing.*] Why, how can I help it when I'm thinking of it always, and—

CHRYSTAL. [*Almost overcome with emotion.*] Get me a chair, I can hardly stand. [NED *gets a chair for her, and during the following scene hovers about her.*] Give me your hand. [*He does so.*] Ned, believe this, that I love you! There's not a thought I have by day, there's not a dream I have by night, but the dream and the thought are of you, Ned.

NED. [*Cheerily.*] Of course, that's just exactly how you ought to feel. [CHRYSTAL *falls into the chair wearily, rests her head in her right hand and is lost in reverie, apparently forgetting* NED'S *presence.*] Why, what are you doing?

CHRYSTAL. [*Dreamily; speaking very slowly and listlessly.*] Looking back into the past, listening to the church bells as they toll for the poor folks dying all around, of the awful cholera plague. [*A pause.*] And all this time I am seeing a little orphan child staring in blank amazement, while her parents are being hurried into one coffin, to be as hurriedly buried in one common grave.

NED. [*Carried away by her manner.*] That child was you, Chrystal!

CHRYSTAL. [*Without moving.*] Wait, for I was just gazing on the dark eyes of a sailor lad, peeping through the window. The little child is all alone, for the neighbors are afraid to enter the place where the plague has set its awful seal. [*With deep feeling.*] But he came, God bless him! He came, and bade the child come to him, to be the care of his young life, the one object of his toil. [*Turning and looking slowly at* NED.] Ned, what was that lad's name?

NED. [*Warmly.*] Why, Terry Dennison, of course! [*He comes to her and she takes his hand and clings to it.*]

CHRYSTAL. [*In the same manner.*] And now, Ned, look back and tell me what you see.

NED. [*Cheerfully, scratching his head thoughtfully.*] I see a little bit of a motherless boy, in a little bit of a shirt, and a little bit of a tarpaulin breeches, piping his eyes out ashore for a father as never came back from the sea. And when he's nigh on to done up, there comes a lad—

CHRYSTAL. A lad with dark eyes!

NED. Yes—and he lays his hand on the boy's shoulder and he says: "What are you crying for, rascal? Think there ain't more than one being in the world? You come along with me," he says, "and if I can't be your father, I'll be your friend. And my home shall be your home, and the crust I earn you shall have a share on." The boy went home with him, and there found you sitting like an angel at the fireside. [*Turning and taking both her hands in his.*] You asked me and now I ask you—this sailor lad, what was his name?

CHRYSTAL. [*Brokenly.*] Terry Dennison.

NED. [*Warmly and buoyantly.*] Oh, Chrystal! If we could always make his life as happy and as contented as he has ours!

[*The music stops.*]

CHRYSTAL. [*Moved by his enthusiasm. Quickly.*] We can, Ned, we can, but only by doing what he himself has taught us—our duty.

NED. Aye, his very words. "Duty—steer by that," he said, "and 'twill guide your bark of life safely through the roughest sea."

CHRYSTAL. Yes, Ned, and that duty now compels a sacrifice.

NED. A sacrifice?

CHRYSTAL. [*With an effort.*] I—I—can never be your wife.

NED. [*Almost stunned.*] Chrystal!

CHRYSTAL. [*With a despairing cry.*] For Terry loves me!

NED. [*Dazed.*] Terry, Terry? Has he told you so?

CHRYSTAL. Yes. [*Bows her head.*]

NED. Say no more. Oh, Chrystal, have I come back only to hear you say— "Ned, I can never be your wife, because I am loved by another!"

CHRYSTAL. [*Going to him; with deep emotion.*] And that other, he who sheltered and protected us when we were friendless and alone, he whose big heart would break at the thought of losing me. Shall we blast the life of him who taught us how to live? Ned, I love you! [*He starts as if to take her in his arms, but she stops him.*] Oh, so well, that the decision shall rest with you. [*Sobbing.*]

NED. [*Joyfully.*] With me?

CHRSTAL. Yes, you must give Terry my answer. [*Enter* TERRY *through the door left. There is a pause, then she whispers to* NED.] Speak to him. [CHRYSTAL *goes to his desk, right, and picks up* NED'S *cap which is lying there. During the next scene, she fondles it and holds it tenderly against her breast.*]

[NED *looks sadly at* CHRYSTAL, *struggles with himself, recovers, goes to* TERRY *who is still standing left, and extends his hand heartily.*]

TERRY. [*With a glad cry is about to take it, then draws back.*] Wait, Ned, it don't seem to me as if I was quite fit to take you by the hand as yet. I've been wrestlin' with myself, heart and soul, and oh, what a fight it's been! But the good within me has conquered at last and so I came to tell you of my resolution—my— [*He almost breaks down. He crosses to* CHRYSTAL, *right.* NED *remains standing on the left.*] Chrystal, I told you the one secret of my life yesterday evenin', do you remember?

CHRYSTAL. [*Hesitating and looking at* NED.] Why, perfectly.

TERRY. [*Looks at her sadly, smiles slowly, takes the picture from his breast, and hands it to her.*] I found this on the beach after you'd gone.

CHRYSTAL. [*Places her hand quickly to her heart as if to find the picture there, starts, but quickly recovers. She watches both men; she is frightened, and laughs and cries at once.*] Have you never seen that before? [*Confused.*] Why, Terry. [*Pause.*] Husband! [*Laughs.*] You're not jealous, before marriage too? Look, Ned, look! Your picture, our hair entwined as our hearts are, as I hope our love shall ever be; the love of sister and brother.

TERRY. [*Starting down to her.*] Ned your brother? And Terry your husband! Oh, be sure, be careful! Don't crush the risin' joy in my heart. Speak you, Ned, you—

NED. [*Has a short struggle with himself, then quick as lightning he crosses to* TERRY, *forcing himself to laugh heartily.*] What, me marry Chrystal? Pshaw! I wouldn't marry her— no, not if she was shod with gold!

[CRYSTAL *presses and kisses* NED'S *hand as he turns towards her.*]

TERRY. [*Turning and grasping him by the hand and shaking it warmly.*] Oh, what a load you've taken off my mind!

NED. Of course, Terry, as a brother I always did love her, and always, always shall. And if I was to be shot for it the next minute, I can't help it, though she's to be your wife, giving her a brother's kiss. [*Kisses and embraces her.*]

TERRY. [*Dashing down his hat, gives a joyous shout.*] Tawdrey!

[TAWDREY, *a gawky, slatternly servant girl, enters right.*]

TERRY. [*To* TAWDREY.] Call the mill hands! Call the mill hands, quick! [TAWDREY *hurries off, left.* TERRY *calls excitedly,*] Owen! Aunt Betsey! [OWEN *enters left, and* AUNT BETSEY, *right. They are both surprised.* TERRY *crosses to the door, right.*] And Dad, wherever is Dad? [UNCLE DAVY *enters quickly, right.*] He's just in time! [*The mill hands, and* TAWDREY *enter left.* TERRY *faces them all.*] I'm goin' to be married!

ALL. [*Surprised and delighted.*] Married?

TERRY. So cheer for the new firm of Dennison and Fairweather! Cheer for my wife, Chrystal, my darlin' forever more, and cheer for me, the happiest man in all the world! [*They all give a rousing cheer.*]

NED. [*Aside.*] And may God help me, the most wretched!

[*There is a scene of general animation.* DAVY *shouts in* BETSEY'S *ear, she screams and faints in his arms.* TAWDREY *jumps on* OWEN'S *back, takes his hat and cheers. The mill hands then return to work, singing the same song as in the opening of the act.*]

CURTAIN

ACT THIRD

"THE BABY"

THE *living room of* TERRY'S *home.*

An evening in early spring, two years later.

SCENE: *A comfortable, cosy room, quaint and old-fashioned, half parlor, half dining room. There is a large, curtained window at the back, to the right of centre, through which can be seen the mill wheel, and, beyond it, a stretch of picturesque landscape, bathed in moonlight. The entrance to the room from out of doors is through a door at the back, to the left of centre. Between the door and the window stands a small worktable, on which is a lighted lamp.*

[NOTE: *This lamp must be practical.*]

A door at the lower left-hand side of the room leads to the kitchen. Above this door, against the left wall, is an old-fashioned piano. Doors at the upper and lower right-hand side of the stage lead to other rooms. [*All the doors have latches, not knobs.*] *Just above the fireplace, against the right wall, is a cupboard, holding some fine old china, a carving knife and fork, a sugar tongs, and table silver. In the centre of the stage, standing on a square of rag carpet, is a large dining table.*

[NOTE: *A hot supper, complete with tea, potatoes, and bread, and including a large pot of baked beans, a meat pie, and a large plate of buckwheat cakes, must be ready off stage down left for the supper scene later in the act. This scene must be very realistic.*]

At the rise of the curtain, CHRYSTAL *is seated at the piano, left, playing and singing.* AUNT BETSEY *is knitting at the worktable, up centre.* UNCLE DAVY *sits in the armchair near*

282

the fire, mending a small toy ship. TAWDREY, *with her hair done up in curl papers made out of newspaper, is seated on the footstool, with the* BABY *in her arms, keeping time to* CHRYSTAL'S *music. The* BABY *wears long skirts.*

AUNT BETSEY. Chrystal.

CHRYSTAL. [*Stopping her playing and turning towards* AUNT BETSEY.] Yes, Aunt.

AUNT BETSEY. Owen is comin' to supper to-night, isn't he?

CHRYSTAL. Yes, Aunt. Terry wants to show him Baby. You know Owen hasn't seen her since the day of her birth. He went away on a coasting voyage and only got back today. And Terry is so proud of Baby, he wants all creation to see her. How late they are!

AUNT BETSEY. Well, if they don't come soon, we'll not wait for them—I'm not goin' to have the supper sp'iled—

CHRYSTAL. Certainly not, Aunt. [*Resumes playing very softly.*]

AUNT BETSEY. David! [UNCLE DAVY *pays no attention. She speaks louder.*] David! [*Shouting at him.*] David!

UNCLE DAVY. Yes—

AUNT BETSEY. Take Baby—and let Tawdrey set the table.

UNCLE DAVY. But I—

AUNT BETSEY. Did you hear me?

UNCLE DAVY. Yes, I heard you—and wonder why I wouldn't hear you. You speak loud enough to be heard all over the house.

AUNT BETSEY. Then take Baby.

UNCLE DAVY. Here, Tawdrey.

TAWDREY. Yes 'um!

UNCLE DAVY. Bring Baby to Gran'dad.

[TAWDREY *hands the* BABY *to* UNCLE DAVY. *While he holds*

the BABY, *she shakes her curl papers in the child's face, play-ing with her.*]

TAWDREY. Ketchy! Ketchy! Ketchy!

UNCLE DAVY. Stop that!

TAWDREY. [*Repeating the business.*] Ketchy! Ketchy! Ketchy!

UNCLE DAVY. [*Remonstrating.*] Stop that I say, do you want to blind Baby?

TAWDREY. [*Continuing her game.*] Ketchy! Ketchy! Ketchy!

UNCLE DAVY. Go along into the kitchen where you belong. What are you doin' here in the parlor anyway? Perhaps you think you're an ornament, but you're not. [*She shuffles off lower left, with offended dignity.*] That girl has got my eve-nin' paper on her head. I suppose that when I want to read my paper, I've got to send for her head. [*To the* BABY.] Now my lady, I'm going to talk to you. [*He puts his finger in the* BABY'S *mouth. The* BABY *is supposed to bite it.*] Ouch! [*He is greatly excited and calls,*] Chrystal, come here!

CHRYSTAL. [*Alarmed.*] What is it, Uncle Davy? [*She runs to* UNCLE DAVY, *and kneels beside him looking anxiously at the* BABY.]

UNCLE DAVY. Baby's cut a tooth.

CHRYSTAL. [*Looks in the* BABY'S *mouth; and then laughs.*] Nonsense, she's only trying to cut one—bless her!

UNCLE DAVY. Well, she needn't try to cut it on me. Does she take me for a gum ring? [CHRYSTAL *goes back to the piano.* UNCLE DAVY *resumes talking to the* BABY.] Now my lady I want none o' your tricks. I haven't forgot the trick you played on me yesterday. [*He laughs; then he begins to play "patty cake" with the* BABY, *repeating as he does so,*]

> "Patty cake, patty cake, 'baker's man!
> Bake me a cake as fast as you can!
> Pat it and roll it and mark it with T
> And bake it in the oven for baby and me!"

[*He takes out his handkerchief.*] Let's play peek-a-boo. [*He plays peek-a-boo with the handkerchief. After that game is over, he sings, holding the* BABY *up in front of him, so she can see and reach his spectacles.*]

> "Ring a ring a rounder
> Daddy catch a flounder
> Hop scotch—hop scotch.
> Hurroo!"

[*The* BABY *takes his spectacles.*] Hello, there, what are ye tryin' to do, take the eyes out of your grandad's head? [*The* BABY *tries to put on the spectacles.*] Oh! you want to try 'em on, eh! [*He puts them on the* BABY, *and turns her face to the audience. Then he sings.*]

> "She was her grandad's jewel
> Baby mine, baby mine.
> She shall share her grandad's gruel
> Baby mine, baby mine.
> She's as lovely as a rose,
> From her head down to her toes,
> Oh! My gracious how she grows,
> Baby mine, baby mine.
> Oh! My gracious how she grows,
> Baby mine."

[*Laughs.*] Speakin' about your toes, reminds me I've not seen your toes lately. Let's have a look at 'em. [UNCLE DAVY *tries to find the* BABY's *feet, and cannot on account of her long skirts.*] Where in the name of common sense do you keep 'em? [*He finally finds the* BABY's *feet. They are encased in red socks.*] There they are. Why they're as red as a couple of boiled lobsters! Let's see you dance, will you dance for grandad? [*He puts the* BABY *down, so that her feet just touch the floor. Holding her clothes up so that her legs are free, he hums a lively jig, making the* BABY's *feet keep time to it. He laughs heartily.*] You're a great baby, a great baby— [*Tossing the child in the air and catching her again.*] Ketchy! Ketchy! Ketchy!

AUNT BETSEY. [*Still knitting at the worktable up centre.*] There—there—David—don't plague Baby.

UNCLE DAVY. [*Almost dropping the* BABY.] Who's a-plaguin' of her?

AUNT BETSEY. You are.

UNCLE DAVY. I aren't neither.

AUNT BETSEY. Look how you're holdin' of her—you hold her as if you never saw a baby before. [*She puts down her knitting, rises and crosses to* UNCLE DAVY.] Give her to me.

UNCLE DAVY. I shan't do it, you go and sit down.

AUNT BETSEY. Give me Baby, I say.

UNCLE DAVY. I tell you I won't do it.

AUNT BETSEY. [*Coaxingly to child.*] Come to its auntie, dear! Come to its auntie!

UNCLE DAVY. [*Mimicking her.*] No, it won't go to its auntie dear.

AUNT BETSEY. [*Peremptorily.*] David, give me that baby.

UNCLE DAVY. You go and sit down. What do you know about babies anyway?

AUNT BETSEY. Well I do declare— if I ever— [*She returns to her work in a huff.* UNCLE DAVY *laughs.*]

UNCLE DAVY. [*Calling.*] Tawdrey!

TAWDREY. [*Entering lower left.*] Yes 'um.

UNCLE DAVY. [*Giving the* BABY *to her.*] Take Baby into the kitchen and give her the yellow kitten to play with. Take care the kitten don't scratch her. [TAWDREY *takes the* BABY, *slings her over her shoulder, and shuffles towards the kitchen, down left.* UNCLE DAVY *calls to her in protest.*] Look how you're holdin' of her! [TAWDREY *pays no attention to him; she goes off down left with the* BABY. UNCLE DAVY *shakes his head in disapproval.*] It's astonishin' how some folks in this house do handle babies! [*He goes back to the armchair and resumes work on his boat.*]

[TERRY *and* OWEN *appear outside the window at back.* OWEN *points to* CHRYSTAL. TERRY *motions him to be quiet, climbs in the window, creeps behind* AUNT BETSEY, *and steals down towards* CHRYSTAL. *As he gets near her,* UNCLE DAVY *accidentally turns and sees him. He rises and is about to speak, but* TERRY *waves his arms wildly at him, motioning him to be silent and to sit down.* UNCLE DAVY *sinks back in his chair, dumbfounded, with his mouth wide open. During all this* OWEN *has started to climb in the window after* TERRY; *he is big and awkward, and falls into the room with a crash.* AUNT BETSEY, *who has been turning the lamp up and down as if gauging it, utters a scream, and turns it down, leaving the room in complete darkness, save for the moonlight shining in through the window. She drops to the floor and crawls under the centre table.* CHRYSTAL *gives an exclamation, and attempts to turn around, but quick as lightning,* TERRY *seizes her in his arms and puts his hands over her eyes. This is all done quickly and simultaneously.* AUNT BETSEY *peers from beneath the table,* CHRYSTAL *struggles with* TERRY, OWEN *sits cross-legged on a chair, centre, surveying the scene with a grin of satisfaction. There is a slight pause.*]

CHRYSTAL. [*Endeavoring to release herself.*] Let go! Who is it? Take your hands away!

AUNT BETSEY. We're all murdered!

OWEN. [*In a hoarse voice.*] Shiver my timbers—who's turned out the lights?

CHRYSTAL. [*Laughing.*] Ah, I know who it is. [*She turns up the lamp. At the same time* OWEN *and* TERRY *lift up the centre table and reveal* AUNT BETSEY, *hiding beneath it.*]

AUNT BETSEY. [*Frightened half out of her senses.*] Don't shoot! Don't shoot! Murder! Help! [*They all roar with laughter.* TERRY *kisses* CHRYSTAL *who boxes his ears. He runs behind* OWEN.]

CHRYSTAL. Terry—and Owen!

AUNT BETSEY. [*Recovering herself.*] The vagabonds! Well—I never!

OWEN *and* TERRY. Forgive us! Forgive us!

CHRYSTAL. You don't deserve it.

AUNT BETSEY. [*Getting up.*] Never. [TERRY *pushes the table back into place.*]

UNCLE DAVY. [*Getting up.*] Never—never—never—

CHRYSTAL. [*Shaking hands with* OWEN *and laughing.*] Why, Owen, how glad I am to see you back! Welcome, old friend, welcome! But next time please come in by the door! [*She crosses to* TERRY, *takes his coat and hat, and hangs them on a peg beside the door, upper right. Then, during the scene between* AUNT BETSEY, UNCLE DAVY, *and* OWEN, CHRYSTAL *pushes the armchair nearer the fire, and seats* TERRY *in it. She brings him his slippers which have been warming at the fire. He takes off his boots and puts on the slippers.* CHRYSTAL *places the boots beside the fire as if to dry. During this action they converse in dumb show.*]

AUNT BETSEY. [*Crossing to* OWEN, *and speaking very sternly.*] I've a good mind not to give you one mouthful of supper, you good-for-nothin'— [*Suddenly smiles at him affectionately.*] Owen, I'm glad to see you back! There— [*She extends her hand, which he shakes heartily; both are laughing.* AUNT BETSEY *turns away, takes off her spectacles and wipes her eyes, goes up to the worktable and busies herself, with putting away her knitting. As she goes,* OWEN *wipes his eyes too.*]

UNCLE DAVY. [*Crossing to* OWEN *and addressing him with comic severity.*] Owen—Owen—you grampus! You—you old salt sea shark! You whale! You hip-po-pot-*to*-mus! You rhi-no-sea-horse! [*During this tirade* UNCLE DAVY'S *voice increases in dramatic intensity, and he advances upon* OWEN *as if to demolish him.* OWEN *shows fear, and squares off, as if to defend himself.* UNCLE DAVY *suddenly breaks off, laughs, and says,*] I'm durned if I ain't glad to see you! There— [*He holds out his hand,* OWEN *grasps it, and they both laugh heartily.*] But the next time, please come inside and fall *out.* It'll be more convenient for the family, especially if they happen to be at tea. [UNCLE DAVY *goes to the fireplace, sits on the footstool below* TERRY, *and resumes work on his boat.* OWEN *also crosses to the fireplace and stands above* TERRY, *leaning on the mantelpiece.*]

TERRY. Well darn me for my know-nothin', empty skull, if I hain't forgot all about Baby!

OWEN. Bless my soul—so had I. And that's principally what brings me here.

TERRY. [*With playful anger.*] You piratical lubber! You hear him, Chrys? Shall I knock him down? [OWEN *laughs loudly.*]

CHRYSTAL. [*Laughing.*] Well, he's not very complimentary to the parents of the baby—I must say.

OWEN. I axes pardon, Mrs. Dennison, but babies is a novelty with me, which parents isn't—that's all. [*They all laugh.*]

CHRYSTAL. [*Crossing to the door down left, and calling.*] Tawdrey! Tawdrey!

[*While* CHRYSTAL *is speaking,* AUNT BETSEY *puts her knitting away in the cupboard, draws the curtains on the window, and proceeds to set the centre table for supper.*]

TAWDREY. [*Speaking off stage, left.*] Yes 'um.

CHRYSTAL. Bring Baby.

TAWDREY. [*As before.*] Yes 'um—comin' 'um—

[*During this,* OWEN *has got his eye on the piano, and crosses over to it.* TAWDREY *enters with the* BABY, *and gives her to* CHRYSTAL. *During the next scene,* TAWDREY *goes back and forth from the kitchen, helping* AUNT BETSEY *with the supper.*]

CHRYSTAL. [*Giving the* BABY *to* TERRY.] There, now, don't

make her cry. [*She busies herself helping* AUNT BETSEY *to set the table.*]

TERRY. [*Holding the* BABY *up proudly.*] Oh, no fear of squalls in this quarter. This is a fair weather baby.

[*By this time* OWEN *is seated at the piano, and he now breaks into a loud discordant strumming, that has no time or tune.* CHRYSTAL *and* AUNT BETSEY, *who are spreading the table-cloth, stop, and put their fingers to their ears.* UNCLE DAVY *drops his boat, crosses quickly to* OWEN, *and clasps him about the neck to silence him.* OWEN *wheels about on the piano stool, facing front, and laughing heartily, with his hands still in action, as if on the keyboard.* AUNT BETSEY *and* CHRYSTAL *resume their work. During all this,* TERRY *is playing with the* BABY, *and pays no attention to what is going on.*]

UNCLE DAVY. Owen! Owen! You'll put our pianner out o' tune.

OWEN. [*With childish delight.*] I say—Dad—that's the first one, I ever played on.

UNCLE DAVY. It ought to be the last.

OWEN. I didn't know I could play so well. I'll give you another tune. [*He turns and starts to play again;* UNCLE DAVY *stops him.*]

UNCLE DAVY. No! No! After supper, Owen! After supper! [*They both turn to cross the stage and see* TERRY, *who has placed the* BABY *"on horseback" on his foot, and is giving her a ride and singing a merry tune to her.* UNCLE DAVY *and* OWEN *are infected with the merriment of the scene, and break into a comedy dance. They dance across the stage to* TERRY, *while everyone laughs.*]

TERRY. [*Proudly, holding up the* BABY *for him to see.*] There, Owen, what d'ye think o' that 'ere?

[OWEN *stands with his hands on his knees, his face a broad grin, his eyes staring with delight;* UNCLE DAVY *is seated on the footstool, all smiles;* TERRY *is the proudest man in the*

*world; all three look as though there never had been such
a baby as this baby since the world began.*]

OWEN. A stunner, Terry, a stunner! Look! Look at it, laughing at me! I believe it knows me! Yes, I'm your Uncle Owen!
Ketchy! Ketchy! Ketchy! [*At each "Ketchy! Ketchy!
Ketchy!"* OWEN *makes a dig at the* BABY'S *ribs, and* TERRY
wards him off.]

TERRY. [*After* OWEN *has repeated this three times.*] Hold
on, Owen! You're too rough.

UNCLE DAVY. What d'ye want to do, Owen, break it?

OWEN. Stop a bit—I've brung it something. [*He takes out a
stick of candy.*] There, you young pirate.

TERRY *and* UNCLE DAVY. Oh! A stick of candy!

[*In showing the candy to the* BABY, OWEN *gets it near* UNCLE
DAVY, *who reaches over and bites off a piece of it.*]

OWEN. Avast there! That aren't for you. [*Laughs.*] It's for t'
other baby! [*The* BABY *takes the candy. They all laugh.*]
Smart baby, Terry! Hold on—it shall have its Uncle Owen's
watch. [*He takes out an enormous, old-fashioned silver watch
and gives it to the* BABY.]

TERRY. Oh, Dad, look, Uncle Owen's watch for Baby.

UNCLE DAVY. Here, give it this hammer. [*Offering his hammer to the* BABY.]

OWEN *and* TERRY. No! no! no!

[*They all laugh.*]

[NOTE: *All this business can be elaborated as the* BABY *gets
used to the stage and to the people. Whatever the* BABY *does
must be acted upon by the actors and taken advantage of, as
it is impossible to set down in so many lines just what the*
BABY *will or will not do, so watch out for the star's humor.*]

OWEN. [*Suddenly stops, his face changes, he looks around at*
CHRYSTAL, *then in a loud whisper to* TERRY, *he says,*] I say,
Terry, my memory is a leetle treacherous. How is the craft
rigged?

TERRY. [*Looks at* UNCLE DAVY, *puzzled.*] Rigged?

OWEN. Is it a bark—brig—ship—whaler or man o' war?

TERRY. What in the name of Davy Jones do you mean? [*He looks at* UNCLE DAVY, *who beckons, he leans over,* UNCLE DAVY *whispers in his ear.*] Oh! [*Then he says to* OWEN *with a loud laugh in which* UNCLE DAVY *joins.*] It's a girl—you lubber—a girl!

OWEN. [*Points to* CHRYSTAL.] Hush—it's all right, only I wanted to be sure, that's all. Say, Terry, let me hold her, won't you? [*He attempts to kiss her.*]

TERRY. No—no— [*He and* UNCLE DAVY *express horror at the idea.*] You don't know how to hold a baby, you never was a father.

UNCLE DAVY. [*Proudly, with an air of proprietorship.*] No —no—don't let him touch her! He'd drop her into the fire.

OWEN. Say, Terry, call her after me—call her the Owen, will you? Will you? Say— [*Delighted.*]

TERRY. Call her Owen? [*Laughing.*] Why how can I, you swab?

OWEN. [*Scratching his head.*] Oh, I forgot, no more you can't.

UNCLE DAVY. No—she ain't that kind of a baby.

OWEN. She's kind o' scuddin' under bare poles too, ain't she? Where's her hair?

TERRY. Gone to meet yours, I reckon, eh Owen? [*He laughs.* OWEN *ties his handkerchief over his bald head as if he had forgotten it and had been suddenly reminded of it.*] Chrystal, here's Owen makin' fun of your baby.

OWEN. No, I ain't nuther—I think it's just the sweetest baby I ever seen.

[*By this time* CHRYSTAL *and* AUNT BETSEY *have finished setting the table, and have placed the chairs around it.* TAWDREY

*has been coming and going, bringing food from the kitchen—
a large dish of hot meat pie, a dish of potatoes, tea, and bread
and butter.]*

CHRYSTAL. There—there! Come to supper. Owen, you sit
there.

*[She indicates his place which is at the lower right-hand
side of the table. They all take their seats.* TERRY, *holding the* BABY *on his knee, sits at the upper left-hand side,
next to* CHRYSTAL, *who is at the head of the table.* AUNT BETSEY *is seated on* CHRYSTAL'S *right.* UNCLE DAVY *sits left, next
to* TERRY, *and opposite* OWEN. *As soon as they are all seated,*
UNCLE DAVY *bows his head and they all do likewise.]*

UNCLE DAVY. My children, let us thank Him, that we are
still together, and, blessing Him for what His bounty has
placed before us, commit the absent to His care.

CHRYSTAL. *[After a slight pause; calling to* TAWDREY *who is
off stage.]* Tawdrey, bring in the bean pot!

TAWDREY. *[Speaking off stage.]* Yes 'um. *[She shuffles on
from the kitchen, left, with an enormous pot of beans. She
places the pot on the table, between* OWEN *and* UNCLE DAVY,
and goes off.]

TERRY. Now, Owen, help yourself, don't stand on ceremony.

OWEN. *[Rising.]* Thank ye, Terry, I'm at home here. I never
stand on ceremony here.

*[He helps himself to three large spoonfuls of pie; then he
sees the bean pot and takes three heaping spoonfuls of beans.
He sits down.* UNCLE DAVY *starts to help himself to beans;
the spoon strikes against the side of the pot with a hollow
sound.* UNCLE DAVY *looks into the pot, then, meaningly at*
OWEN'S *plate.* OWEN *is quite unconscious of this.* OWEN *takes
the pepper bottle from the castor, and helps himself liberally
to pepper, thumping the bottle hard as he does so. This causes*
UNCLE DAVY *to sneeze violently.* UNCLE DAVY *reaches for a
potato with his fork,* OWEN, *unintentionally takes the same*

one. UNCLE DAVY *reaches for another one, and again* OWEN *takes it. After this has happened a third time* UNCLE DAVY *looks at* OWEN, *who pays no attention.* UNCLE DAVY *picks up a potato with his fingers, as if to say "You'll not get this one," and places it at the side of his plate.* AUNT BETSEY *reaches over and takes it with her fork.* UNCLE DAVY *takes another potato, and places it on the other side of his plate, and is satisfied he has it safe. During all this,* CHRYSTAL *has been pouring the tea and passing bread and butter.*]

CHRYSTAL. How much sugar in your tea, Owen?

OWEN. No sugar, thank ye. I'm sweet enough.

CHRYSTAL. [*Passing the bread to him.*] A piece of bread, Owen.

OWEN. [*Taking a large piece from the top.*] Thank ye. [*He butters the bread with the carving knife, then he doubles it over; it opens, and he doubles it over again. It opens once more and this time he sticks the carving fork in it, pinning it together.*]

[TAWDREY *enters with a plate of very large buckwheat cakes; she places them on the table between* OWEN *and* UNCLE DAVY *and goes off left.*]

CHRYSTAL. Owen! Help to buckwheats, please.

OWEN. Yes'm. [*He rises, picks up two buckwheat cakes with his fingers, puts them on a plate, and passes the plate to* AUNT BETSEY. *He helps* CHRYSTAL, *and* TERRY *in the same way. Then* OWEN *picks up one cake, puts it on a plate, hesitates, looks at* UNCLE DAVY, *then hands the plate to him.* UNCLE DAVY *takes it, looks at it, and holds out the plate for more.* OWEN, *without noticing* UNCLE DAVY'S *action, takes a plate, helps himself to three buckwheat cakes, picks up the molasses jug, and pours molasses liberally over them.* UNCLE DAVY *holds out his plate for some molasses.* OWEN *licks the mouth of the jug.* UNCLE DAVY *is disgusted.*]

UNCLE DAVY. Stop! Stop! Bless me, I almost forgot Ned's

chair. [*He gets up and puts a chair at* NED's *place at the foot of the table.*] There, that's it.

OWEN. [*Surprised.*] Ned's chair?

TERRY. Yes, Dad's got a notion that some fine evening about suppertime Ned'll walk in, so he allus keeps his chair and plate ready for him. [CHRYSTAL *rises and goes to the window to conceal her emotion.*]

OWEN. He's been gone over two years now, hasn't he?

TERRY. Over two years.

OWEN. And you've never heard from him?

TERRY. Never.

OWEN. Sing'lar, ain't it? [CHRYSTAL *stifles a sob. They all turn and look at her.*]

OWEN. Why! What's the matter with Chrystal?

TERRY. [*Very gently.*] Hush! She can't help thinkin' of him —her brother Ned as she loved to call him. Owen, hold Baby, will you?

[TERRY *gives the* BABY *to* OWEN, *and goes up to* CHRYSTAL. OWEN, *who is delighted to get the* BABY, *takes her gently in his arms, swings her to and fro, as if in a hammock, and sings some old sailor song.* TERRY *gently brings* CHRYSTAL *back to the table.*]

TERRY. There, Owen, that'll do, give me Baby.

OWEN. Oh, no, leave her where she is—she's swingin' all nice and comfortable in her little hammock.

TERRY. [*Good-naturedly, but determined.*] Give her to me, I say! Here, Chrystal, make him give me that baby! She's my baby—and I want her—so give her here.

OWEN. [*As* TERRY *attempts to take the* BABY.] Oh, don't be mean, lend a fellow a baby, won't ye? [*As* TERRY *holds out his arms insistently.*] Oh, take your old baby! [TERRY *takes the* BABY *and goes back to his place at the table.*]

[*Sailors are heard in the distance, off right, singing "The Heaving of the Lead." The song grows louder as they approach, then dies away again. All the characters listen, eating silently.*]

TERRY. [*As the song dies away.*] What's that, I wonder?

OWEN. [*With his mouth full.*] Some ship's crew just dropped anchor I reckon.

UNCLE DAVY. If it should be Ned!

[CHRYSTAL *starts.* TERRY *gives* UNCLE DAVY *a warning look.*]

TERRY. That's just like you, Dad! Always talking about Ned —and him not within a thousand miles.

NED. [*Calling outside; as if from a distance.*] Hillio! Hillio! Aboard the Terry and Chrystal, ahoy!

[*At the sound of his voice, they all listen, then spring up with joy.*]

ALL. It's Ned!

[NED *runs past the window, from the right, and dashes on through the door at back. They all rush to greet him, crying excitedly.*] Ned!

NED. [*Embracing* CHRYSTAL *who is the first to meet him.*] Chrystal! Aunt Betsey! Terry! Owen! [*He embraces* AUNT BETSEY, *turns and clasps* TERRY *by the hand, then goes down stage to* OWEN *who greets him heartily.*]

UNCLE DAVY. [*Who has risen at* NED's *entrance, and now stands for a moment as if dazed and stunned.*] My God—my boy—alive! Alive! my boy—my boy! Thank God! Thank God! [*He bursts into tears, then laughs.*] Alive—I knowed it—I allus said as how he'd come back to supper. Sit—sit down—ye must be nigh on to starved. [NED *sits in the chair at the foot of the table. As soon as* NED *is seated, they all rush to wait on him, each one offering him something.* UNCLE DAVY *gets very excited, pushes and forces them all back.*] Don't touch him—don't touch him—let him alone. [*Very loud.*] Damn it, I say, let him alone!

OWEN. Hello—hello—mutiny!

UNCLE DAVY. Oh! I don't care a continental cuss—

AUNT BETSY. [*Shocked.*] David!

UNCLE DAVY. [*Thoroughly aroused, seizes the bean pot and brandishes it threateningly.*] Aunt Betsey, if you open ye mouth, I'll strangle ye with the bean pot; I tell ye I've kept this place for him over two years, and nobody shall wait on him but me.

TERRY. [*Soothing him.*] All right, Dad—no one *shall* wait on him. [*To* NED.] Ned—don't you eat a blessed mouthful 'cept what Dad gives you.

NED. [*With his mouth full.*] Not a blessed mouthful. [UNCLE DAVY *is satisfied. He helps* NED *to food.* CHRYSTAL *takes the* BABY *from* TERRY, *and comes over to* NED, *holding the child up for him to see.*]

CHRYSTAL. Ned, you haven't noticed Baby!

[NED *notices the* BABY *for the first time. He stops eating, turns his chair about, and gazes from one to the other, astonished.*]

NED. Baby! What baby? Whose baby? Aunt Betsey's?

AUNT BETSEY. [*Confused.*] Ned! [*She goes up to the window, indignant.*]

UNCLE DAVY. [*Aside to* NED, *digging him in the ribs.*] Ned —decency—decency. [UNCLE DAVY *goes up and brings* BETSEY *down to her seat.*] Aunt Betsey, come and sit down. The boy didn't mean nothin'. Besides, you may be happy yet.' [*Laughs.*]

CHRYSTAL. [*Hurt and pouting.*] Aunt Betsey's indeed—mine, of course.

NED. Yours! Well—who'd ever thought of your having a baby? Give it here. [*He takes the* BABY.] Let's have a look at it. Well, I do declare! Here is a surprise! I say, Chrystal, what is it?

OWEN. [*Laughing.*] Why, it's a girl, you lubber.

TERRY. I thought any fool would know that, Ned!

OWEN. [*Proudly.*] I knowed it the very first clatter.

NED. If it ain't the very image of you, Chrystal.

TERRY. No—no—me—me—

NED. [*Looking again.*] Yes, it's got your nose.

OWEN. And that's the only bad feetur on its face.

TERRY. [*Pretending to be angry, and threatening* OWEN *in fun.*] What?

NED. But she's got Chrystal's mouth—and so I'll kiss it. [*He does so.*] Ah, ha! my young lady, we shall have many a romp just as your mother and me used to have when she wasn't much bigger'n you are now. [*He looks kindly, yet sadly at* CHRYSTAL, *who drops her head unnoticed by the others. There is a loud knock at the door at back, left.*]

TERRY. Who can that be?

UNCLE DAVY. I'll bet it's that Smith's boy come to borry our axe again.

TERRY. Come in.

[MR. ELLINGHAM *enters. He is a gentlemanly elderly man. He wears an old-fashioned business suit.*]

ELLINGHAM. Pardon me, Mr. Dennison?

TERRY. Yes, sir. Step in.

ELLINGHAM. [*Coming down.*] Excuse me, but business compels me to intrude upon your little family circle.

TERRY. [*Rises, offers his seat to* ELLINGHAM.] Sit down.

ELLINGHAM. First permit me to introduce myself; I am Charles Ellingham, attorney for the house of Headway and Lynden, grain and flour merchants, Boston, as you may see by this letter. [*He gives* TERRY *a letter.*]

TERRY. [*Shaking hands.*] Glad to see you, sir. [*Indicating the others.*] These are my folks; father—aunt—old friend —wife and baby. [*They all rise and bow as* TERRY *introduces them.*] Quite a family party, won't you join us? [*He indicates a place at the table.*]

OWEN. Yes, sit down and have a bean.

ELLINGHAM. No, I thank you, but I will, with your permission, interrupt your meal a moment only.

TERRY. All right, sir—no hurry, sit down—

ELLINGHAM. Thank you. [*Does so.*]

TERRY. Now fire away.

ELLINGHAM. I regret to inform you, Mr. Dennison, that our firm is in a very crippled condition and unless it is able to call in all outstanding debts by this day week, it must close its doors; it holds your note for three thousand dollars, and I have called to ascertain your intentions regarding it.

TERRY. My intentions—why I never had but one intention, and that was to pay it.

ELLINGHAM. [*Rising, as if to go.*] Ah! I see—quite satisfactory. You have three days' grace, I will report all O. K. [*He starts to go.*]

TERRY. Stop—you can make a better report than that while you're at it.

ELLINGHAM. [*Smiling.*] How so, pray?

TERRY. Chrys, just bring me my pocketbook, will you?

CHRYSTAL. Yes, Terry. [*She goes off, lower right, and reenters after a moment with a pocketbook full of bank notes which she gives to* TERRY.]

TERRY. Have you the note?

ELLINGHAM. No, but I will give you a receipt annulling it and will mail you the cancelled note tomorrow.

TERRY. Pen and ink, Chrys. [CHRYSTAL *gets pen and ink*

from the small table up centre, and brings them down to
ELLINGHAM. *Then she goes down to* NED *and takes the* BABY
from him. ELLINGHAM *writes out a receipt and signs it.*
TERRY, *meanwhile, takes a roll of bank notes from the pocketbook and counts them.* ELLINGHAM *gives the receipt to* TERRY,
*who takes it, laughing heartily as he holds out the bank notes
to* ELLINGHAM.] And now, there's your money, and that, I
believe, makes a clean slate—all spic-and-span new notes of
the Traders' Bank of Boston, M-a-s-s.!

ELLINGHAM. [*Starting and looking at the notes.*] The Traders' Bank did you say? Why friend, you are surely joking
with me—the Traders' Bank failed at noon yesterday.

ALL. [*Stunned.*] Failed! [*They all rise except* NED, *who
squares his chair around so as to face* ELLINGHAM.]

ELLINGHAM. These notes are worthless.

TERRY. I'm ruined.

ALL. Ruined!

[UNCLE DAVY *staggers to the armchair right, and falls
heavily into it.* AUNT BETSEY *goes to him, and leans over the
chair, soothing him.* OWEN *stands transfixed,* NED *stares
blankly.* TERRY *sinks into* OWEN'S *chair. The notes and the
receipt drop from his hand to the table.* CHRYSTAL *crosses
to him quickly, kneels at his side, and places the* BABY *in his
arms, looking up at him pleadingly, as if to say "You still
have your wife and baby."* ELLINGHAM *takes his hat as if
to depart.*]

TERRY. [*Stopping him and holding out the receipt to him.*]
Take back your receipt, sir, every dollar I have in the world
is there. [*He points to the notes on the table.*]

[*Music.*]

CURTAIN

ACT FOURTH

"The Lane"

A LANE *near Whalers' Wharf.*

Several weeks later.

SCENE: *A picturesque, shady lane with a glimpse of the harbor in the distance, where a fleet of whaling vessels lies at anchor. To right and left, at the upper and lower ends of the lane, narrow footpaths wind off through the trees. Before the curtain rises, a chorus is heard singing "Hearts of Oak." The song is heard faintly at first, as though at a distance, gradually increasing in volume as the singers come nearer. When they are well into the second verse, the curtain goes up.*

At the rise of the curtain, a group of sailors, singing "Hearts of Oak" passes across the stage from right to left. They finish the song away in the distance.

As the song ends, NED *enters hastily from the right. He is greatly perturbed, and crosses the stage rapidly. When he reaches the centre,* CHRYSTAL'S *voice is heard off right.*

CHRYSTAL. [*Calling anxiously, from off stage, right; a sharp, breathless cry.*] Ned! Ned! [NED *pauses, takes one or two steps towards the left, then dashes down right, as though to make an exit.* CHRYSTAL *enters hurriedly, upper right, and sees* NED.]

CHRYSTAL. [*Calling peremptorily.*] Ned!

NED. [*Sullenly.*] Why have you followed me here? [*He turns his back on her.*]

CHRYSTAL. [*Starting centre.*] Because *I* believe it best to end what we have begun—believe that we should no longer deceive— [*He turns quickly and looks her straight in the face.*]

301

no longer lie, *lie* to ourselves. [*He hangs his head.*] That having opened the grave of the past, we should look boldly upon our buried love within. Oh, Ned, *you* were mad to ever have returned here. I, wicked to have so prayed—so watched for your coming. I might have known—I might have known.

NED. I was mad. [*With a passionate cry.*] I thought I could rejoice in Terry's happiness; fondle his child as if it were my own; but I cannot, Chrystal. I see you, and—

CHRYSTAL. [*Frightened.*] Hush— Hush!

NED. [*His passion increases.*] I love you, Chrystal—*love* you. I have struggled—have fought against it, because—

CHRYSTAL. Because—you—must not love me.

NED. [*Quickly.*] Must not love *you?* [*Music.*]

CHRYSTAL. Ned, listen to me, and I will tell you what I have scarcely dared breathe even to myself. I will tell you—because you love me, [*She looks steadily at him*] and I trust you. Ned, when I hear your step—I tremble all over—when you approach me, I feel the hot blood rush into my face— if you touch me—my pulse quickens—and when I pass your dear old room I can't keep back my tears. Sometimes I go to the lane—see—[*Looking around*] this very lane in which you first told me you loved me, and I sit down and live it all over again. Oh, [*As if in a dream.*] such a cold day it was, and yet we were so warm; such a snowy, frosty, wintry day, and yet I was so glad, [*Sobbing.*] so happy. I never knew how much I loved you until then, and then I knew, oh, in a moment—I knew, that in all the wide world, there could be no other man for me than Ned Fairweather. [*Pause.*] And yet I married—married Terry. [*He is greatly affected.*] And I love him. [*He starts as if jealous, facing her.*] But not in that way— [*Quickly.*] not in that way. I can give him my hand without trembling—can see him come and go without changing color—without my pulses beating faster—and he is my husband—the father of my child. [*She crosses down left, then turns and approaches him.*] Now you see *why* you must go away—why we must never meet again. You must not love me—you must give me up—

NED. [*Turning suddenly and fiercely.*] I cannot—I will not.

CHRYSTAL. [*Recoils with a frightened cry.*] Ned!

NED. [*Taking her in his arms.*] I say, you are mine—you belong to me—do you hear—to me—*and I will not give you up.*

CHRYSTAL. [*She continues to recoil before his passionate and determined advance.*] You frighten me.

NED. [*As before.*] What do I care for any other man?

CHRYSTAL. [*Terrified.*] Hush!

NED. There is no man on earth dares tear you from me again.

CHRYSTAL. Stop! Stop!

NED. I tell you I will not give you up. [*His manner now changes to one of low intensity.*] Chrystal! Do you remember the afternoon in the old mill when, although it was like *tearing* out my heart, I gave you up to him! You said it was our duty, our sacrifice, and we did it. And the portrait—*my* portrait which he found upon the beach—*you* told him was only a brother's gift to a sister. [*Very strong.*] Oh, that lie! That lie! Better the truth—the fearful truth at once, than to let him marry a girl whose whole love was given to his dearest friend. It was not a sacrifice—it was a *crime*. [*He crosses down right and then comes back to her.*]

CHRYSTAL. [*With sudden energy, facing him.*] Silence—I say—silence! I will not listen—you shall not say another word. [*Then, all her indignation melting into a deep and tender pity, she speaks very rapidly.*] Why, man—man—what would you have me do? [*Hysterically.*] Would you have me go to Terry Dennison and tell him that I loved you before I married him—that I— [*He turns as if divining what she would say.*] Yes! That I love you still! [*He turns away abashed.*] Speak! Tell me what to do! And out of my weakness I will pluck strength to cry out, "Terry! Husband —friend! Come to me—help me—save me from myself!"

NED. [*After a pause; he comes centre, and speaks very resignedly; he is broken and ashamed.*] Chrystal, forgive me. You have shown me the dangerous reef that I so nearly ran afoul of. I must about ship or we are wrecked forever. [*Reverently.*] Oh, how noble, how fine you are! But don't despise me—for if I can't command, I can at least obey, and I do, Chrystal—I do. I give you up,—a second time— I give you up—to him.

CHRYSTAL. [*Goes to him. Full of gentle affection and confidence.*] Brave—honest— [*Lays her hand on his shoulder.*] Ned! [*He turns slowly and sadly—looks half dazed upon her. She takes his hand and kisses it. At that instant the sailors singing "Hearts of Oak" are heard in the distance. They both listen;* NED *stands as if looking into the future.*]

CHRYSTAL. [*Following his gaze and in a second understanding his determination; in a horrified whisper.*] Oh!

NED. The sailors bound for a cruise with Captain Hearthaway. [*He crosses right.*]

CHRYSTAL. [*In terrified pleading.*] Not with them—not with them!

NED. Yes—with them. [*He turns and holds out his hand to her.*] Chrystal—come *home.* [*She takes his hand and they walk slowly down right.*[

CHRYSTAL. [*As he leads her off.*] It is right—it is just—it is holy. But—my heart—my life, go with you. [*They go off, lower right.*]

[*There is a pause, Then* TERRY *comes slowly on from the left. He is pale, haggard, older, and altogether changed from the light-hearted man of the previous acts. He staggers down right, as if to follow* NED *and* CHRYSTAL. *Then, unable to*

stand, he leans, overcome, against a tree, on the right. OWEN
GARROWAY *follows* TERRY *on, and stands left, as if thunder-
struck. The sailors' song dies away in the distance.*]

TERRY. My God! My God! My God!

OWEN. [*Takes one step towards him.*] Terry—Terry—

TERRY. [*Stops him.*] Hush! Owen—hush! Disturb not the
dead.

OWEN. The dead!

TERRY. Yes; for all the sunshine and brightness of my life
have passed away. I am no longer of this world—my soul
goes out for *them*. [*He gazes after* NED *and* CHRYSTAL.]
For them—and I am dead—dead—dead. [*Extending his
arms as if towards* NED *and* CHRYSTAL; *then letting them
fall heavily at his sides.*]

OWEN. Courage—man—courage.

TERRY. [*Raising his head.*] Why, I have no need of courage,
Owen, all the pain is gone. [*Endeavoring to recover his man-
hood.*] A strange calm has come over me, and lookin'—
[*Turning towards the sea*] towards the broad, blue sea—
I feel that I could—that I could— [*He tries to finish the
sentence, then gives way to his grief and weeps.*] Oh, Owen!
I can't—I can't—my heart is breakin'—

OWEN. I can't bear this, Terry. It's been all my fault, I
deserve a hundred on the bare back this 'ere blessed minute,
that's what I do. [*Wipes the tears from his eyes.*] I deserve for you to come to me and say, "Owen Garroway—
you're a damned scoundrel! Your I. O. U. was like yourself, false—to the core—and from this minute, we're stran-
gers."

TERRY. [*Gently.*] Your fault, Owen! Your fault, ah! No!
It's been mine I tell ye, mine all along; what right had I,
I'd like to know, to ever dream that a chick of a girl like
that, could love a great, rough bear like me? I tell you I
should 'a' knowed better—I should 'a' knowed better—

[*Pause.*] Did you hear them? How they'd suffered—the sacrifices they'd made—and all along o' their steerin' by that one word, I taught 'em when they were little children, a danglin' on my knees! And Ned—a-tearin' out his heart, givin' up his little girl-wife to me, and she, Chrystal the darlin'—comin' to me with a smile on her lips—comin' like a lamb to the slaughter, and I, coward and thief that I was, took her from him—blighted their young lives—wrecked their future—drove Ned from his home and broke my Chrystal's heart. Oh! What a villain I've been—what a villain I've been!

OWEN. Terry—be a man.

TERRY. A man! A man! Would a man have done what I have done? It's only within the past few minutes that I've seen myself in my true colors—seen myself—in all my selfishness and wickedness.

OWEN. [*Solemnly.*] All my blunder—all my mistake. My I. O. U. was out o' gear, that time—and I'll never risk another.

TERRY. [*After standing in a reverie, suddenly comes to a resolution.*] Yes, they must live for the livin'.

OWEN. What d'ye mean, Terry?

TERRY. That I must—go away—forever. That I must repay sacrifice for sacrifice—[*The song of the sailors is heard in the distance*] heart for heart—tear for tear.

OWEN. Where will you go, Terry?

TERRY. [*Quietly but firmly; pointing in the direction of the song.*] With them.

OWEN. The Arctics!

TERRY. Yes, the Arctics; there I may get the swash out of my ears, the burnin' sun out of my brain—there I may lay my head down, not on the mother earth—but upon the lifeless ice—that so resembles my end—my end.

OWEN. [*Shaking his head and murmuring to himself, heart-broken.*] Poor Terry!

TERRY. [*Taking* OWEN's *hand between both of his.*] And Owen—you must teach them to forget me. [OWEN *makes a movement as if to remonstrate;* TERRY *stops him.*] Not one word, to alter or stay my course—it is the only thing for me to do.

OWEN. [*With bowed head.*] So be it.

TERRY. And now, Owen, I want you to go to the mill—[*He endeavors to stifle his tears but cannot*]—break the news gently, gently—you—know—for I dare not. Pack me up a few things—you know what—say good-bye to the old folks. Don't let them come here—I couldn't bear the sight of their white faces. And then, Owen, take my little baby in your arms—and kiss her for me, and bring me a tiny lock of her hair. Then find Chrystal and Ned and send them here to me. But not one word to let 'em know that they were overheard, they must never know that—you understand?

OWEN. I understand. [*He crosses down right:*]

TERRY. Then—go— [OWEN *goes slowly off, lower right.* TERRY *turns down left. There is a pause.*] And now let me go out of the world, out of the world—that they may be happy— that they may be united. Yes, out of the world—for I shall never come back into it again. [TERRY *turns up stage and starts to go off, upper left. At the same time* NED, *carrying his sailor's dunnage, enters, upper right, and the two come face to face.*]

NED. [*Starting back.*] Terry!

TERRY. [*Stepping forward and offering his hand with a frank, open smile. There is deep silence for a moment, as they stand with their hands clasped, looking into each other's eyes as if to say, "I have wronged you, but, I would lay down my life to serve you."*] Where are you steerin', lad?

NED. To the Company's office. [*The scene is bathed in the rosy glow of sunset.*]

TERRY. Have you seen Owen?

NED. No!

TERRY. [*With a sigh of relief.*] So much the better, so much the better. Ned—I'm goin'—away—

NED. Away! Where?

TERRY. To the Arctics.

NED. [*Dumbfounded.*] The Arctics!

TERRY. Yes, you see that affair of the bank well-nigh ruined me, and I see no way out o' it but a venture.

NED. [*Completely astonished and taken aback.*] But—Terry —what need for you to go? There's me as—

TERRY. Duty! That's the word I always steered by—and it teaches me never to take from another the bread I can earn myself. [*He turns away.*]

NED. [*Trembling with emotion and surprise.*] In taking such quick sailing orders, have you thought of your wife and child?

TERRY. [*Turning and looking at him kindly.*] Thought of them—ah, yes. There's the only sting—the thought of partin' with my wife and child. [*A gun is fired from the fleet.*]

NED. [*Starts at the sound of the gun, then says with energy.*] No—no—*you* must not. I will go!

TERRY. Ned—give me your two hands. [*He does so with head bowed.*] Look at me— [*He does so.*] Now hear me well— by the memory of the past—I charge you to remain home, —to be a protector to my Chrystal, a father to my child!

[NED *tries to avoid his look. The gun is fired once more.*]

NED. [*Hesitating.*] I—I—

TERRY. [*With all his strength.*] Man to man—grasp to grasp —promise it!

NED. [*Slowly.*] I promise—

TERRY. [*With a grateful grasp.*] Good! And now another— [NED *looks into his face imploringly and wonderingly, as if to say, "What more can you ask?"*] If anything should happen to the fleet—if anything should happen to me— [NED *starts.*] We don't know what may happen, we can only guard against the worst. So if it should be, that after waitin' five years, there comes no word or token from me, I want you to make *Chrystal your wife.*

NED. Oh! Terry—not that—not that—

TERRY. [*Very calm.*] Answer me!

NED. But—

TERRY. Answer me!

NED. [*In a low voice.*] Yes! [*The gun is heard again, sounding almost like a funeral knell and at the same moment* CHRYSTAL *is heard off right, calling.*]

CHRYSTAL. [*Calling off right, in an agonized voice.*] Terry —Terry!

TERRY. [*To* NED.] Hush! Not one word!

[CHRYSTAL *enters lower right, pale and haggard, her hair streaming in the wind. She is followed by* OWEN.]

CHRYSTAL. [*Flinging herself passionately in* TERRY'S *arms, and clinging to his neck.*] Oh! Terry—Terry—it can't be true—you will not leave me—alone!

TERRY. [*Tenderly.*] Hush, my darlin', I'm goin' for your sake and for the sake of—our child. Besides, you will not be alone. See, here's Ned. Ned will be with you. [*He releases her and goes up to* OWEN, *right.*]

CHRYSTAL. [*After a quick glance from one to the other, aside to* NED.] Have you told him?

NED. Nothing—he knows nothing.

CHRYSTAL. Then he shall, for I will tell him everything. [*She starts towards* TERRY.]

NED. [*Stopping her.*] And drive him away forever?

CHRYSTAL. God pity me—God pity me! [*She stands perfectly motionless. At the same moment, the last gun is fired from the fleet. A group of sailors, with their dunnage, crosses the stage at back, from right to left.*]

OWEN. The last gun!

CHRYSTAL. [*Rushing to* TERRY *and clinging to him; frantically pleading.*] Oh, Terry! Terry! Don't go—please don't go!

TERRY. Courage, Chrystal, courage! I'm not leavin' you alone. You have our child and see—here is Ned who will love and guard you always. [CHRYSTAL *with a cry of revulsion, turns from* NED, *and throws herself on* TERRY'S *breast.*]

CHRYSTAL. No, no, Terry! Don't leave me. Don't go! [TERRY *drags her arms from about his neck, kisses* CHRYSTAL *passionately and passes her over to* NED.]

TERRY. Take her, Ned, take her! [CHRYSTAL *faints in* NED'S *arms.* TERRY *grasps* NED'S *hand.*] And now, Ned, I charge you, as God is our witness—keep your word to me!

NED. I will.

TERRY. Good-bye! God bless you both! [*He rushes to* OWEN *and takes his hand.*]

OWEN. [*Whispering hastily.*] The lock of hair!

TERRY. [*Clutching it in his hands.*] Hush!

CURTAIN

ACT FIFTH

"The Wedding"

A country *churchyard.*

Six years later. A morning in early summer.

SCENE: *A quaint old country churchyard. On the right stands the church, covered with vines, and with flowers and shrubs growing about the steps. The yard contains a number of tombstones, and at left centre stands a large monument with a high, wide base, on which is carved the following:*

Sacred to the Memory
of
TERRY   DENNISON
Erected by
CHRYSTAL
and
NED

A very large weeping willow overhangs this stone.
The main entrance to the churchyard is at the upper left-hand side of the stage, and beyond can be seen a view of picturesque country. There is a walk or path leading off through the trees at left first entrance, and another one at left second entrance.
At the rise of the curtain, birds are singing, and the church bells are ringing; this continues at intervals during the act. The choir can be heard singing a wedding hymn inside the church, to the accompaniment of the organ.
Enter along the path at left first entrance, NED *and* CHRYSTAL, *hand in hand.* CHRYSTAL *is dressed quietly, but becomingly, as if for a second wedding, in a silk dress of some light color. She is pale and calm.*

NED. Do you hear, Chrystal? Our wedding bells! Oh! I don't believe there's such a happy time in the world as when those bells are ringing. Do you, Chrystal? [*She drops her head and does not answer.*]

[LITTLE CHRYSTAL *runs on from the left second entrance. She is a lovely, golden-haired little girl, about six years old, the embodiment of happy, joyous childhood. She wears a simple but very dainty little white dress, and carries a small bunch of flowers. She runs directly to her mother.*]

LITTLE CHRYSTAL. Oh, Mama! Mama!

CHRYSTAL. [*Turns and kneels beside her tenderly.*] Well, darling?

LITTLE CHRYSTAL. Look! [*She holds out the flowers.*] Such pretty flowers, I found them growing over there. [*Pointing off left.*] Smell them. [*She crosses to* NED *and offers the flowers as he stoops to smell them.*] Ain't they nice?

NED. [*With a smile.*] Yes, very.

LITTLE CHRYSTAL. [*Crossing to her mother.*] You smell, Mama. [CHRYSTAL *does so.*] What do you call them?

CHRYSTAL. Roses and forget-me-nots.

LITTLE CHRYSTAL. [*With delight, about to run away.*] Oh, then I'll get some more and put them there on Papa's grave. [*Pointing to the monument.* CHRYSTAL *turns away affected.* NED *turns halfway up stage.*] Good-bye! [*Kissing her hands to both,* LITTLE CHRYSTAL *runs to the entrance, left, then runs immediately back almost out of breath.*] Oh! I'd almost forgot, don't let Uncle Ned be my new papa till I come back, will you, Mama? 'Cause I never had a real papa, and I want to see how they make 'em. Good-bye, I'll run all the way. [CHRYSTAL *has turned away, very much affected.*] Kiss me, Mama! [CHRYSTAL *turns and lays her hands upon the child's head and looks steadily into her face. She does not speak, but weeps silently; the child sees it.*] Oh, Mama, have I been naughty?

CHRYSTAL. No, my child, no.

LITTLE CHRYSTAL. Then why don't you kiss me?

CHRYSTAL. [*Kissing her.*] There, run and pick your flowers, run and pick your flowers.

LITTLE CHRYSTAL. [*Kissing her.*] I'm so glad! [*Running off left second entrance.*] I wouldn't like to be naughty to-day, I'll soon be back, Mama. [*She goes off.*]

NED. [*Coming down right.*] Chrystal! [CHRYSTAL *turns her face towards him. He holds out his hand.*] Come!

CHRYSTAL. [*Does not take his hand, but looks steadily at him.*] Is this right?

NED. Chrystal, when Terry left you to my care, I never spoke a word or made a sign; at last came the black news. [*Both are visibly affected.*] Still I never opened my lips. Five years passed, then when I approached you I seemed to hurt you, and I waited another year. At last you consented. If you think it right to marry me—here's my hand. But if you think it is not—why—I'll just step in there and tell 'em, for I'd rather a thousand times break my promise to the dead— [*Points to the monument*] than ever you should feel regret that you became my wife. What is it to be? [*There is a slight pause.*] I want to make you happy, Chrystal. And then, remember, it is Terry's wish. Have you forgotten his parting words? "When I am gone, Ned will care for you and love you. I leave you and our child to him."

[CHRYSTAL *stands a moment in thought, then calmly gives* NED *her hand. He puts his arm about her waist and leads her slowly into the church.*]

[*A pause. Music. Then* TERRY *enters through the churchyard gate, upper left. His eyes are sightless, his hair is perfectly white, his face haggard. He wears a sailor's suit, old and worn, and a faded bandanna is wound about his head. He walks with slow, uncertain gait, feeling his way with a stick. When he is well down stage he pauses, and stands perfectly still, leaning heavily on his stick.*]

TERRY. [*In a quiet, flat, colorless voice; the voice of a blind man.*] This must be the churchyard and there should stand the old church. How sweet the air is, how fragrant the flowers— [*As if catching a long breath*] and how bright the glorious sun seems to shine. What a strange feelin' of peace; can it be that the wish of my heart is about to be answered? It must be—it is. For six long years I have hoped for, prayed for this hour—prayed that I might once again stand in their presence, and listen to the sound of their voices. Not to be known—not to speak—not to move—only to listen— [*With a peaceful smile.*] And for six years I have been longin' for one clasp of my baby's arms. Oh! My Father, can this be? Thou blessed Saviour Who hath guided the sightless, shattered wanderer's footsteps thus far in safety—grant *this—only this*—I ask no more in this world or the next. Amen.

[*A pause. He drops his head. After a moment the organ is heard playing the prelude to the chant which is then taken up by the choir. At the sound* TERRY *turns, lifts his head slowly towards the church, and listens with rapt attention. As it proceeds he walks in the direction of the sound, sinking upon the church steps, as it finishes.*] The weddin' service— the same they sang the day I led poor Chrystal to this very altar. [*The organ continues playing after the chant is sung.*] Happiness and endless joy attend your wedded steps through life, whoever you may be. [*The organ stops.* LITTLE CHRYSTAL *enters left, running, her apron filled with flowers; she goes directly towards the monument, sees* TERRY *and stops suddenly, half frightened at his appearance.*]

LITTLE CHRYSTAL. Oh! What a poor old man! [*He raises his head and turns it towards her at the sound of her voice. She continues, curiously.*] Are you a beggar man? [*She seats herself and busies herself with the flowers she has brought, looking at* TERRY *occasionally then at the flowers as she puts them together, holding them off a bit to observe the effect.*]

TERRY. No!

LITTLE CHRYSTAL. [*Pleased and smiling.*] You look like one

then, you look so old and poor. Oh, I know! You're a sailor! I can tell! My poor papa was a sailor—Mama says. Does all sailors and soldiers be beggars, when they get old?

TERRY. [*Smiles, amused.*] What put such an idea as that into your head, child?

LITTLE CHRYSTAL. 'Cause I see lots, and Mama gives me money to give them. So if you'll just stay here, I'll run and call her. [*She runs to the steps as if to go into the church.* TERRY *puts out his hand and stops her. She pauses, drawing a little away from him.*]

TERRY. No! No! No! You need not call your mother, child, I do not want for anything.

LITTLE CHRYSTAL. [*Surprised.*] No!

TERRY. No!

LITTLE CHRYSTAL. [*Disappointed.*] I'm so sorry. [*She goes back to her flowers.*] 'Pon your word?

TERRY. 'Pon my word.

LITTLE CHRYSTAL. Ain't you fooling?

TERRY. No, my child, I have all I want. When I was discharged from the hospital they gave me some money.

LITTLE CHRYSTAL. [*In awe and wonder, as if it were some dreadful place.*] Was you in the hospital? [*She has hard work to pronounce the word.*

TERRY. Yes.

LITTLE CHRYSTAL. [*In the same tone.*] What did you steal?

TERRY. [*Smiling.*] I didn't steal anything.

LITTLE CHRYSTAL. Then you must 'a' killed somebody, didn't you?

TERRY. [*Smiles.*] No—I didn't kill any one.

LITTLE CHRYSTAL. Then what made them put you in the—the—the—what did you say?

TERRY. The hospital.

LITTLE CHRYSTAL. Yes—that's it, the hospital—what—made them put you in the hospital for?

TERRY. I had been very sick and poor, I had no money.

LITTLE CHRYSTAL. Why didn't you go home? [*She grows interested, and quite inquisitive and talkative.*] Didn't you have any? [TERRY *shakes his head.*] No friends? [*He shakes his head again.*] No mother? [*He shakes head.*] No nothing in the whole wide world?

TERRY. [*Slowly.*] Nothin' in the whole wide world.

LITTLE CHRYSTAL. [*A pitying look crossing her face.*] Ain't you awful poor? Oh! I know, you're an orphan, ain't you?

TERRY. [*Holding out his hand.*] Come here—little one—take my hand— [*She draws a little away.*] Don't be frightened. I won't harm you, my child. [*She gains courage and slowly crosses to him.*] I'm very fond of little children—come—take my hand, won't you? [*She draws closer and closer and finally takes his hand.*]

LITTLE CHRYSTAL. There, I've got it. [*Laughs.*] I ain't a bit afraid now. Come! [*She tries to pull him to his feet.*]

TERRY. [*Rising.*] Where?

LITTLE CHRYSTAL. Just a little ways—over by my flowers.

TERRY. [*Moving with her towards the monument.*] Have you been picking flowers?

LITTLE CHRYSTAL. Yes.

TERRY. Will you give me some?

LITTLE CHRYSTAL. Yes. [*As they get to the monument.*] Now sit down!

TERRY. Sit down?

LITTLE CHRYSTAL. Yes. [*Pulling him down.*] Sit right—down—there—

TERRY. [*Sitting on the base of the monument.*] You're a good little girl. God bless you. [*He puts his arm around her; she stands, leaning against his knee, with her face partly towards him, partly towards the audience.*]

LITTLE CHRYSTAL. [*Patting his hand and playing with his fingers.*] Oh! What a big—rough hand you've got—twice as big as mine, see? [*Measures hands, then laughs loudly.*] Oh, what dirty nails you've got, why don't you clean 'em? Mama says you must always keep your little finger nails clean. Do you live here? [*Looking over her shoulder into his face.*]

TERRY. Once I did, but that's a long time ago. And when I think of that, I can scarcely speak, my throat gets so hot and parched.

LITTLE CHRYSTAL. Poor man—he's thirsty! I'll go and get him a drink of water. [*She runs off, right.*]

TERRY. [*Feeling for her.*] You've gone—child—ah—you were a bit frightened after all!

[*Re-enter* LITTLE CHRYSTAL *with a tin cup of water.*]

LITTLE CHRYSTAL. Here, poor man—I've brought you a drink of water. [*Puts it in his hand.* TERRY *drinks, then gives her the cup.*]

LITTLE CHRYSTAL. [*Takes the cup, looks into it, then up at him.*] Do you want any more?

TERRY. No! [*She places cup on the ground near the monument.*] But I want you to come here and let me talk to you of my own little girl.

LITTLE CHRYSTAL. [*Getting between his knees and looking up into his face.*] Have you got as nice a little girl as me?

TERRY. [*Smoothing her hair.*] I hope so—but I haven't seen her since she was a tiny thing in her cradle.

LITTLE CHRYSTAL. I wish you would go and find her and bring her to my house to play with me. Won't you please?

Oh! I'm so glad I met you! I like you awful lots now. What made you come here—tell me—what made you come here?

TERRY. Partly to find out if some fresh stone would tell me what I have not the courage to ask. The name of the newly dead beneath.

LITTLE CHRYSTAL. Then why don't you look?

TERRY. Because, my child, I am blind.

LITTLE CHRYSTAL. [*Awed.*] Blind! [*Looks up into his face.*] Why, your eyes is open.

TERRY. Yes, but I cannot see.

LITTLE CHRYSTAL. [*After passing her hand across his eyes.*] Oh, ain't that dreadful? [*Full of pity.*] Can I do something for you?

TERRY. You can take my hand, lead me around, and spell me out the names. You can read?

LITTLE CHRYSTAL. I can read this one—my papa's.

TERRY. Your father's?

LITTLE CHRYSTAL. Yes.

TERRY. Is this your father's grave?

LITTLE CHRYSTAL. Yes, you've been sitting on it all this time.

TERRY. [*Aside.*] Poor child, she has lost her father. [*Aloud.*] You haven't told me your name, yet—little one—what is your name?

LITTLE CHRYSTAL. My name is Chrystal, same as Mama's.

TERRY. [*Trembling all over.*] Chrystal! How old are you?

LITTLE CHRYSTAL. Six—going on seven.

TERRY. And what was your father's name?

LITTLE CHRYSTAL. I'll read it to you. [*Reads the inscription on the monument.*]

"Sacred to the mem-or-ory of Terry Dennison. Erected by Chrystal and Ned."

[*While the child is reading,* TERRY *sits transfixed. As she finishes, he rises slowly.*]

TERRY. [*In a hushed, agonized voice.*] My God—My God! My own grave—my own tombstone—and read to me by my own child! [*Completely overcome, he falls on his knees, his head bowed across the base of the monument.*]

LITTLE CHRYSTAL. [*Moving away frightened.*] Did you know my papa—

TERRY. [*Raising his face with an effort.*] No—no—my child— [*Restraining himself from embracing her. Aside.*] No—no—I must—not—dare not—breathe to her who I am— [*Pause.*]

LITTLE CHRYSTAL. [*Seeing him cry, goes to him and as she speaks, kneels and puts her arm around his neck.*] Did I make you cry, I'm so sorry—what did I do?

TERRY. [*Stifling his feelings, gets back to his seat on the monument.*] Nothin', my child, you have done nothin'. Chrystal, I want you to sit on my knee a moment— [*Takes her on his knee, and caresses her face and hair tenderly.*] You know, my darlin', that I shall soon have to go away, and then you will never see me again and I will never talk to you any more. [*Aside.*] My own little girl, my darlin' baby girl at last!

LITTLE CHRYSTAL. When you find your little girl, you won't be able to see her, will you?

TERRY. [*Choking.*] No! I shall *never* see my child again. [*Takes her face in his hands and stares at it, as if to read it with his sightless eyes.*]

LITTLE CHRYSTAL. But you can make it up in kisses, can't you?

TERRY. [*Taking a lock of hair from his breast and kissing it.*] Yes—

LITTLE CHRYSTAL. What's that?

TERRY. A lock of my baby's hair.

LITTLE CHRYSTAL. Let me kiss it too. [*Takes it, kisses it several times.*] Poor little baby—poor little baby! [*Gives it back, looks up at him.*] Kiss me, and when you find your little girl you can kiss her and say that little Chrystal sent it. [*Clapping her hands in childish glee.*] Won't that be nice? [TERRY *kisses her, forgets himself, and is too forcible. She pushes him away, pettishly.*] Oh, you hurt! What makes you kiss me so hard?

TERRY. Chrystal, I want you to put your arms around my neck—you put your little arms around my neck—[*She does so*] and try—try hard—Oh—so hard—to make believe that I'm your father. Only let me hear your little voice call me father once—only once! Try my child—try for God's sake—try—hard—hard—hard! [*He clenches his hands imploringly, almost beside himself.*]

LITTLE CHRYSTAL. Oh, I can't! You ain't a bit like my papa. Mama says he was so strong, and big and tall and brave and handsome—oh—*so* handsome! And you ain't big and tall and handsome. And every night I see him—just as Mama says he used to look!—see him in my dreams. And every night I kneel down at Mama's feet and pray for him—pray that he may be happy, up there in his new home among the stars! [*He kisses her; she feels the tears fall on her face, wipes them from his eyes, smooths his hair and kisses him, taking his face in her hands.*] Poor man, don't cry any more. Please don't. I'll tell you where my Mama is if you won't cry. [*Laughs and chuckles.*]

TERRY. Where is your mother, child?

LITTLE CHRYSTAL. [*In great glee.*] She's in the church there—

TERRY. [*Starts.*] In the church there?

LITTLE CHRYSTAL. Yes— [*Chuckles.*] She's gettin' married.

TERRY. Gettin' married? [*Trembling.*]

LITTLE CHRYSTAL. [*Chuckling.*] Yes—! She—is.

TERRY. [*Almost afraid to ask.*] To whom?

LITTLE CHRYSTAL. To my new papa of course.

TERRY. [*Fearfully.*] What's his name?

LITTLE CHRYSTAL. Guess!

TERRY. [*Almost afraid.*] N—ed Fairweather !

LITTLE CHRYSTAL. [*Astonished.*] How did you know?

TERRY. [*Falling on his knees.*] Thank God—Thank God! [*The organ is heard playing a wedding march.* TERRY *rises.*] But hark! They're comin'! They will find me here. That must not be. My child—I must leave you— [*Kisses her fervently.*] I must go away.

LITTLE CHRYSTAL. [*Stopping him.*] But I won't let you go! not till you've seen my mama—and wished her joy, like everybody else.

TERRY. [*Trying to release himself.*] No! No! I dare not.

LITTLE CHRYSTAL. [*Holding him.*] You must! [*Enter* NED *and* CHRYSTAL *from the church. Little* CHRYSTAL *runs to her mother.* TERRY *sinks on the monument, hiding his face.*] Look, Mama, here's a poor old sailor man, and he's blind!

CHRYSTAL *and* NED. Blind!

LITTLE CHRYSTAL. [*Pointing to* TERRY.] Yes, Mama!

CHRYSTAL. [*Going to* TERRY *and putting her hand on his shoulders, says gently,*] Poor man! [*To* NED.] He looks very poor and wretched. Ask him to come home with us.

NED. [*Good-heartedly and cheerily.*] Indeed I will. Come along old fellow—[*He claps* TERRY *on the shoulder.* TERRY *shivers.*]—and eat a bite of the wedding turkey. [NED *crosses down left.*]

CHRYSTAL. [*Crossing left.*] Bring him with you, Chrystal dear. Bring the poor man with you, child. [*As* CHRYSTAL *crosses the stage she keeps her eyes on* TERRY, *as if drawn to him by some strange, subconscious sympathy.* NED *is waiting down left for her. She extends her hand mechanically to him. As he leads her slowly off, she looks back at the kneeling figure of* TERRY.]

LITTLE CHRYSTAL. Yes, Mama, I won't let him go. Come along poor man,—[*She takes* TERRY *by the hand, and tries to pull him to his feet*]—you don't need your stick, I'll lead you. Come along! [TERRY *rises.* LITTLE CHRYSTAL *has his left hand in her right, and points off with her other hand. She looks up steadily into his face, and he stares blankly ahead, as they move very slowly off, down left.*]

CURTAIN

ACT SIXTH

"The End"

OWEN GARROWAY'S *hut.*

Late afternoon, the same day.

SCENE: *The cabin of an old ship which has been turned into a hut, but which still retains its quaint, nautical atmosphere. The whole scene is fishy to a degree, but spotlessly clean. The wooden floor is scrubbed white, like a well holystoned ship's deck. There is a small, square window at back centre, with a deal table beneath it. There is another window on the left-hand side of the stage. Between these windows, set diagonally in the wall is a neatly made bunk. Below the window on the left, is a stove, with a shelf above it. The entrance to the hut is through a door on the right. Above the door, against the right-hand wall, is a ship's locker. Down right, below the door, is a stool holding a pail of water. Picturesquely distributed about the walls hang a lantern, a sou'-wester, an oilskin coat, sea boots, and a ship's glass. Some nets are piled in the upper right-hand corner, and several oars are leaning against the wall. Down stage at left centre, stand an old armchair, covered with a patchwork quilt, and a footstool. Above the chair is a small table on which are a bottle of medicine, a glass and spoon, and some loose flowers.*

[*NOTE: The scene is very shallow, and runs only about half the depth of the stage.*]

A bit of the seashore can be glimpsed from the windows, and also through the door when it opens.

At the rise of the curtain, TERRY *is lying in the armchair, left centre. He wears a clean white shirt, and a pair of* OWEN'S *trousers. He is very ill.* OWEN, *his face all sympathy,*

*is tending him. The setting sun shines through the window,
left, on* TERRY's *face.*

TERRY. [*In a faint voice.*] Thank you, Owen, that's better.
I'm glad I can sit up; the doctor said I might, didn't he?

OWEN. Yes, he said so.

TERRY. What else did he say?

OWEN. [*Evading the question.*] He said— [*Giving him medicine.*] Here, Terry, it's time to take your medicine.

TERRY. Ah! Owen, I heard him. How long did you say I
had been here?

OWEN. Since mornin'.

TERRY. How did it come about?

OWEN. Why, it appears as how little Chrystal was a-leadin'
of ye, when just as she got ye to the door step, ye went off
in a dead faint, kerplunk.

TERRY. The joy, Owen, the joy at my heart was too much
for me.

OWEN. I s'pose so! Well, there was a great to-do. The child
cried as if her heart would break. She thought you was
dead. They wanted to bring you right into the old house
whether or no, but I knew that'd never do.

TERRY. You had recognized me?

OWEN. In the twinklin' of a marlinspike. Ye might lose
yer arms and both yer legs, and yer hair might be sky-blue
instead o' white—but ye could never deceive me, Terry
Dennison, never!

TERRY. [*Deeply moved.*] Owen, friend! [*He holds out his
hand.* OWEN *clasps it warmly.*]

OWEN. So I makes an excuse as how it might throw a damper
on the weddin' party and managed to have you brung here
by promisin' 'em they might call.

TERRY. [*Eagerly.*] And have they?

OWEN. Yes, but so far I've managed to keep 'em from seein' you, tellin' 'em the doctor's orders was so strict. But I'm afraid I can't hold out.

TERRY. It won't be necessary much longer, Owen. I can't last through this, I feel it, I know it—

OWEN. Don't talk that way, Terry.

TERRY. I must, it's the truth. [*His groping hands touch the flowers on the table.*] Who brought these flowers?

OWEN. [*Choking.*] The child. She followed ye all the way here, knocked at the door, and asked "How is the poor blind sailor man?" Then when I told her, she gave me a bunch of flowers, and says: "Give him these, and tell him little Chrystal plucked them for him." Then she turned sadly away. But as far as I could see her she kept a-lookin' back as though afraid the house would go out of her sight forever.

TERRY. [*Wistfully.*] And didn't she see me?

OWEN. Forgive me, Terry, but I couldn't help it, she begged so hard, an' ye were fast asleep. I lifted her up to ye, she kissed yer cheek so softly and smoothed yer hair, and then turnin' to me, her eyes full o' salt water, she says "Be good to him, won't you, Uncle Owen, for my sake, for I love him." I tell you what, Terry, that set my pumps a-goin'. I'll never let her in again, I couldn't stand it. [*Wipes his eyes.*] I tell ye, Terry, ye were wrong to have come back at all.

TERRY. I know it, Owen, I know it, but I couldn't help it. If ye only knew how hard I've tried. The thought of my baby haunted me day and night till at last her face, always lookin' into mine, became a torture worse than life itself; I pictured to myself how she'd grown, how she looked, whether she was like her mother, or whether she resembled me, how tall she was, what she did, what she said. Then came this cravin' for the sound of her voice,—just to hear that child call me father. That was a happiness I never dreamed of till now. Owen, when I'm gone, bury me there in the old churchyard—that'll be the sweetest restin' spot on earth for me.

OWEN. Terry, have ye no other wish?

TERRY. Other wish, what do you mean, Owen?

OWEN. Why, I've thought all day I read a longin' in yer face.

TERRY. [*Who has followed every word.*] Yes!

OWEN. To see Ned?

TERRY. [*Quickly.*] Ned!

OWEN. Was I right?

TERRY. Yes, yes, but I dared not ask it. [*His voice trembling with emotion.*] Can it be that you have done so?

OWEN. I've sent for him, and told him; I thought it best.

TERRY. And he will come? [*At that moment* NED *crosses the window at back, from the left.*] Speak, man, is he comin'?

[OWEN *silently opens the door, right.* NED *enters. Instinctively* TERRY *knows him, and with a superhuman effort, rises to his feet.* NED *rushes to him and they are clasped in silence in each other's arms.* OWEN, *overcome, turns away and stands at the centre window with his back to them.*]

NED. [*Puts* TERRY *back in the chair; he stands on* TERRY'S *right.*] Terry, Terry, we believed you dead.

TERRY. Yes, yes, I know—Owen has told me everythin'. You've kept your promise, you're a brave lad—Ned—a brave lad!

NED. [*Deeply affected.*] And now, Terry, tell me, why did you go? Did you suspect, did you know?

TERRY. Hush! I loved you both, I stood between you and happiness, that was all. Be kind to her and love my little girl. Never let them know,—let my child remember me only as her mother has pictured me to her, only as she sees me in her baby dreams. [*At this moment distant bells chime six o'clock.* TERRY *starts and listens intently.*] Ah! [*With a start.*] Who's that? [*Turns his head quickly.* OWEN *who has been at the window, at back, comes down left quickly.*]

OWEN. [*In a frightened whisper.*] Chrystal!

NED. [*Startled; in a whisper.*] Ah! [CHRYSTAL *crosses the window at back from the left;* LITTLE CHRYSTAL *is with her.*]

TERRY. Hush! Fear not for me. Stand between us and hide me from her sight. [CHRYSTAL *enters, right, carrying a small basket, and leading* LITTLE CHRYSTAL, *who has some flowers in her hand.* NED *turns and meets* CHRYSTAL, *right centre, and during the scene he stands between her and* TERRY.]

CHRYSTAL. Pardon me for intruding, but the doctor told me you were up, so I have come to bring you a bottle or two of old wine and some fruit, and to ask if I can be of any service to you. [*Owen, who has crossed, takes the basket and puts it on the table, left. He remains standing, left.*]
[*Aside to* NED.] I'm glad you were so thoughtful, Ned.

LITTLE CHRYSTAL. And here's some flowers I picked for you.

[*She crosses to* TERRY *and gives him her flowers.*]

TERRY. [*To* CHRYSTAL.] May I kiss her? [OWEN *checks him.*] May I kiss her child?

LITTLE CHRYSTAL. [*Climbing into his lap.*] Yes, you may kiss me all you want to. [TERRY *kisses her.*]

CHRYSTAL. You are a stranger here?

TERRY. Not altogether. Six years ago I sailed from this port with Captain Hearthaway.

CHRYSTAL. [*Starting.*] With Captain Hearthaway?

[NED *starts.*]

OWEN. [*Aside, to* TERRY.] For Heaven's sake!

TERRY. [*Aside, to him.*] Do not fear; all's safe.

CHRYSTAL. Then you must have known my husband, Terry Dennison?

TERRY. Terry Dennison! Was he your husband?

CHRYSTAL. Yes. Did you know him?

TERRY. Know him! He was my messmate. He died in my arms!

CHRYSTAL. [*Looking up as if thankful for positive news of* TERRY's *death.*] You were with him when he died, then?

TERRY. Yes. We arrived in the Arctics all safe, everythin' went well, till, homeward bound, we were caught between two mountains of ice; our shipmates one by one succumbed to cold and hunger; rescue came at last, but too late for poor Terry. He was dead, and I, the only survivor, frozen, my eyesight gone forever.

[*All are deeply affected. The chorus of the "Mill Song" is heard off stage, very distantly, increasing in volume as the scene progresses.*]

CHRYSTAL. Did he leave no word, no message?

TERRY. Yes. When he found his time had come, he dragged himself to my side and said, "If ever you live to return to Marblehead—I want you to find out Chrystal—that's my wife," he says, "and give her this." [*Holding out the lock of hair.*] "It's a lock of my baby's hair. Owen placed it in my hand the day I parted from them all. Kiss her for me and say I sent it; she'll believe you. And if you find her married, why Ned'll be her husband, and he won't mind!" [*He turns his face pleadingly towards* NED. CHRYSTAL *looks at* NED. *He nods his head in consent, crosses to* TERRY, *and stands at his left.* CHRYSTAL, *deeply moved, crosses to the right of* TERRY's *chair, and sinks on her knees beside him.* OWEN, *with bent head, leans against the shelf down left.* TERRY *stares steadily into* CHRYSTAL's *face, as if his sightless eyes could read it, then puts his hand around her neck and draws her face to him, giving her one long, fervent kiss. During all this, she never raises her eyes to his face.*] And then he said, "Tell my little baby to put her arms around your neck and call you father. It is my last wish."

[*The child, who has listened to this with wonder and childish awe, throws her arms around his neck and clasps him firmly.*]

LITTLE CHRYSTAL. Father!

TERRY. [*With a deep sigh.*] At last! [*Kisses her. His face is full of joy and bliss. His arm falls from* CHRYSTAL'S *neck and he dies.*]

CHRYSTAL. [*Who, at the exclamation of the child, has looked up startled and now realizes all, cries in an agonized voice,*] Terry! [*To* NED, *sobbing.*] Oh, Ned, Ned! Why did you not tell? [*She throws herself on* TERRY'S *breast.*]

NED. [*Pointing upwards.*] Hush, darling, He willed it so.

[*The chorus, singing the "Mill Song," dies away in the distance as the curtain slowly descends.*]

THE END OF THE PLAY

www.ingramcontent.com/pod-product-compliance
Lightning Source LLC
Chambersburg PA
CBHW021214090426
42740CB00006B/215